British Studies Series

General Editor JEREMY BLACK

Published

John Charmley **A History ... 1996**
David Childs **Britain ...**
John Davis **A History ... 5–1**
David Eastwood **Government and Community in the English Provinces, 1700–1870**
W. Hamish Fraser **A History of British Trade Unionism 1700–1998**
Brian Hill **The Early Parties and Politics in Britain, 1688–1832**
Kevin Jefferys **Retreat from New Jerusalem: British Politics, 1951–1964**
T. A. Jenkins **The Liberal Ascendancy, 1830–1886**
David Loades **Power in Tudor England**
Alexander Murdoch **British History, 1660–1832: National Identity and Local Culture**
Anthony Musson and W. M. Ormrod **The Evolution of English Justice: Law, Politics and Society in the Fourteenth Century**
Murray G. H. Pittock **Inventing and Resisting Britain: Cultural Identities in Britain and Ireland, 1685–1789**
Andrew Thorpe **A History of the British Labour Party**

Forthcoming

D. G. Boyce **Britain and Decolonisation**
Glenn Burgess **British Political Thought from Reformation to Revolution**
J. B. Christoph **The Twentieth-Century British State**
Gary De Krey **Restoration and Revolution in Britain**
Jeremy Gregory **The Long Reformation: Religion and Society in England *c.* 1530–1870**
Katrina Honeyman **Women and Industrialization**
Jon Lawrence **Britain and the First World War**

(*List continued overleaf*)

F. J. Levy **Politics and Culture in Tudor England**
G. I. T. Machin **The Rise of British Democracy**
Allan Macinnes **The British Revolution**
Thomas Mayer **Britain, 1450–1603**
Michael Mendle **The English Civil War and Political Thought**
W. Rubinstein **History of Britain in the Twentieth Century**
Howard Temperley **Britain and America**

British Studies Series
Series Standing Order
ISBN 0–333–71691–4 hardcover
ISBN 0–333–69332–9 paperback
(*outside North America only*)

You can receive future titles in this series as they are published by placing a standing order. Please contact your bookseller or, in case of difficulty, write to us at the address below with your name and address, the title of the series and the ISBN quoted above.

Customer Services Department, Macmillan Distribution Ltd
Houndmills, Basingstoke, Hampshire RG21 6XS, England

A History of British Trade Unionism 1700–1998

W. Hamish Fraser
Professor of Modern History
University of Strathclyde

First published in Great Britain 1999 by
MACMILLAN PRESS LTD
Houndmills, Basingstoke, Hampshire RG21 6XS and London
Companies and representatives throughout the world

A catalogue record for this book is available from the British Library.

ISBN 0–333–59610–2 hardcover
ISBN 0–333–59611–0 paperback

First published in the United States of America 1999 by
ST. MARTIN'S PRESS, INC.,
Scholarly and Reference Division,
175 Fifth Avenue, New York, N.Y. 10010

ISBN 0–312–21857–5

Library of Congress Cataloging-in-Publication Data
Fraser, W. Hamish.
A history of British trade unionism 1700–1998 / W. Hamish Fraser.
p. cm. — (British studies series)
Includes bibliographical references and index.
ISBN 0–312–21857–5 (cloth)
1. Trade-unions—Great Britain—History. 2. Labor disputes—Great Britain—History. 3. Labor movement–-Great Britain—History. I. Title. II. Series.
HD6664.F757 1999
331.88'0941—dc21 98–29187
CIP

This book is printed on paper suitable for recycling and made from fully managed and sustained forest sources.

10 9 8 7 6 5 4 3 2 1
08 07 06 05 04 03 02 01 00 99

Printed in Hong Kong

Contents

Abbreviations

ACAS	Advisory, Conciliation and Arbitration Service
AEU	Amalgamated Engineering Union
APEX	Association of Professional Executive, Clerical and Computer Staff
ASCJ	Amalgamated Society of Carpenters and Joiners
ASE	Amalgamated Society of Engineers
ASLEF	Associated Society of Locomotive Engineers and Firemen
ASRS	Amalgamated Society of Railway Servants
AUEW	Amalgamated Union of Engineering Workers
BSA	British Small Arms Co.
BSC	British Steel Corporation
CBI	Confederation of British Industries
COHSE	Confederation of Health Service Employees
CPGB	Communist Party of Great Britain
CPSA	Civil and Public Services Association
CSEU	Confederation of Shipbuilding and Engineering Unions
CWC	Clyde Workers' Committee
DATA	Draughtsmen and Allied Technicians' Association
EEF	Engineering Employers' Federation
EETPU	Electrical, Electronic, Telecommunication and Plumbing Union
ETU	Electrical Trades Union
GCHQ	Government Communications Headquarters
GMBATU	General, Municipal, Boilermakers and Allied Trades' Union
GMWU	General and Municipal Workers' Union
GNCTU	Grand National Consolidated Trades Union
GPMU	Graphical, Paper and Media Union
ISTC	Iron and Steel Trades Confederation
MFGB	Miners' Federation of Great Britain

MSF	Manufacturing, Science and Finance
NACODS	National Association of Colliery Overmen, Deputies and Shotfirers
NALGO	National Association of Local Government Officers
NASDU	National Amalgamated Stevedores and Dockers' Union
NATSOPA	National Association of Operative Printers
NEDC	National Economic Development Council
NGA	National Graphical Association
NUCPS	National Union of Civil and Public Servants
NUGMW	National Union of General and Municipal Workers
NUJ	National Union of Journalists
NUM	National Union of Mineworkers
NUPB&PW	National Union of Printing, Bookbinding and Paper Workers
NUPE	National Union of Public Employees
NUR	National Union of Railwaymen
NUS	National Union of Seamen
NUTGW	National Union of Tailors and Garment Workers
NUVB	National Union of Vehicle Builders
PCS	Public and Commercial Services' Union
SDF	Social Democratic Federation
SOGAT	Society of Graphical and Allied Trades
TASS	Technical Administrative and Supervisory Union
TGWU	Transport and General Workers' Union
TUC	Trades Union Congress
UCATT	Union of Construction, Allied Trades and Technicians
USDAW	Union of Shop, Distributive and Allied Workers

1 Learning the Game

A number of historians have tried to make a distinction between early forms of workers' organisations emerging in the eighteenth century and the later forms, using epithets like 'primitive' to describe the earlier activities and following the Webbs in perpetuating a Whig interpretation from 'barbarism' to 'a more civilised society'.[1] There is little justification for such an interpretation. There are very few aspects of modern trade unionism which are not apparent in the earliest years of its existence. Journeymen craftsmen combined to provide mutual aid in the form of cash payments in sickness or for widows and orphans. They devised mechanisms to assist those who were out of work to find a new job. They combined to exert pressure on employers to protect earnings and, occasionally, to try to improve hours of work or push up wages, while also trying to devise rational and fair procedures for settling differences. They sought to control who could enter the craft and be employed. They joined workers in other crafts to campaign for or against legislation and, occasionally, they took to the streets to protest and demonstrate. By the end of the eighteenth century they were providing financial support to one another across craft divisions in industrial disputes.

Early Organisations

Trade unions emerged not as a product of the factory system but amongst artisans, the shoe-makers, cabinet-makers, tailors, building workers, weavers, operating in small workshops or in their own homes. They were there whenever a merchant or master craftsman was employing or organising groups of producers and, therefore, some kind of employer/employee relationship was developing. Many craftsmen were self-employed, selling directly to the public, but, as markets began to widen in the eighteenth century, a few master craftsmen would extend their business by taking on assistance in the form of apprentices and journeymen. In other cases, merchants would organise the purchase of goods from the producers and, in time, would seek to control the supply of raw materials. Independent domestic craftsmen found themselves gradually converted into controlled and employed workers, losing much of their autonomy. In either of these situations tensions between the employer or merchant and the journeymen were likely to arise over quality of work, over pace of production, over rates of payment or over hours of work. The aggrieved would look for mutual support from other craftsmen. Trade unions were a product of what Karl Marx dubbed the 'period of *manu*facture', the time of early capitalist organisation of largely domestic crafts in order to increase production to cater for widening markets, but before any substantial mechanisation.

Independent craftsmen had formed guilds from earliest times and, although Sidney and Beatrice Webb in their great *History of Trade Unionism* tried to make a clear distinction between the guilds and the emerging trade union movement, there is a blurring between their functions. Guilds were about controlling entry into the craft to ensure that the trade was not overwhelmed by numbers. They were about providing mutual aid to dependents and they were often about controlling prices. Not surprisingly, there were attempts to break their monopoly and to control their operations. They were organisations of master craftsmen, time-served artisans who had acquired a requisite level of skills through apprenticeship and experience. They were about protecting the quality of craft work by ensuring that only those with the necessary expertise could participate in the craft. Most craftsmen could expect to progress to being a master of his craft. It is when that began to change and when some masters began to employ others on a full-time basis, or when middlemen began to organise the distribution, that journeymen's organisations, separate from the guilds but, in many cases, modelled on them, began to appear. Such bodies were generally about defending the customs and practices of the craft and maintaining control of entry into the craft. In other words, they were about trying to preserve those features of regulation which craftsmen had long recognised as giving them protection from the cold blast of an unregulated market.

The pressures against restriction and regulation of the world of work either by guilds or by the state were clearly growing by the end of the seventeenth century. As towns grew in size and spread beyond the traditional boundaries it was more difficult to keep records of who were qualified craftsmen with the right to practise in the town. In Glasgow there were complaints about the large number of 'straingers', wrights and masons, who had flocked into the town in the aftermath of the great fire there in 1652 and no doubt the same happened in London after its great fire of 1666. The more enterprising, seeing opportunities and profit amid adversity, were prepared to defy customary restrictions. The Elizabethan Statute of Artificers of 1563 had given Justices of the Peace in England the power to regulate what artisans could charge and what journeymen and apprentices should be paid. By the end of the seventeenth century these were powers that were being less used. In Scotland as early as 1426 magistrates in the merchant-dominated royal burghs could fix the prices that craftsmen could charge, and this right was reaffirmed at various times over the next two centuries. There, a still-dominant landowning class was less than sympathetic towards a slowly emerging business middle class and concerned most of all with maintaining social stability. The gentry retained control of politics and society and such regulation was to continue in Scotland until beyond the end of the eighteenth century.

Both regulation and deregulation encouraged organisation. In a regulated system some form of occasional organisation was necessary to petition for or against changes in conditions or earnings. Thus Gloucestershire woollen weavers united across the county in 1755–6 to petition Parliament to enact new legislation to ensure that the Justices acted to regulate wages annually.[2] In an increasingly deregulated situation, as in most of eighteenth-century England, the need for organisation was equally necessary to present the journeymen's case to employers. None of this required the *continuous* association which the Webbs regarded as essential for a definition of a trade union. But it usually meant that there were known practices and procedures amongst groups of journeymen which could be called into play when required. There were also known people who could be relied upon to act as spokesmen when required. H. A. Turner points out,

> people of the same occupation, who were regularly brought together in the same workplace or town, may acknowledge regular leaders, develop customs of workplace regulations and systematic 'trade practices', and can produce a disciplined observance of the latter without embedding these procedures in formal records.[3]

What was more likely to create the shell of some continuous organisation was the development of mutual-aid organisations, an area which has been vastly under-researched. Part of the function of guilds' mutual aid was to provide support for widows and orphans, to contribute to infirmaries, occasionally to bulk-buy foodstuffs and to assist those who had fallen on hard times. Eighteenth-century journeymen sought to develop parallel organisations. Sick and burial 'box' clubs provided continuity of organisation and required trusted officers. They could, if required, provide the basis of organisation for industrial purposes. The Society of Woolcombers at Tiverton in the West Country had a benefit society in 1700.[4] Edinburgh tailors formed a 'Charitable Concert of Journeymen Taylors' in 1714. Shoe-makers, skinners and a number of other crafts followed in the 1720s. Leith Shipwrights had a society for the relief of those 'who are sick and infirm' dating from 1731 and Glasgow tailors, stay-makers and upholsterers soon after raised a fund by voluntary subscription 'to be applied for the relief of such of them and their widows, as should happen to be reduced to indigent circumstances'.[5] As early as 1727 master tailors in Edinburgh were claiming that the charity box was a fund 'out of which refractory persons might be maintained, till their masters should be compelled to yield to their demands, however extravagant they might be'. Aberdeen woolcombers deposited their money with an employer and banker, but when in 1759 they fell into dispute he refused to release the funds and the Court of Session declared 'That such combinations of artificers, whereby they collect money for a common box, inflict penalties, impose oaths and make other by-laws are a dangerous tendency, subversive to peace and order, and against law'.[6]

A third root of organisation was the establishment of houses of call. These were in part a further extension of mutual aid. At least some journeymen craftsmen could expect to spend time in their youth tramping not just to find work, but to extend their skills. Hobsbawm suggests that formalised tramping for the latter purpose was relatively limited in Britain and that there was nothing comparable to the French artisans' *tour de France*.[7] None the less, journeymen did move around and looked to their craft to assist them in finding work. Tailors in London and Dublin had houses of call from the 1720s, Edinburgh had ones from 1742, as an alternative to 'cookshops and ale houses', as the source of information about available work. Both workers and employers were required to register to make use of these, which might be run by an old member of the craft who could be expected to go out in search of available workers when employment was available. But call houses could develop into a protection for workers. An increasing pressure in many town crafts was the inflow of workers from other towns and from the rural areas coming into rapidly growing cities and presenting themselves, despite possibly very limited skills, as tailors or shoe-makers or masons. Call houses could be the means of regulating who could be available as an acceptable journeymen. Under the older system, based on a public house, the complaint was that those journeymen who spent the most money had the best chance of getting a job even if they were 'the greatest bunglers just from the country'. Call houses, it was hoped, would ensure that only those who could prove they had the necessary skill would be registered.[8] Skill could be proved by some documentation from the place of origin, a 'note' or 'blank' from the equivalent organisation, or by some kind of test.

Tramping clearly encouraged the development of country-wide links between workers in similar crafts and could be the means of spreading organisation and ideas. Hobsbawm shows how West Country woolcombers were among the first to organise a tramping system in the early 1700s. Aberdeen Woolcombers' Society, formed by a dozen journeymen in 1755, having sent a delegate to make contact with similar societies in England, introduced a tramping system a year or two later. Aberdeen employers were soon complaining that it produced 'a factious and mutinous spirit'.

But many organisations appeared as the result of disputes over conditions and wages and there was no shortage of these. C. R. Dobson counted 383 between 1717 and 1800,[9] but there is no doubt that those he noted were a mere fraction of the total. Industrial conflict was a significant feature of eighteenth-century town life. Adrian Randall is undoubtedly right to suggest that it is quite artificial to make a distinction between protests over the price of bread, the much-studied meal riots, and protests over reductions in rates of payment.[10] Both could equally stem from a perception of, in E. P. Thompson's classic phrase, a 'moral economy', a just and fair pattern of regulation, be it of prices or wages. When the rules of that 'moral economy' were breached by farmers, merchants or employers then riot, protest or strike or a combination of all three could result. Gloucestershire weavers went on strike and rioted over a period of six weeks in 1728 against a unilaterally imposed cut in piece rates by some clothiers. Forty Edinburgh tailors struck in 1734, complaining that the master tailors were taking higher profits than masters in other crafts. Paisley linen weavers in 1754 reacted to a reduction of their rates with a 'resentment . . . chiefly vented against their masters' windows'.[11]

But as Dobson's study showed, many strikes were not defensive, but were intended to increase earnings or to reduce hours. Tailors in particular had learned to use the occasions of rush orders for new clothes from the well-to-do – coronations, sittings of Parliament, royal mournings – to threaten strikes to push up wages. They could also use a sudden demand for military uniforms at the outbreak of war, just as shipwrights in the royal dockyards would seize the same moment when ships were being fitted out for battle. There are numerous other examples of aggressive as opposed to defensive striking. Edinburgh masons and joiners struck in 1764 for a rise, the former claiming that their wages had not been increased for a hundred years. They also petitioned the courts, arguing that the masters were combining to hold down wages, which the journeymen claimed ought to be ruled by the 'rate of viveris', the cost of living.[12] Four years later a group of Edinburgh shoe-makers were pressing for a rise on the grounds that they were having to wait so long at the employer's to collect the cut-out leather and to return the finished work that they were having to extend their working day up to fifteen hours in order to make a living.[13] Employers responded by agreeing with Glasgow employers not to take on any Edinburgh men. Workers were also learning to make comparisons with those in a similar position in other towns. After London and Westminster tailors were granted a reduction in hours to 12 hours per day by Act of Parliament in 1769, the Edinburgh tailors successfully pressed for a similar reduction. Elsewhere, workers learned the tactic of the rolling strike, or the 'strike in detail', tackling one employer at a time, and when the demand was refused, going on strike, supported financially by workers of other employers.[14]

Population growth, increasing urbanisation and the rapid development of newer capitalist forms of organisation all had a major effect on groups of workers and, therefore, regulation of entry into crafts became a central aim of many workers' organisations. There had long been resistance to employers taking on too many apprentices and so eventually overstocking the craft. Spitalfield weavers in 1719 complained of the 'covetousness of both masters and journeymen in taking so many 'prentices for the sake of the money they have with them; not considering whether they should have employment for them'.[15] As Edward Thompson argued, journeymen tried to maintain the traditional limitations on numbers and length of apprenticeships just as the guilds were succumbing to the pressures of many employers to waive such restrictions on the growth of their labour force. Similarly, journeymen tried to keep control over adult workers, perhaps country-trained workers coming into their crafts. Attempts to enforce restrictions on entry by legal means were, by the middle of the eighteenth century, increasingly being overturned by the courts as a threat to the 'necessary subordination' of man to master. Houses of call remained one mechanism for trying to maintain regulation of entry and Edinburgh journeymen tailors in the 1780s battled with their employers to control, first of all, who should be entered on the call list as available for work and then how far the employer should be allowed a free choice from the list. On other occasions direct action could be taken to harry 'strangers' whether employers or journeymen.

Direct action to ensure solidarity was another feature of disputes. John Rule writes of ritualistic shaming and punishing of strike breakers in the West Country by 'cool staffing', fixing the culprit to a pole and parading him through the village before dropping him in the duckpond.[16] Handloom weavers would generally ensure that all came out during a strike by removing all the webs from the looms and ritualistically carrying them through the streets. Attacks on machinery can be seen as part of a similar pattern. The smashing of spinning jennies in Lancashire in the late 1760s and of knitting frames in Nottinghamshire at the end of the 1770s was action against new workers and against employers who were deviating from the traditional relationship.

Unions and the Law

During the eighteenth century both employers and journeymen resorted to Parliament and the courts for their own purposes. James Moher has identified 30 pieces of legislation between 1305 and 1799, twenty of them between 1720 and 1799, banning combinations among specific groups of workers.[17] After an extended dispute of London tailors in 1720–1 Parliament was persuaded to ban combinations of journeymen tailors in London and Westminster and, at the employers' behest, to fix hours and wage rates. A 1725 law specifically banned combining by woolcombers and weavers. Irish combinations seem to have caused particular concerns and were regularly banned. Edinburgh employers in the early eighteenth century often applied to the magistrates for the arrest of journeymen who combined to press for a rise in piece rates, although they were permitted to present petitions to the magistrates. During the first half of the eighteenth century it was generally employers who supported legal regulation of prices and hours as an effective barrier against journeymen's demands, although they did not always find gentry JPs entirely sympathetic. They also made use of the Statute of Artificers, which demanded long notice for leaving employment, against breaches of contract. By the later eighteenth century things had changed. Employers now wanted the minimum of restriction on their freedom of action, whether to cut pay rates in order to compete or to increase rates to attract the best skilled labour. It was journeymen who looked to the courts as a protection against the destructive effects of market forces on their craft.

Gloucester weavers successfully petitioned Parliament in 1755 for a new Act confirming the JPs' duty to fix wages, only for it to be overturned two years later after a lobbying of parliamentary opinion by the master clothiers. Increasingly employers were arguing that prices paid had to depend 'as in reason it ought, on *the demand of the market*'.[18] In a number of areas journeymen found that both Parliament and the courts were not hostile to the idea of workmen retaining some legal protection. Magistrates were often most concerned to maintain social order and stability and saw new work methods as threatening such stability. Spitalfield silk weavers were successful in getting mechanisms for regulating and enforcing wage rates in 1773 and the Act was extended to include manufacturers of mixed cloth in 1792. In the highly volatile situation in Scotland in the 1790s and early in the new century when political radicalism was around, JPs became in fact *more* interventionist. They raised the piece rates for Edinburgh tailors in 1793. In 1795 they ruled that, because of the high price of provisions, Leith shipwrights should be granted a wage increase. In 1796 they ruled that rates on certain articles should 'be settled by the mutual agreement of masters and men, and not at the discretion of masters alone'. In 1803 the same body of Justices mused that since the price of the staple oatmeal was not high there *might* be a case for a reduction in the wages of carpenters; but, since the price of clothing and house rents had gone up, they should in fact be granted a backdated increase. In 1805 printers in Edinburgh were granted a rise after an accountant was appointed by the court to examine employers' wages books.[19]

By the end of the eighteenth century, however, there was a clear hardening of attitudes towards workers' organisations.

In England the master paper-makers got an Act to suppress the Journeymen Papermakers' Society, which had successfully resisted a lock-out, and there was no clause in the Act allowing for regulating of wages. A similar Act followed in 1799, aimed at London millwrights and it was quickly followed by the General Combination Act of 1799 which was amended in the following year. On pain of up to three months in jail, the Acts forbade any attempt to interfere with 'manufacture, trade or business in the conduct or management thereof', or any attempt to persuade workers not to take work or to strike. The 1799 Act allowed judgment before a single Justice of the Peace; the 1800 amendment required two Justices and allowed for review by a higher court. Both Acts applied only to England. In Scotland, where judge-made law was more significant than statute and where courts had continued to be involved in wage-fixing, the right to combine was still recognised as long as it was not against the public good. The Scottish supreme court declared in 1800

> that it is only when workmen combine to raise their wages beyond their due and legal rate, or seek a rise in wages at their own hands, without submissive, regular lawful applications to the proper tribunal, or when they proceed to acts of violence, and breach of the peace that they are obnoxious to the laws.[20]

By 1808, in a case involving Edinburgh paper-makers, the issue was much more debated, with some of the younger judges asking 'what it is that fixes the rate of reasonable wages, except a free market'. But the right to combine for an approach to the courts was still allowed.

In England the Combination Act seems to have been used very rarely to suppress unions and the authorities tended only to intervene when there was the whiff of sedition around a combination. Journeymen's societies clearly continued to exist and to resist some of the changes in work methods and employment practices which employers were trying to introduce. Engineering employers complained that the Acts had had 'no effect at all among engineers and millwrights in restraining combinations'.[21] On the other hand, the shadow of illegality hanging over unionism must certainly have deterred many from associating with a journeymen's club and pushed the weight of advantage more firmly to the side of the employers. The readiness of the state to intervene to take harsh measures against machine smashing was another deterrent. The Luddite disturbances in Nottinghamshire, Yorkshire and Lancashire in 1811 and 1812 thoroughly frightened the authorities because they had a radical political element in them and the brutal response to these events made clear that the state was now firmly on the side of capitalist development.

It was particularly employers in the expanding and highly competitive textile industries who were at the forefront of trying to push through new work patterns and who most resented any hindrance to these. In Scotland, where unions could still operate with some impunity, these issues were fought out. Handloom weavers had for some years been trying to control the increased flood of workers into their trade and launched a scheme to establish an effective apprenticeship system. To do this they set up a General Association of Operative Weavers in 1809. By the following summer a Glasgow committee claimed to be in touch with some 100 districts, containing 40 000 looms, both north and south of the border. The Association began to develop proposals for its own factory to provide work for unemployed weavers and so keep them out of the labour market. At the same time there were strikes by other groups of craftsmen and calls from employers for legislation to suppress combinations. The factory-based master cotton spinners complained that recent court decisions in Scotland had made it impossible for employers to resort to law against combinations and there were demands for the Combination Acts to be applied in Scotland. The threat was enough to bring about a meeting in February 1811, in an unprecedented display of workers' solidarity, of delegates from a range of different journeymen's societies in Glasgow and the West of Scotland. It agreed to petition against any Combination Bill should it be introduced.

The Glasgow weavers, with the backing of 'the whole of the trades of any consequence in the town', also made another attempt to get Parliament to accept a bill for the limitation of numbers of apprentices. When this failed they turned to the magistrates and submitted a table of prices for the many different kinds of weaving to the Lanarkshire Justices. Their case was that employers had a legal obligation to provide a wage that was 'proportioned to the rate of provision' and that 'wages that will not afford a moderate subsistence, is [sic] highly unreasonable as well as illegal'. When the JPs granted a list which was close to what the weavers demanded, the employers took the matter to the Court of Session where five judges once again debated the appropriateness of wage regulation. They reaffirmed that the power to regulate lay with the Justices, who duly declared that the new rates should be paid. The merchant-manufacturers refused to pay these and tried to instigate criminal proceedings against the Weavers' Association. The weavers struck across most of central Scotland with all the accompanying ritual of carrying webs through the streets.

The authorities were, not surprisingly, extremely anxious, especially since there were disputes in many other places among other groups of workers. The outbreaks of machine smashing in England added to a sense of crisis. There were also food riots in a number of areas and signs of a revival of political radicalism during the winter of 1811–12. Eventually, pressed by the business leaders in Glasgow, the legal authorities acted against the Weavers' Association and arrested the leading members. Eight of them were brought to trial and sentenced to between two and eighteen months. The judgment seemed for the first time to make simple combination a crime in Scotland.

The Scottish employers had been pressing the Home Secretary, Lord Sidmouth, to legislate against unions and these events in Scotland formed the context of his decision to remove, once and for all, any possibility of judicial interference by repealing the old statutes. Four months after the trial the Acts on wage regulation in both England and Scotland, dating back to at least the sixteenth century, were swept away. In the following year, the Statute of Artificers of 1563, laying down the requirements of apprenticeship, was also repealed. It was the end of the last remnants of an older, regulated, paternalistic order in the face of increasing pressure for economic growth within a *laissez-faire* society. It was a major victory for the new industrialists. A London employer rejoiced that it would mean the end of control of machines by millwrights and allow the emergence of a new cheaper class of engineering worker.[22]

A campaign for repeal of the Combination Laws began almost immediately after 1814 and attracted support from a number of different directions. Clearly some politicians, like the radical Joseph Hume, felt that the law was now too heavily weighted on the side of employers and that in a liberal society the state's role ought to be an even-handed one. Some employers also recognised that there was some value in being able to deal with journeymen's organisations, which palpably continued to exist in defiance of the law. Others were confident that, if illegality were removed, most unions would fade away. Finally, Francis Place, the London breeches-maker and indefatigable political operator, who was confident that workers would gain from the development of an unregulated capitalist system, persuaded a parliamentary select committee to recommend repeal. The 1824 Act went further in granting immunity from legal action to workers in unions than most of the politicians, perhaps bamboozled by Hume and Place, had ever intended and, when repeal was followed by a spate of strikes, a new measure was introduced. This restricted the right to combine only for specified actions over the regulation of hours and wages, not for any other interference with management. It also introduced new offences covering intimidation and molestation of other workers.[23]

Responses to Capitalism

By the time the Combination Laws were repealed trade unions were established across a range of occupations. Crafts in many towns had societies of some kind which lent themselves to united industrial action. More scattered groups such as handloom weavers, often based in rural areas, were trying, generally less effectively, to keep organisations going. But, in the developing cotton industry of Lancashire and Lanarkshire, they were negotiating over price lists from at least the 1760s and, in both places, some form of association had a more or less continuous existence from the 1790s. New factory workers like the cotton spinners and calico printers implanted traditions of craft organisation in the developing mills. Mule spinners by the end of the Napoleonic Wars were among the most effectively organised of workers in both cotton regions. Occasional unions of coal miners, sometimes linking workers across coalfields, also appeared.[24]

Almost all the unions were small and local but there were frequent attempts at creating wider nation-wide links between societies in the same craft. Paralleling these were the appearance of, usually short-lived, employers' associations. But there were also signs that craft consciousness was giving way to a wider working-class consciousness. Glasgow workers had come together to campaign against hostile legislation and there was often mutual financial support in disputes. In 1819 the Deptford shipwright, John Gast, was the moving force behind a proposal for an inter-union organisation, the 'Philanthropic Hercules' and a pioneering workers' paper *The Gorgon*, while in Manchester a 'Union of all Trades called the Philanthropic Society' was launched. By 1824 committees of trades' delegates existed in Glasgow and Edinburgh and no doubt elsewhere.

Attempts to achieve more effective organisation also intensified in the aftermath of repeal. Pattern-makers, smiths, filers and turners engaged in steam engine and textile machinery construction in the North of England – the workers who were embodying the craft of engineering – formed a number of friendly and tramping societies in 1824. Two years later, rules of a Steam Engine Makers' Society were approved in Manchester by delegates from a number of different societies and a Friendly Union of Mechanics appeared about the same time. The activities of the Lancashire cotton spinners' leader, John Doherty, helped to create a General Union of Cotton Spinners in 1829, linking English, Scottish and Irish spinners' unions. There had been rapid technical developments in the cotton spinning mills in the mid-1820s, which had led to bitter struggles over the management of the work-place. Disputes were much more frequently over issues of management than over wages. Employers, through their overseers, were anxious to impose discipline, control, good time-keeping and flexibility on a workforce which had imported the rather casual work patterns of domestic industry. They made extensive use of fining, dismissal and sometimes violence against vulnerable younger workers. Workers tended to resist and in both Lancashire and the West of Scotland there were many struggles in the 1820s over the prerogatives of management. As Maxine Berg has argued, 'workers adapted their own culture and rhythms of work to new contexts so that the factory never became the capitalist controlled and utterly rational form of work organisation' that employers would have wanted.

It was at the end of years of tension over such issues that major strikes broke out in Lancashire. In January 1829, 10 000 workers in Stockport were on strike for six months. There were lock-outs in Manchester, as employers got together to defeat the unions, and the secretary of the Manchester Union, John Doherty, hoped to make his Spinners' Union the nucleus of a general union of all trades. Through the *United Trades' Co-operative Journal*, later the *Voice of the People*, he campaigned throughout the North of England and the Midlands for a National Association for the Protection of Labour. He marketed this as a practical organisation to provide mutual support during strikes but, like many of the most active union leaders in the early 1830s, he was influenced by the ideas which are generally included under the umbrella of Owenism. Many workers had come to identify the competitive nature of capitalism as a major cause of the deterioration in their status and their conditions of work and looked for an alternative. Robert Owen's ideas of co-operation, even to the extent of opting out of the capitalist system into co-operative communities, had an appeal, particularly for those craftsmen who felt that they were losing out as a result of the changes wrought by industrialisation. For others, co-operative workshops were a mechanism for providing work at times of unemployment and a means of discouraging undercutting of wages by those desperately seeking work.

Meanwhile, the struggles for control in the cotton mills came to a head. The Lancashire spinners were active again at the end of 1830, trying to recover the reductions of the year before, by systematically organising mills to strike in turn. The united employers in the Ashton and Stalybridge area responded with a lock-out of 52 mills and the imposition of a further wage cut. Doherty attempted to get a general strike of spinners, but the Scots and Irish, among whom the technological changes were less advanced, refused to join in. In Lancashire, the disputes erupted into violence and Thomas Ashton, son of one of the leading mill-owners, was shot dead. Eventually starvation forced the strikers back to work by March 1831. The Grand General Union of Spinners collapsed in some acrimony in the aftermath of the strike, as not only the Scots and Irish but other spinners in nearby towns like Preston and Bolton were accused of failing to support the cause.

The improved economic conditions of the early 1830s, after a long economic recession in the late 1820s and a very sharp rise in bread prices in 1830–1, encouraged other groups of workers to try to claw back some of the ground most of them had lost in the difficult years. There were numerous attempts to link unions of different trades. In Glasgow a committee of trade societies produced their own journal which pushed plans for a general trades' union. In London, unions formed a federal Metropolitan Trades' Union in March 1831, which quickly got caught up in the campaigns for parliamentary reform and for factory legislation. In Yorkshire the Leeds Union spread among woollen and worsted workers, after a strike at Gott's mill in Leeds lasting 33 weeks from February to October 1831. Gott's was the most technologically advanced mill and it was here that there were the most crucial struggles over the issues of managerial control of work patterns.

Organisation began to filter to other groups of workers; there were the first signs of organisation among women workers. Female powerloom weavers, powerloom tenters and powerloom dressers in Glasgow united in a union 'for their mutual protection against the encroachment of tyrannical overseers'. In Aberdeen, despite denunciations by local clergy, a Female Operatives' Union successfully resisted wage cuts at local mills. Tommy Hepburn inspired a short-lived union among miners in Northumberland and Durham to campaign against truck shops, fines and the length of the working day. A strike in 1831 brought concessions, but in the following year the employers got together to fight back and the union was crushed. Employers also collaborated to break the Builders' Union, which loosely united a number of existing builders' unions of stonemasons, plasterers, plumbers, glaziers and carpenters in the North and Midlands, and which had emerged largely in response to the spread of bigger firms of *general* building contractors as opposed to the specialist crafts.[25] Lancashire building employers introduced the 'document' by which workers were required to renounce union membership. In Yorkshire the woollen and worsted employers drew up a 'bond' in which each pledged themselves not to employ any union members.

The late 1820s and early 1830s had also seen the spread of co-operative societies among groups of workers, as a means of coping with the sharp price rises but also holding out some hope of finding an alternative to the developing capitalist system. It was through these that unionists and Owenite-inspired co-operators probably made their links. Owenites had initially looked to wealthy philanthropists as the best hope of financing their co-operative activities and Owen himself had no great enthusiasm for trade unionism and certainly did not see unions as an essential part of industrial relations. But in the early 1830s at least some Owenites hoped that trade unions could be the means by which workers themselves might raise the necessary resources to lay the foundations of the 'New Moral World'.[26] Owenite activists worked assiduously to gain support. Owen himself addressed numerous meetings and persuaded, among others, the Operative Builders' Union to back schemes for co-operative production. Owen's long-established support for the shortening of factory hours also gained him credit among the textile unions.

Spreading social tension in many different parts of the country came to a head in the spring of 1834, first of all in Derby. There, a trades' union linking a number of different trades, probably a left-over from Doherty's National Association for the Protection of Labour, had been winning localised strikes. The Derby employers responded with a general lock-out and clearly saw themselves as fighting the nation's battle against trade-union power. The unions tried to respond by setting up their own co-operative businesses and the whole event attracted attention throughout the country. It was while this was going on that a conference met in London in February 1834 from which emerged the Grand National Consolidated Trades' Union. It was intended as a federation of existing unions, with separate trade divisions. Its main strength lay among the tailors, including women tailors and bonnet-makers, and shoe-makers in London and, although there were contacts with unions in the Potteries and in the North of England and Scotland, it was never effective in attracting general support, although some 11 000 paid dues to it in April 1834.[27]

The high-point of the influence of the Grand National was the great demonstration held in London in April 1834 to protest against the arrest and sentences of six agricultural labourers in Tolpuddle in Dorset, to which 40 000 turned out. The six were members of the Friendly Society of Agricultural Labourers set up months before the Grand National was established and owing nothing to it, although it is possible that George Loveless, the moving spirit behind the Society, had read a pamphlet issued by the Yorkshire Trades' Union. Rural workers were extremely difficult to organise, scattered as they were in farms and villages. Collective action did occasionally explode into strikes and demonstrations, usually over wages or poor relief. The coming of the threshing machine, reducing the demand for labour at harvest time, led to major protests (inevitably described as riots) in East Anglia in 1822 and, most spectacularly, in the 'Captain Swing' rick-burning and machine-smashing protests across the southern counties in 1830. Farming, too, was going through a major transformation with the growth of large-scale capitalist farming. As unionism gathered pace among craft workers in the towns of the area, it is not surprising that the idea should have spread to farm labourers. But the reaction to the Tolpuddle union was as much to do with a panic among landowners as about a reaction to trade unionism as such. They were sentenced for the taking of illegal oaths. There was nothing unusual about oaths of loyalty to an organisation. It had long been the core of freemasonry as a means of ensuring solidarity and secrecy. But there were advantages in attacking the union through that route. While it was difficult to attack a friendly society, since these had long been held up as models of self-help, by focusing on the issue of oath-taking the authorities were able to brand the organisation as sinister, conspiratorial and threatening. The harsh sentences of transportation on the labourers were ammunition for middle-class radicals in their attacks on the landed aristocracy and it was they who initially set up the protest committees before other unionists began to take up the cause.

This was a time of immense social agitation and unions were faced with pressure and advice from many different directions. Some were urging them to press for political reform and universal suffrage. Others were trying to entice them to republicanism, while yet others were talking about a class-conscious revolutionary stance. Owen was only one of those trying to latch on to the spreading union movement, but he managed to capture public attention, leading the members of the Grand National Consolidated Trades' Union on his white horse in the Tolpuddle demonstration in London. However, the defeat of the London tailors in a strike later in the year effectively meant the end of the Consolidated Union. Other defeats followed as employers rallied in a counter-attack. A general strike in Oldham was comprehensively broken in April; Yorkshire weavers were defeated in May; London building workers in July. Only in Staffordshire did the Potters' Society manage to see off an attempt to impose the 'document' requiring the renunciation of union membership.

Both contemporaries and the Webbs and others, writing of these events, have seen the period of the early 1830s as potentially revolutionary. The shoe-maker, William Benbow, had issued a call for a 'grand national holiday', a general strike against capitalism. The Owenite and millennialist press built up expectations of confrontations which would bring some kind of social revolution. The discontents against the 'competitive system' were widespread. But the evidence of practice is that few unionists had the high hopes and utopian expectations of the Owenite missionaries and set themselves more limited goals. The Glasgow unionists' newspaper, while sympathetic to the ideals of Owenism, had a distinctly pragmatic approach and argued that there were dangers in 'intermingling metaphysics with the every day purposes of life'. It was a view that was probably held by most trade unionists.

Surviving and Consolidating

With the failure of the experiments in general unionism and the deeply hostile atmosphere of the mid-1830s, most trade unions entered a difficult period of cautious consolidation. The

Builders' Union, for example, broke into its disparate parts and only the stonemasons managed to maintain some kind of national organisation. That too crumbled when it became bankrupt in 1841 after a disastrous strike against Peto's, the building contractors, during the rebuilding of the Houses of Parliament and the erection of Nelson's Column. A national organisation of plasterers disappeared entirely and the painters remained as local clubs until the 1860s.

The onslaught against unions had not been so pronounced in Scotland in the early 1830s, where employers seemed less confident in challenging the spread of organisation, but it came in 1837. Strikes of miners and iron workers in Lanarkshire were broken by importing Irish labour and unionists were barred from the bigger coal and iron companies. It was left to the civil authorities to seize the opportunity of the shooting of a strike-breaker during a strike of cotton spinners in 1837 to arrest the officials of the strongest of the unions, the Associated Cotton Spinners. Led by the Sheriff of Lanarkshire, there was a deliberate policy, on the scantest of evidence, to identify the spinners' union with violence and assaults dating back over three decades. Secret oaths were cited as further evidence of the sinister nature of the organisation and the spinners' case never gained the sympathy from the middle class accorded to the Dorchester labourers, but in practice there was little difference in aim. The arrest and trial was a stage-managed exercise intended to break unionism in the West of Scotland and the sentence of seven years' transportation was meant to deter others. Eventually, largely through the action of other trade unions, the outcry was such and the nature of the legal proceedings so questionable that, unlike the Tolpuddle Martyrs, the five unionists were never actually sent to Australia and instead languished in the Thames prison hulks until pardoned in 1840. But the trial and sentences had effectively served the purpose of branding unionism with the mark of violence and intimidating potential members. Membership of what had been a strong and well-organised union movement melted away.[28]

Workers were in a weak bargaining position in the late 1830s and early 1840s as the country experienced what was to be the worst economic depression of the century. For some the Chartist movement offered hope and all recent work points to the involvement of trade unionists in Chartism. It is hardly surprising that activists who had got caught up in trade unionism and remained committed to it in difficult times, should also be the most politically aware. Those craftsmen whose position was being threatened by the expansion of their crafts through the influx of new labour were the most likely to pin some hopes on political power. But it was a second string to the bow of protecting and improving working conditions. Few saw it as a solution to economic problems and, as a tailors' delegate to a Manchester trades' conference in the aftermath of the widespread strikes of 1842 observed, 'Although the majority voted for the Charter . . . they were not able to carry into effect the vote they had given' and few of the 'delegates, or the trades they represented, had the courage, the energy, or the determination'.[29]

Chartism did little to address the economic plight of many. By May 1842 more than a million people out of an English population of 16 million were in receipt of poor relief. Firms collapsed. In Stockport, for example, more than half the master manufacturers were said to have gone out of business in the six years since 1836. The long, exceptionally hot summer brought an explosion of unrest, despite the economic depression. In June there were strikes in the Midlands, Cumberland and in Glasgow. In July Staffordshire coal miners struck after a wage cut and stopped most of the pits by pulling the plugs from the steam boilers which pumped out the water. They claimed a nine-hour day, including an hour for food, 4s (20p) a day wage payable in cash and a supply of coal. Meanwhile further north in Ashton and Stalybridge three firms threatened their weavers with a 25 per cent reduction. The determination of one of the employers to make an example of the matter to drive home the issue of authority, the presence of some Chartist activists and the fact that some of the Lancashire employers were deep into the campaign against the Corn Laws and were not averse to stirring up agitation to embarrass the government, all contributed to the development of what came very close to a general strike throughout Lancashire,

Cheshire and parts of the Midlands. (These were the so-called 'plug' strikes where solidarity was ensured by sabotaging the steam engine boilers.)

Later that same year a Miners' Association of Great Britain and Ireland was formed after a meeting in Wakefield. Miners in the North of England had two particular grievances: the extensive use of the truck system, forcing miners' families to purchase from the mine shop; and the yearly hiring bond. The latter had once given some guarantee of wages, but this had been eroded and now miners were tied to a particular company and forced to work for an employer when needed, but without any assurance that work and wages would be provided. There were unsuccessful strikes in Northumberland in 1836–7 against the bondage system. The late 1830s and early 1840s saw an expansion of the coal industry to satisfy a growing demand from new industries and the emerging railways. By the early 1840s there were signs of county-wide miners' unions in Durham, Northumberland, Lancashire, Yorkshire and Staffordshire and it was these, perhaps encouraged by the Chartist, Feargus O'Connor, and his paper, the *Northern Star*, who were represented at the Wakefield meeting. The two key figures in the Association were Martin Jude of the Northumberland Union and David Swallow of the Yorkshire Miners.

One thing that miners were continually up against was the master and servant legislation which made it a criminal offence for a worker to break his contract of employment while for employers it was only a civil offence. With yearly contracts, miners were particularly vulnerable, and the new Association hired a legal adviser, W. P. Roberts, at a salary of £700 a year to fight such cases. Generally, there was a desire to avoid precipitate strikes although a conference held in Glasgow in 1844 tried unsuccessfully to co-ordinate a national strike of miners. Northumberland and Durham miners did come out in a four months' strike. The owners, led by Lord Londonderry, were determined to break the unions, however, and imported strike-breakers from Cornwall, Wales and Ireland. Strikers' families were evicted from their homes but barred from admission to the poor-law workhouses, and shopkeepers were intimidated into refusing credit. Eventually the strike was broken, but there were some gains and the yearly bond gradually disappeared to be replaced by a monthly contract. The Association and the county unions then faded away in the sharp depression in the coal trade in 1847–8.

The struggles in mining, as in many other industries, were not just about wages, but over the whole pattern of work. Alan Campbell, Fred Reid and others have written of the tradition of the 'independent collier' who saw himself as a free tradesman contracting to produce coal at a pace which suited himself. The new coal companies wanted a different kind of work-force, one which operated to the discipline of the owners. Rules and fines were brought in to force the miners to work for a full week. In Lanarkshire they were actively forbidden to keep poultry and dogs, lest it encourage a casual approach. In other words, discipline was being imposed outside as well as inside the work-place to bring about a cultural transformation.[30] It was a pattern that was being repeated in many different industries.

Other groups of workers were clear about the importance of co-ordinated action and mutual support. They had plenty of evidence from the struggles of the 1830s that employers were ready and capable of uniting to break unions both through their own actions and in cahoots with allies in political authority. But there were always tensions over how far control and resources should be in the hands of a central executive and how far it should remain with local unions and branches. The Stonemasons' Union was rent by internal struggles over this issue and the question of whether the union should be exclusively craft-based or should try to include other building workers. In 1838 the largest engineering unions of Yorkshire and Lancashire combined in the Journeymen Steam Engine and Machine Makers' Friendly Society with around 3000 members and tried to tighten central control. A part-time general secretary was appointed in 1839 based in Manchester and in 1843 the post was made full-time. But a hostile court case in 1847 against the secretary and the executive of the Society made them back away from centralisation of finance and of industrial policy. There were various efforts in the 1840s to unite different societies of trades involved in engineering in a defensive alliance against a united front by some of the employers, so that if one group of workers were in dispute 'the whole of the trades of that shop shall strike'. They were particularly hostile to the use of the 'quittance paper', a character and wages note from an employer which was required when a worker moved jobs. Millwrights, engineers, smiths and iron founders united in various struggles in Lancashire in 1844 and 1845 against the 'document' and the 'character note'.[31]

Other groups were responding to the changing conditions and trying to devise effective structures. The Friendly Society of Ironmoulders moved in 1846 to a more centralised structure with the final authority on strike action vested in the executive committee and a full-time secretary was appointed in 1853. The Friendly Boiler-Makers' Society, which had been formed in 1834 and had been extending its membership in the 1840s, became the *United* Friendly Boiler-Makers' Society and tried to impose some measure of central control over its branches. It elected its first full-time secretary in 1845 and extended its funds for sick, funeral and disablement benefits. At the same time, it spelled out more clearly its trade purposes, particularly the regulation of apprentices. Richard Harnott became full-time secretary of the Operative Stone Masons' Society in 1847, a post he was to hold for the next quarter century, and began to pull decision-making to the centre. A new federation of Lancashire cotton spinners was formed in 1842, embracing both the older hand-mule spinners and the new minders of self-acting machines. It was a shrewd new tactic that had been learned from hard experience, that to resist new technology was futile and what needed to be done was for existing workers to retain control of it. A great deal of later craft unionism was precisely about gaining control of new machines for union members. The printers also tried to consolidate with the formation in January 1845 of the National Typographical Association, linking the various societies of London, provincial and Scottish compositors. The idea here, too, was to have a central authority which could co-ordinate strike action, conserve resources and deploy industrial pressure to the best advantage. It broke up in 1848 with the reappearance of a London Society of Compositors and a separate Provincial Typographical Association and, eventually, a Scottish Association emerged.

By 1850 most of the features of trade unionism and industrial relations which were to shape the next century were in place. The central issue of the power of management and the power of workers to control the labour process was a recurring cause of dispute as was the issue of how the gains of technological change should be distributed between employer and workers. Unions had had to tackle difficult issues of structure – how far decisions should be centralised and how far they should be left to those on the spot – and of collaboration between crafts and within industries. Unions had to confront the issue of politics and how to operate most effectively in a state which was increasingly placing its weight on the side of capitalism. Despite the many set-backs, unionism had emerged in some ways strengthened from the struggles and set-backs of the 1830s and early 1840s. They had learned of the need for mutual support against employers, who had shown a readiness to combine where necessary against unionism. There was an increasing number of examples of support given across craft and union boundaries and trades delegates' meetings were an established feature in many cities. Unions had learned the need to be aware of public opinion and politics. They had distanced themselves from many of the wider social and political movements and determined to focus their activities on the industrial struggle. There was less of a belief that the advance of capitalism, 'the competitive system' as it was referred to, could be halted by direct confrontation, which had generally led to defeat and the break-up of nascent unions. Instead, increasingly, groups of workers had recognised the need for effective organisation, where possible on a national basis, to offer protection within the system. They were striving to achieve stability. They were learning to operate within capitalist systems of production. As Hobsbawm says, they had learned the rules of the game.

2 The Rise of National Unions, 1850–80

As economic conditions picked up towards the end of the 1840s a number of unions were putting in hand changes to make their organisation more effective. But such changes were not easily achieved. Local societies did not like to abandon their independence and branches did not like to lose control over their own funds. It was difficult to persuade workers with grievances of their own to subordinate themselves to the needs of other workers at the other end of the country. Yet, faced with growing signs of employers' collaboration and, in almost all industries, pressure for change in work patterns, there was a recognition that co-ordination was necessary.

Amalgamations

There is no doubt of the immense importance of the amalgamation of the Manchester-based Journeymen Steam Engine Makers', Machine Makers' and Millwrights' Friendly Society, the 'Old Mechanics', as it was known, with the Liverpool-based Steam Engine Makers' Friendly Society, some branches of the Smiths' Benevolent, Friendly Sick and Burial Society, some London Smiths and some other small societies in September 1850.[1] The resulting Amalgamated Society of Engineers (ASE) was larger than any other union. It started with only 5000 members but had 12 000 at the end of its first year and sustained growth over the next quarter century to nearly 40 000. Even more significantly, it organised the key skilled fitters and turners in the expanding industries of machine-making and machine tool-making on which so much of the mid-Victorian boom was to depend. Of great significance for the future, however, was the failure to incorporate other key groups of skilled metal workers, the foundry men, the pattern-makers, the smiths, who were determined to cling to a distinct craft identity. It left engineering workshops as places where different workers struggled against one another for control of changing labour processes. Amalgamation of unions or tasks was never an easy process.

The two key figures behind the amalgamation, were the Ulster-born Scot, William Allan from Crewe, and the Cheshire engineer and publican, William Newton. Newton was the inspirer and publicist, Allan the organiser and administrator. Both had been working towards amalgamation for half a decade or more; both had a fairly clear conception of what they wanted the new organisation to achieve. Like other unions of craftsmen before them, their concern was to devise a union which would regulate entry into the trade and ensure that the various engineering crafts were not flooded by poorly skilled, low-paid new workers whose presence would push down the level of wages. Observation of what had happened to handloom weavers, tailors, shoe-makers and others, who over the decades of industrialisation had failed to control entry into their trades and found their status and earnings undermined, made the dangers inherent in an industry which was expanding by leaps and bounds fairly obvious. New recruits were being pulled in from the ranks of country blacksmiths and woodworkers; new machinery provided opportunities for employers to try to push down labour costs, by using less than time-served workers to operate the machines. The Society's first concern was to 'prevent a surplus labour in our trade' (as the 1851 Rules declared) by maintaining strict control of the system of apprenticeship, over how many apprentices per skilled journeymen and over the length of training. But apprenticeship was difficult to maintain and difficult to check and therefore there was the fall-back position that the union would only accept those workers who were paid the standard wage, i.e. the wage acceptable in the district for a fully skilled turner or fitter.

Secondly, the ASE was concerned with establishing 'a well-regulated organisation', one which was stable and permanent. The history of many of the early unions had been brief, with workers flocking to them at times of industrial unrest and flocking out of them when the moment of confrontation had passed. The much more successful models of stability were the friendly societies, where workers subscribed for future benefits and where failure to pay dues would result in loss of savings. Those organisations which managed to combine friendly-society benefits and industrial activities were the survivors. It was this pattern which the ASE incorporated into its organisation, drawing on elements from its constituent bodies. For 1s (5p) weekly due a member was eligible for up to 10s (50p) per week unemployment benefit for 26 weeks and 7s (35p) for a further twelve weeks; 10s (50p) a week for up to six months' sickness benefit; a lump sum of £100 on permanent disablement; £12 funeral allowance; and when unemployment was particularly high, up to £6 emigration assistance.

A further feature of the new organisation – still part of the desire to ensure both effectiveness and national identity – was the annual equalisation of funds between the different branches. The theory was to maintain some central control over funds, with branches being discouraged from substantial expenditure without the approval of the executive. In practice, this proved very difficult to achieve, since the branches held the money until the end of year redistribution and were, therefore, able to retain a great deal of autonomy. The supreme body of the Society was the delegate meeting which had to approve all rule changes. General policy matters were left to an executive council of 37, initially elected by the London district, and day-to-day matters were in the hands of a full-time general secretary, William Allan, from 1850 until his death in 1874.

It was not the first attempt at forming a nation-wide union. But the rapid development of railways in the 1840s and the coming of the penny post made effective national organisation more feasible than ever before. Yet it was to take a couple of decades or more before most unions were able to achieve lasting national structures. Despite the ASE, throughout the 1850s almost all trade unions remained small and localised and only a few other attempts at amalgamating succeeded. It always proved difficult in the textile industry. The large spinning areas of Bolton and Oldham refused to associate with the attempted amalgamation of cotton spinners in 1853. The weavers opted for district associations following the Blackburn

Weavers' Association in 1854, one based in Padiham in 1856, Darwen in 1857, Accrington, Preston and Haslingden in 1858. It took 30 years to pull such associations together into an effective county-wide organisation. In mining, there were only traces of trade unionism in some of the most important coal-fields, like Northumberland and Durham, appearing at times of industrial unrest. In other fields, organisations existed but were reaching only a tiny proportion of a rapidly expanding work-force. Early attempts at national links had been short-lived. However, in 1855, Alexander McDonald, a university-educated miners' agent from Lanarkshire, succeeded in persuading the remnants of organisation in the Scottish coal-fields to associate in a General Association of Coal and Iron Miners, but control still remained with the districts. Three years later, some of the Yorkshire miners succeeded in creating a South Yorkshire Miners' Association, still only county-based, but linking many pits in an expanding coalfield. The Northumberland and Durham Miners' Association was revitalised in the 1860s when some employers tried to go back to yearly contracts.

To the Webbs the ASE was the 'New Model' for modern unionism. Since then, the extent to which it was either new or a model has been regularly questioned.[2] Indeed, the Webbs themselves recognised that a great deal of what they highlighted had already existed for some time in the pre-amalgamation trade societies. The 'Old Mechanics' had had an elected executive committee and a full-time general secretary since 1843 and William Allan had developed his administrative skills in that position since 1847. The combination of benefit and industrial funds had been a feature of the Journeymen Steam Engine Makers' Society, which as well as out-of-work pay, provided funeral benefit, accident disablement benefit and a travelling allowance. In 1846, it had extended its benefits to include a sick allowance and a superannuation scheme. Other societies had started to link benefits and industrial activities. What was new was the size, the extent of benefits and the efficiency with which the organisation was run.

The Amalgamated Society of Carpenters and Joiners, formed in 1860, was one of the few societies which consciously took the ASE as a model and neither ever became in any sense typical of trade-union organisation. The ASCJ brought together a number of small local woodworkers' societies and when the remarkable Hull joiner, Robert Applegarth, took over as full-time general secretary in 1862 it began to grow rapidly from the original 600 members to 3320 in 1865 and over 10 000 by the end of the decade. Despite this, many joiners' societies remained outside the Amalgamated, some purely local, like George Potter's London Progressive Society with 130 members, others regional like the Manchester-based General Union and the Scottish Associated Union.

Other traditional crafts began to create nation-wide organisations, from the local societies which in many cases had existed for decades. The cabinet-makers, organised in the old Friendly Society of Cabinet-Makers, made major changes to their organisation between 1864 and 1874 by becoming more centralised and extending friendly society benefits with high contributions. On the other hand, the rival Alliance Cabinet-Makers, formed in 1865, attracted members by asking for lower contributions.[3] It spread out from London, but both organisations continued to face competition from small local societies. Many tailors' societies with their long history came together in the Amalgamated Association of Tailors in 1866 with its headquarters in Manchester. Scotland had its own Amalgamation. London and Provincial shoe-makers united in the Amalgamated Cordwainers' Society in 1863. Henry Broadhurst, the future general secretary of the TUC, persuaded the Operative Stonemasons' Society to adopt a more centralised system in the 1870s but keep their friendly society side and their trade section separate. Members were permitted, if they wished, to join only the trade section, which gave them funeral benefit, retirement benefit and strike support. Most trade unions had no alternative but to leave a great deal of autonomy at local level, preferring federal structures. Hardly any Scottish trade union offered friendly society benefits other than death benefit, surviving on the basis of their cheapness. A number of other societies, like the Friendly Society of Ironfounders, the United Society of Boilermakers (which from 1852 included 'and Iron Shipbuilders' in its title) and the Flintglass Makers' Society, offered a similar range of substantial benefits in return for high dues, but their friendly society side long predated the formation of the ASE. The societies like the ASE, the ASCJ, the Ironfounders and the Boilermakers, which offered a full range of benefits, were the exception rather than the general rule. It remains highly questionable then how far the ASE can be regarded as a model. None the less, its success and stability inevitably influenced others in due course.

Even when a national organisation seemed to have been successfully created, there was always the danger of schism. The very capable general secretary, Charles Williams, could not hold together the National Association of Operative Plasterers formed in 1860. Most of the London branches broke away to form a Metropolitan Association in 1870. The same secessionist tendencies were just as apparent in the expanding iron industries. The puddlers and millmen of Staffordshire formed a union in 1863, which became the Associated Ironworkers of Great Britain. Within two years it had split, with the Teeside and Yorkshire workers forming their own National Amalgamated Association of Ironworkers, under the presidency of John Kane. Once separate organisations were established in different areas it proved extremely difficult to persuade them to abandon independence. Most Scottish unions insisted on independence from their English brethren and when some of the big English societies began recruiting in Scotland the Scottish local organisation would fight for survival by undercutting the subscription rates.

The Webbs made much of the centralised control and uniform trade policy of the ASE, but Keith Burgess's studies have undermined this view.[4] Power in shaping trade policy remained pretty firmly at branch and district level and a failure by executives to recognise this could result in defiance of the leadership and even breakaways. An elaborate system of friendly benefits did much to encourage centralisation of authority, but a variety of administrative structures persisted and decentralisation was much more common than centralisation. It was usual for the executive of the union to be made up of delegates of the locality in which the headquarters sat. So for decades the London district was responsible for the ASE and selected the general secretary. In some cases, the headquarters and the executive moved between main cities. The Boilermakers' executive was chosen by the twenty lodges (as its branches were called) of the important Tyneside district, with lodges selecting in rotation one member of the seven-man committee. The appointment of full-time secretaries and the extension of union bureaucracies increased the pressure for stability and an end to rotation, but there was a strong attachment to democratic control in various forms. Usually, a general meeting of delegates could overrule the executive and the officials and through the 1870s there was a consciousness of the need to sound out members' opinions. Any rule changes required wide membership approval. In some cases the general secretaries were elected by a direct vote of the membership, often on an annual basis but, as the Webbs pointed out, far from leading to change, it 'invariably resulted in permanence of tenure exceeding that of the English civil service'.[5]

These were unions of craft workers which were about protecting the position of those with certain skills from the greatest threat to their position. This was from other workers who, with less skill or greater need, might be prepared to take on a job at less than the going rate. Insisting that only the time-served could do particular tasks was the most effective way of protecting themselves. There was no tradition of apprenticeship in the coal-mining industry or in most of the textile industry, but this did not prevent workers trying to control who could enter the key jobs. The hewers had an element of control over who could come into the work gang and in older collieries they tried to recruit from within the family and community. They could not do this in the new pits in South Wales and elsewhere where largely new communities were being created. They had to find other means of trying to maintain their earnings, usually by trying to restrict production in order to keep up the price of coal. Variations in the traditions and markets of different coalfields meant that miners generally stuck to county organisations. John Normansell provided a vigorous leadership for South Yorkshire miners from 1864. Northumberland Miners' Mutual Confident Association came into being in the same year to resist the reintroduction of the yearly bond, and the Durham Association five years later. Staffordshire Miners' county organisation appeared in 1863. Alexander McDonald, leading a loosely linked Scottish Miners' Association persuaded them to come together in a British-wide federation, the National Association of Coal, Lime and Ironstone Miners, in 1863. It was mainly intended to lobby Parliament for legislation to improve mining conditions. But in 1869 a rift occurred with the Lancashire miners, led by Thomas Halliday, breaking away to form a more centralised Amalgamated Association of Miners, which was intent on pursuing a more aggressive industrial policy.

The Lancashire cotton mill workers were organised mainly in local societies. There were frequent efforts to link them, but the relatively loose federations which were created generally failed to survive for very long. An Association of Operative Cotton Spinners, Twiners and Self-Acting Minders was formed in 1842, which sought to unite both hand-mule spinners and self-acting mule minders, but it faded after 1857 when the big areas of Bolton and Oldham withdrew. A renewed effort in 1853 barely survived the great Preston strike of that year, and again failed to attract Bolton and Oldham. Not until 1869 was a permanent Amalgamated Association of Cotton Spinners, Self-Acting Minders, Twiners and Rovers of Lancashire and Adjoining Counties formed. The powerloom weavers' unions gradually clustered around a number of district organisations from the 1850s. In 1858 a number of district associations were linked in the East Lancashire Powerloom Weavers' Association, the so-called First Amalgamation, which survived through various vicissitudes until it was reorganised in the late 1870s. Across the Pennines in Yorkshire among the woollen workers, apart from some small societies of overlookers, unionism barely took hold before the end of the century.

A Labour Aristocracy?

Over the past thirty years, the debate over the concept of the 'labour aristocracy' has generated a considerable literature. The Webbs' analysis of trade union development was a useful weapon for those who sought to emphasise a discontinuity sometime around mid-century. The 'New Spirit and the New Model' was contrasted with the earlier 'Revolutionary Period'. Raymond Postgate, writing thirty years after the Webbs on *The Building Trades*, entitled his chapter on the mid-century decades, 'The Servile Generation'. The implication was that not only had the new structures and new leaders of the 1850s and 1860s reflected changes in working-class attitudes and the demise of revolutionary attitudes, but had in fact helped to create these attitudes by means of bureaucratic restraints on worker militancy, by an obsessive caution over the use of funds, and by a greater concern for maintaining friendly-society benefits than pushing for advances on the industrial side.

The modern debate dated from E. P. Thompson's *Making of the English Working Class* in 1963. If Thompson was right that a working class, 'conscious of itself as a class', had indeed been made by the 1830s and 1840s, then, from a Marxist point of view, it was necessary to explain why that class had not lived up to its 'historic' revolutionary potential over the succeeding decades. The parameters of the debate go well beyond the boundaries of trade unionism, but E. J. Hobsbawm and John Foster both accepted Friedrich Engels's argument that factory workers protected by the Factory Acts and the large unions had created 'an aristocracy among the working class'. While Hobsbawm, in a seminal essay on 'The Concept of a Labour Aristocracy', added many nuances to the concept, he went along with the view that 'the boundaries of the aristocracy and of trade unionism were normally . . . believed to coincide'.[6] Royden Harrison asserted that 'from their head offices in London, they could concert and direct policy in quite a new way' and create 'a Trade Unionism concerned with its public image'.[7]

For those who rejected a Marxist analysis, the concept of a labour aristocracy was a *deus ex machina* to explain something which did not require explanation, the lack of a revolutionary class consciousness among workers. Henry Pelling famously repudiated the concept as doing 'more harm than good to historical truth'.[8] A. E. Musson argued that the contrast between the militancy of the second quarter of the century and the moderation of the third quarter has been painted too sharply, so that 'they grossly inflate the importance and even distort the character of "revolutionary" Owenism, while, on the other hand, they greatly exaggerate the novelty and pacifism of the so-called "New Model"'.[9]

Most aspects of the debate on the labour aristocracy go well beyond trade unionism but there is little doubt that trade union leaders did contribute to the cultural change which has allowed the mid-century years to be described as 'an age of equipoise'. But there was never any question of abandoning the main purposes of trade unionism, to defend their members against encroachments and to push for improvements. The change was in the tactics being deployed to achieve these ends. It was not just in terms of the organisation of the ASE that there was continuity with past practices. The rules of the Society, the pages of Newton's journal, *The Operative*, and the monthly and annual reports of the journal all reflect perceptions and attitudes which would have been perfectly recognisable to the trade unionists of the 1830s. There was a clear sense of the craftsman's responsibility for the craft. 'It is our *duty*' [my italics], said the 1851 Rules, 'to exercise the same control over that in which we have a vested interest as the physician who holds his diploma or the author who is protected by his copyright.' Both Allan and Newton believed that the ideal social structure was one based on co-operation rather than competition. They believed that co-operative workshops were a way of keeping the unemployed out of the labour market. Before the funds were decimated in the lock-out of 1851, £10 000 had been earmarked for the setting up of co-operative workshops in London. This was not some conversion to classical political economy, an acceptance of the immutable 'laws' of supply and demand as propagated in the numerous crude popularisations of John Stuart Mill's *Principles of Political Economy*. Trade unionists had long recognised that the long-term unemployed would always be tempted to accept a wage cut in order to find work and, therefore, it made sense to keep them out of the labour market, whether by finding alternative work for them or by providing the means for them to migrate. The cotton spinners of Glasgow had had an emigration fund since the 1820s and, by the 1850s, there were numerous emigration societies supported by trade union activists. The ASE's emigration fund fitted this tradition. In principle, it was no different from the travelling benefits which had encouraged tramping in search of work.

At the same time, there is no doubt that by the end of the 1850s there was among many trade unionists a growing acceptance of a great deal of the economics of *laissez-faire*. A decade of propaganda from the Anti-Corn Law League and the economic upturn of the late 1840s and early 1850s had been enough to convince most that the moves towards free trade were creating the conditions for economic prosperity. The few who tried to argue for protectionism or that the state had a responsibility to provide work for the unemployed found themselves increasingly isolated. But, of course, trade unionism by its very existence was a rejection of the argument that the effect of market forces on labour could not be modified and there was no acceptance of any 'iron law of wages'. The *Flint Glass Makers' Magazine* bluntly declared, 'it is all very well to talk about the law of supply and demand; we happen to know there is enough for all and to spare'.[10] Accepting the laws of supply and demand did not involve any assumption that nothing could be done, but rather encouraged the effort to adjust the realities by controlling the supply of labour.[11]

Trades Councils

There was still in the 1850s a tendency to look to other local unions for support every bit as much as to other parts of the trade. Local support committees had appeared on numerous occasions in the past. In London, a Metropolitan Trades' Committee had appeared from time to time, at least since 1818 when the Deptford shipwright, John Gast, had urged the establishment of 'a general workmen's organisation, as distinguished from separate trade clubs'.[12] Glasgow had regular meetings of 'Associated Trades' or 'Delegated Trades' or 'United Trades' committees from at least 1812. In the crises-riven 1830s the United Trades' Committee met regularly throughout the decade. In Sheffield there was an 'Alliance of Organised Trades' in 1838. In London, William Lovett was secretary of a Trades' Committee to keep an eye on the Parliamentary Inquiry into Combinations. In Aberdeen there was a 'Delegated Committee of Sympathy' for three or four years from 1846 'to bring together all the organised trades so that they could support each other in the event of a strike of any one of them, or when any general movement was required in support of trade unions'. A committee of Sheffield trades' delegates in 1847, faced with a hostile Manufacturers' Protection Society, advised the local unions to 'obtain a general Trades' Council, composed of delegates from every trade'. In 1848, a Liverpool Trades' Guardians' Association was formed. Metropolitan Trades' Delegates met throughout the 1850s, to co-ordinate pressure on the government over the Friendly Societies' Bill, to campaign against 'systematic overtime' and to assist striking workers.

Permanent trades councils begin to spread from the end of the 1850s. Glasgow and Sheffield both formed councils in 1858, the former after meetings and demonstration in support of the unemployed, the latter after a printers' strike at the *Sheffield Times*. Delegates from London trades met early in 1859 to give assistance to a strike of glass workers in the Midlands against the employers' attempt to introduce the 'document'. A few months later they were meeting to support the London building workers struggling for the nine-hour day. What emerged was the need for an organisation to collate information, to co-ordinate activities and to get the union case across to a wider public. It was William Allan of the ASE who proposed that there should be a 'standing committee of all the trades of London . . . in order to meet crises like the present'.[13] A seven-, later a fifteen-man council was set up in July 1860, elected by a general meeting of delegates. Other councils began to appear. Barrow, Bolton, Bristol, Edinburgh, Greenock, Halifax, Leeds, Nottingham, Preston and Warrington established councils in the early 1860s. The years of industrial unrest, 1865 and 1866, brought councils for Wolverhampton, Birmingham and Manchester and Salford. Between 1855 and 1866 at least 24 trades councils had come into existence and although some of them did not survive into the 1870s, in most of the main cities these became permanent organisations. Most trades councils tried to make themselves the spokesmen for the unions and for the working class generally in their areas. They had two broad roles, which were not always compatible. First, they were intended to be the focus for co-ordinating support in major disputes, both local and elsewhere. They were the means by which delegates from striking workers from different parts of the country collecting financial support could be checked out and put in touch with local societies. Secondly, they all saw themselves as having the task of trying to create a public opinion that was more sympathetic to trade unionism.

Because of its size and the fact that London was the headquarters for a number of the largest societies, the London Trades Council was inevitably especially important. Unions seeking support for industrial action tended to approach London to get 'credentials' from the Trades Council to allow them to appeal to the big unions. The new Council also attracted many, including some former Chartists, who saw it as a possible focus for political activity. But there was deep-seated resistance to trade unions getting involved in political activity. Many saw politics as divisive, as weakening the industrial side of unionism and as possibly attracting hostile political intervention. What the Council did encourage were amalgamations. Its report of 1864 noted,

> It is worthy to remark that societies after they amalgamate, or otherwise become large, steer clear of strikes and yet raise and sustain their wages much easier and with less expense than small societies have done, or, we believe, ever will do. This may be accounted for through the power, in the shape of men and money, which the large societies have at their command, and which never fail to be appreciated by the employers, whenever the contending parties confront each other. We therefore would advise all societies to amalgamate, should circumstances favour them so doing.[14]

Such arguments did not appeal to many of the smaller societies which had stayed out of earlier amalgamations. George Potter of the Progressive Carpenters and manager of the recently launched *Bee-Hive* newspaper, emerged as the leading spokesman of these smaller societies on the Trades Council. Tension became increasingly focused on personal rivalry between him and Robert Applegarth, general secretary of the larger Amalgamated Carpenters.

When, during a strike of Birmingham building workers against the 'discharge note' and for payment by the hour, Applegarth tried to assert the authority of the executive of the ASCJ by condemning unofficial action, Potter's *Bee-Hive* attacked

Applegarth, not because he was advocating moderation, but because he was undermining the position of workers who were already on strike. Potter's argument was that once a strike had been embarked upon then it should be supported and that those on the spot knew better than any central executive what was necessary. By 1865 tension within the Trades Council was threatening to destroy it and there was much bitterness caused by Potter's attempts to create a London Working Men's Association as an alternative to the Council. During 1866 the Council struggled to maintain its affiliated societies and achieve any kind of united voice.

Courting the Public

Probably, the really new feature of the ASE was its high public profile. Partly this was from choice, partly from force of circumstances. Inevitably, a new organisation of the size of the ASE was going to attract attention. It emerged at a time when the press was expanding and strikes were news. But it also courted publicity deliberately. To be a national union it needed good communication and to make itself known quickly. William Allan recognised that the new, cheaper press was creating a public opinion which could influence events and could itself be manipulated. The very fact that it was decided that the headquarters of the union should be in London rather than in industrialised Lancashire was a sign that the Society's advance would depend on power and influence, not just on membership. Other union leaders too recognised the importance of winning public support. Important links were forged by the London leaders with the increasingly influential intellectual class amongst the journalists, lawyers and civil servants, first through the Christian Socialists around F. D. Maurice, then the Positivists, such as Frederic Harrison and E. S. Beesly and, through them, with the wider group of Liberal-Radical politicians.[15]

Trade unions had long faced a hostile press and this continued in the 1850s and 1860s. They were attacked as destructive of British competitiveness, tyrannical in their attitudes towards both management and workers, run by agitators, 'for the protection of the dunce, the drunkard and the unskilful' according to Thomas Fairbairn, the Manchester engineering employer.[16] It was claimed that they intimidated workmen and employers by violence and were against the spirit of the age by trying to maintain a protective system at a time when, it was agreed, market forces should have free rein. They were valueless since they sought to flout the laws of political economy when they tried to alter wages which only supply and demand could really affect. To combat such all-pervasive views trade unionists used a variety of different means. There were sympathetic publications, usually published by Owenites and radicals from earlier decades; papers such as *Reynolds' Newspaper*, *Lloyd's Weekly Newspaper*, the *Glasgow Sentinel* and the *Potteries Examiner*. An important product of the London nine-hours movement was the launching of the *Bee-Hive* newspaper, by George Potter.

But union leaders also set out to win friends who could get access to a wider, middle-class public. Through their interest in co-operation, Allan and the ASE leadership had contacts with the Christian Socialists who proved vital allies when the newly formed Social Science Association investigated *Trades Societies and Strikes*. This report, published in 1860, countered many of the popular assumptions about trade unions. They were not run by agitators, but by men 'superior in intelligence and moderation' to the majority of workmen. Far from causing strikes they were often a restraint upon them, offering 'a cool and moderate view of a question in dispute'. Those who belonged to unions also tended to be the better workmen, 'superior both in ability and steadiness to non-society men'. In the 1860s they found additional allies among the group of Positivists who were trying to challenge some of the basic assumptions of *laissez-faire* and saw unions as a way of assisting the transformation to a society where the interests of the individual would be subordinate to those of the wider community.

Union leaders also began to develop links with influential Liberal-Radical politicians, who were themselves looking for allies in their battles against the continuing aristocratic dominance of British society. A number of union leaders became involved in various radical causes in the 1860s, sharing platforms with middle-class activists on issues like support for Italian and Polish independence. They associated with John Bright, a Rochdale businessman and MP for Birmingham, in support of the anti-slavery cause in the American Civil War and in return Bright came to see them as potential allies in his campaigns against aristocratic privilege. They collaborated in the growing call for parliamentary reform. Many of these middle-class Radicals were, like Bright himself, businessmen; all had links with the local business communities in the constituencies which they represented and contributed to changes in employers' attitudes towards unions. The philosophical underpinning of Liberal Radicalism, classical political economy, was also beginning to change. John Stuart Mill led the way with a revision of his *Principles of Political Economy* in 1862, which accepted that there was a necessary role for trade unions: 'the indispensable means of enabling the sellers of labour to take due care of their own interests under a system of competition'.[17]

The need to win over influential support and public opinion was increasingly apparent to most trade unionists and resulted in a number of national conferences in the 1860s. In 1864, as part of a campaign launched by the Glasgow Trades Council against the Master and Servant Acts, a national conference of trade union representatives was held in London over three days to press for legislation to modify the Acts.[18] There was still pressure for defensive structures. Eighteen sixty-five and 1866 saw an increased incidence of lock-outs by employers' organisations. In response to this, the Sheffield Association of Organised Trades called a conference in July 1866 out of which came a short-lived organisation, the United Kingdom Alliance of Organised Trades, which by the end of the year claimed 60 000 members through 60 affiliated societies. It could not survive the outcry against Sheffield unions which followed attacks on non-unionists in 1866.

The Junta

The Friendly Societies Act of 1855 had provided the means by which some trade unions with extensive friendly benefits and large funds could take action against officers who were

nice neat term which has continued to attract historians. According to the Webbs this group of trade union leaders, Applegarth of the Carpenters, Allan of the Engineers, Daniel Guile of the Ironfounders, Charles Coulson of the Bricklayers and George Odger, secretary of the London Trades Council, had acted together as a kind of committee of trade unions through the London Trades Council since 1864. The Webbs painted them as enlightened modernisers against the backward-looking George Potter. Others have accepted the argument that the so-called 'Junta' provided a national leadership. But this is grossly to exaggerate both their unity of purpose and their influence. Few wanted to get caught in the personal animosity which existed between Applegarth and Potter and at no time, other than in the Conference of Amalgamated Trades, did these leaders act effectively as a 'joint committee of the officers of the national societies'. But the threat to their funds and, indeed, even possibly to their survival as trade unions did bring these key figures together in 1867. They were aware that the attacks on trade unionism from employers and politicians had been mounting over the previous two years. Opponents of the extension of democracy were painting unions as violent and dangerous class conspiracies. Employers in many parts of the country were collaborating with the clear intention of breaking trade unionism. The judgment in the Bradford Boilermakers' case, the *Hornby* v. *Close* decision came on top of this. It dispelled the idea that registration under the Friendly Societies' Act of 1855 ensured protection from dishonest officials and was interpreted as part of a general onslaught on trade unionism. It convinced them of the need to get involved in political action.

The immediate concern of Applegarth and the amalgamated unions was to get protection for those unions who, like themselves, were registered under the Friendly Societies' Act. There is little doubt that they saw their interests as different from those of the smaller societies. The first meeting of the Conference of Amalgamated Trades was held in January 1867, and supported a Private Member's Bill which would have given protection to the funds of registered societies. In this they generally showed an insensitivity towards those unions which were not registered and towards provincial pretensions. George

Potter seized on this and called a national conference of those unions not included in the Conference of Amalgamated Trades and of trades councils, in St Martin's Hall in March 1867. It was intended as a deliberate challenge to Applegarth and to the now much-weakened London Trades Council. Delegates from 30 provincial unions and nine trades councils attended and set up their own committee to prepare for the Royal Commission. It was not a question of Potter's conference speaking for more militant elements. Almost all the delegates favoured conciliation and arbitration for settling disputes every bit as much as Applegarth and his associates, but their interests were different. Most of them, without the large reserves of the ASE and the ASCJ, did not believe that registration as a friendly society was a solution. William Matkin of the General Union of Carpenters believed that 'we shall destroy our objects as a trade union, because by registering, *we shall expose the whole of our financial position*'.[21] Most were there because they resented London claims to speak for all of the country.

Impressed by the effective publicity which the conference achieved and still concerned to win the propaganda debate in favour of trade unionism, S. C. Nicholson, the president of the Manchester and Salford Trades Council, called what is usually taken as the founding conference of the Trades' Union Congress in June 1868.[22] The initial structure was modelled on the Social Science Association whose annual conferences discussed presented papers, but there was an immediate decision by the 34 delegates to turn it into an annual meeting which could act as a pressure group on Parliament and encourage collaboration between unions.

Meanwhile, the Conference of Amalgamated Trades had largely fallen apart. The failure of the Private Member's Bill to protect funds and another hostile court decision which seemed to threaten the right to strike had convinced the Conference that unions needed wider protection than merely of their funds. It forced a reconciliation with Potter and they agreed to act together to support a bill based on the Minority Report of the Royal Commission. But before the Bill was passed the national leadership of the unions now fell to the rather more representative Parliamentary Committee of the Trades Union Congress, with George Howell, a former bricklayer, who had made his reputation as secretary of the Reform League, as its secretary, William Allan as treasurer and George Potter as chairman. Initially there were only three other members, but it was gradually enlarged.

Trade Unions and the Law

It was pressure from the Conference of Amalgamated Trades which ensured that they had at least two sympathetic voices on the Commission: the London barrister, Frederic Harrison and the Christian Socialist writer, Thomas Hughes. Robert Applegarth and William Allan were impressive witnesses before the Commission, arguing that their organisations should be seen predominantly as friendly societies and that far from instigating strikes they were mainly a restraint on these. Harrison's Minority Report powerfully pressed the Applegarth argument that some trade unions had changed and were a force for order and stability in industrial relations and therefore ought to have their funds protected.[23] Harrison argued that the big national societies, 'which possess very large funds and great power over their respective trades, are those against which there exists least cause for complaint'. A relatively sympathetic government came up with a couple of stop-gap measures in response to all this lobbying: first, the so-called Russell Gurney's Act of 1868 which, while carefully not mentioning trade unions, provided the means for action by unions in cases of larceny or embezzlement; second, the Trades Unions' Funds Protection Act of 1869, a temporary measure which allowed a society, even if deemed to be in restraint of trade, to take legal action.

The success of the unions before the Royal Commission had been remarkable. They had not necessarily won the argument, but it was the Minority Report which shaped future legislation. A measure of the success in winning the public case was the way in which the press handled the campaign in Newcastle-upon-Tyne among engineering workers for a nine-hour day in 1870–1. *The Times* denounced the employers' resistance 'as imprudent and impolitic'; the *Spectator* declared that there could be little sympathy for 'masters who reply cavalierly by lawyers' letters to their men's demands'. The *Pall Mall Gazette* found the union demand 'perfectly reasonable'. The *Spectator* also believed that John Burnett, the men's leader, would make a splendid MP.[24]

The substantive measure which emerged was the 1871 Trade Union Act which made permanent the protection of the funds of *registered* unions and apparently removed any liability for being 'in restraint of trade'. Gladstone argued that it was the continuation of a policy of *laissez-faire*, 'in all economic matters the law to take no part', with any taint of criminal conspiracy removed. But employer pressure within the Liberal Party meant that specific criminal offences of 'molestation', 'obstruction' and 'intimidation' by workmen were retained. These poorly defined words had been a feature of legislation affecting unions since 1825. Court cases in 1851 had ruled that it was unlawful, even by peaceful persuasion, to try to get others to leave their employment. The Molestation of Workmen Act of 1859 allowed that 'merely agreeing with others to fix wages or hours or by endeavouring in a peaceable way and reasonable manner to persuade others to cease or abstain from work for that purpose' was not criminal, but it still left room for hostile interpretations. During the 1860s, courts were developing concepts of civil conspiracy, that the existence of a combination might in itself make an action a criminal 'threat' or 'molestation', which if done by an individual was not criminal. This was reaffirmed in 1867 in a case involving London tailors.

An outcry co-ordinated by the third TUC, held in London in March 1871, succeeded in getting the criminal clauses removed from the Trade Union Act although they were incorporated in a separate Criminal Law Amendment Act. Although a mere threat to strike was no longer a statutory offence, in some ways the Criminal Law Amendment Act made the situation worse, since the House of Lords extended the list of the undefined and imprecise illegalities in the Bill by adding 'watching and besetting' and 'persistently following'. This provided the opportunity for hostile judges to interpret 'molestation' as almost any action which could be regarded as 'an unjustifiable annoyance and interference with the masters in the conduct of their business'. Miners' wives in Mountain Ash in Wales and farm labourers' wives in Chipping Norton in

Oxfordshire found themselves jailed for hooting at strike-breakers. It also allowed Mr Justice Brett, in the case of the London gas stokers in 1872, to find that the threat to strike to get an employer to reinstate a worker victimised for trade union activity, was a criminal conspiracy in common law, thus effectively undoing most of the gains of the 1871 Act.

What the separation of the criminal clauses from the Trade Union Act did do, however, was to permit a focused campaign for repeal of the Criminal Law Amendment Act. Over the next three years, there was a demand for equal treatment before the law, something which had been a persistent trade union demand.[25] There were various demonstrations against the Act and workers displayed some of their recently acquired political clout by voting against Liberal candidates who were opposed to repeal. As a result of that and an effective campaign by Liberal Radical friends of Labour such as A. J. Mundella (but also, more surprisingly, by Robert Lowe, no admirer of trade unions), Disraeli's Government substantially modified the Act in 1875 to the trade unions' advantage with the Conspiracy and Protection of Property Act. It laid down that nothing done 'in contemplation and furtherance of a trade dispute' would be criminal unless the action itself was criminal, and it specifically permitted peaceful picketing. The Employers and Workmen Act, replacing the terminology of Master and Servant, gave employer and employee equality before the law in breach of contract cases. Both were now civil causes. The 1876 Trade Union Act Amendment Act also extended protection of funds to all trade unions, not just to those which otherwise would have been 'in restraint of trade'.

The Unskilled and Unorganised

Almost all of the mid-century unions were concerned with organising skilled workers. The initial purpose of most of them had been to limit entry into their particular craft to those who had served an agreed apprenticeship or training or, at the very least, were capable of earning a 'standard' rate of pay. In other cases they were trying to ensure that new technology which replaced tasks formerly undertaken by skilled workers none the less remained in the hands of their members and were not taken by new, less skilled and less well-paid workers. They saw their role as being to hold out those who might threaten the position of their members, hence their hostility to women workers. There was no hostility to women organising once they were well-established in particular jobs, but there was a deep hostility to women trying to penetrate new areas of work. It was seen as an inevitable prelude to a general wage reduction. In resisting women, men's unions were able to play on Victorian perceptions of the centrality of the family. The Bookbinders' Union in the 1860s, for example, accused employers of going against biblical teaching, 'by taking away men's role as breadwinner'.[26] The Scottish Typographical Society argued that allowing women to become printers would 'unfit them for the active and paramount duties of female society'.[27]

There had always been attempts by less skilled workers to organise unions. In most cases such attempts were short-lived. The obstacles to their success were great: the casual nature of much of the work; the ease with which new workers could be trained to a particular task; the pressure on jobs from displaced rural workers; the lack of education and organising skill; the low level of earnings. But one can find examples of general labourers' unions as early as the 1830s. In the 1850s Clydeside had a Harbour Labourers' Society. During the London building lock-out of 1859 there was a Builders' Labourers' Union.

The best opportunities for the less skilled (for few experienced workers are without particular skills) came when economic conditions were good and there was high demand for labour. The generally good conditions in most areas in the late 1860s and the boom conditions everywhere in the early 1870s proved just such an opportunity and many new unions appeared. Many of these were in the ports. London dock workers resisted a wage cut in 1871 with a Labour Protection League, which claimed 30 000 members within a year, and London, Liverpool, Hull and Glasgow all had unionism among dockers in the early 1870s. Scavengers, shop assistants, postal workers, omnibus workers, gas stokers, builders' labourers, among many others, also began to organise. The hitherto only partially and intermittently organised railway workers, with the assistance of the Liberal brewer and railway director, Michael Bass, formed the Amalgamated Society of Railway Servants (an interesting anachronistic term which said much about industrial relations in the railways) in 1871 and a similar Scottish Society was formed in the following year. London gas stokers organised the Amalgamated Gas Stokers' Union during a strike in 1872 and ended with five leaders sentenced to a year in jail under the Criminal Law Amendment Act. At the end of 1872, a conference of lightermen, carmen, railwaymen and members of the left-wing Land and Labour League resulted in the formation of an Amalgamated Labour Union with a central council which had to give approval for strike action, just as in some of the craft unions.

The movement which most caught the public imagination was the so-called 'revolt of the field', when the notoriously poorly paid farm workers began to organise. There had been some abortive efforts to form protective societies in Scotland, in Dorset and in Lincolnshire in the 1860s, but the special opportunities created in the early 1870s, when farm workers were being attracted in huge numbers to the booming industries, thus improving the bargaining position of those who remained, allowed something more substantial to emerge. The remarkable Methodist lay preacher, Joseph Arch, the secretary of the Warwickshire Agricultural Labourers' Society formed in 1872, was able to link it with similar societies in Lincolnshire, Huntingdonshire, Kent and Sussex, all of which had appeared at roughly the same time, in a National Agricultural Labourers' Union. By 1873 it claimed 72 000 members and 982 branches. It faced immense hostility from the landowners and farmers who saw the union as nothing short of a 'communist' challenge to the entire social system.[28]

Much is often made of the hostility between skilled and unskilled workers, with the frequently quoted remark of Thomas Wright, who wrote under the *nom de plume* of 'the Journeyman Engineer', that unions 'have little regard for the unskilled labourers attached to the trades, and are, above all other men, bent on "keeping them in their places", upon seeing them remain unskilled labourers, and not "creep[ing] into the trade", while whatever pity they have for those most to be pitied of all human beings, the agricultural labourers, is largely met with contempt'.[29] As against that, there are numerous examples of skilled workers rallying to the support of the unskilled. A few months after Arch formed his union, a meeting of London unions was called to support it, although the London Trades Council fell out with Arch over his attempt to centralise most of the union funds, and they gave encouragement to the alternative 'Federal Union of Agricultural and General Labourers', which maintained local control of funds. Applegarth assisted Patrick Kenny to form a General Labourers' Union and George Potter and Henry Broadhurst, the future secretary of the TUC, both attended the inaugural meeting of the Gas Stokers' Union. Labourers, seamen and dockers' unions were all represented in the London Trades Council by the spring of 1873. Edinburgh Trades Council invited a Labourers' Association to join the Council as early as 1868. Similar examples can be found in many other towns.

It was middle-class sympathisers who were behind the efforts to organise women workers. In July 1874 Emma Paterson founded the Women's Protective and Provident League, which organised women bookbinders and the sweated workers in feather and artificial-flower work and in shirt-making in the East End of London. It was intended as an umbrella organisation to encourage membership of existing unions or to set up new unions. It grew slowly among laundresses, tailoring workers and weavers. The Scottish Tailors' Union, while determinedly excluding women from their own union and workshops, set up the Benefit Society for Glasgow Working Women in 1876.[30]

Few of these unions of the unskilled survived the economic downturn of the second half of the 1870s. Many had been largely wiped out in industrial disputes. Activists faced victimisation. Agricultural depression decimated Arch's union, which had slumped to 15 000 members by the end of the decade and continued to decline. But it would be wrong to see unionism among the unskilled as entirely disappearing. Little pockets of organisation persisted. Liverpool docks saw mass strike action in 1874 and Hull docks in 1877 and again in 1879. A Liverpool Union of Stevedores, Labourers and Quay Porters and a Birkenhead Amalgamated Dock Labourers' Union were formed in 1879 and peaked in 1881, only to melt away.[31] But, generally, even if there is no clear evidence of union organisation, workers in particular localities knew which leaders to look to for advice. Where there was some particular expertise an element of organisation could survive. The stevedores in the docks, for example, required to load the ships, generally managed to maintain some effective organisation. Railway unions survived, even if not recognised by the employers, and in spite of splits when engine drivers and signalmen formed their own unions in 1880.

The striking feature of the 30 years from the 1850s was undoubtedly the emergence of large national organisation: 44 000 in the ASE, nearly 18 000 in the Amalgamated Carpenters, 13 000 in the Operative Stonemasons, 18 000 in the United Society of Boilermakers by 1880. Improved communications by train and by telegraphy and improved knowledge, with the great expansion of a cheaper press, all made nation-wide organisation easier to sustain. The development of national markets brought common problems and encouraged efforts to achieve standardisation of earnings and conditions. Collaboration between unions was firmly in place through permanent trades councils, providing a forum for debate and publicity. The Trades' Union Congress with its Parliamentary Committee and a permanent general secretary was well established by the 1870s and nation-wide in its coverage. The Mayor of Nottingham gave delegates a civic reception in 1872. But alongside the large organisations there was a plethora of tiny outfits catering for specialist groups of workers, often concentrated in a few localities. Some of these could be very effective precisely because of their specialisation, but many others struggled to survive.

Actual numbers of members in unions and the density of union membership are difficult to come by. It is impossible to be exact and historians tend to repeat the guesses of earlier historians. Henry Mayhew's estimate at the beginning of the 1850s that around 10 per cent of London craft workers were organised readily became converted into a national estimate. Frederic Harrison suggested numbers of 'not short of half a million' in 1865, but argued that in times of conflict they could call on an equal number of men who were not members of the society.[32] At the 1867 Royal Commission the secretary of the Midland Builders' Association suggested a range of levels of unionisation from 6 per cent among brickmakers to 10 per cent of carpenters, 19 per cent of bricklayers and 30 per cent of plasterers. Union membership may have been as much as halved in the second half of the 1870s from a peak in 1873, but even those numbers were still as high as they had been in 1870.[33] George Howell, even in the economically bad year of 1879, believed that among groups like cotton spinners, provincial printers and London bookbinders unionisation was as high as 90 per cent; among boilermakers 75 per cent and even among a group like cabinet-makers scattered in relatively small workshops, 25 per cent.

3 The Coming of Collective Bargaining, 1850–80

It would be ridiculous to deny that there was a marked change in the tone of trade unionism in mid-century. What is debatable is *how* extensive the change was, how far a change of tone covered continuity in tactics and what caused whatever changes there were. As Royden Harrison has pointed out, however, 'whether or not one discerns a basic continuity in trade union history during the second and third quarter of the nineteenth century largely depends on what one is interested in'.[1] An examination of leading trade unionists and employers can come up with a very different picture from a study of the work-place and, as Kitson Clark has said, despite all the protestations of the leaders, at the work-place the squeeze was still applied to employers wherever possible.

When he took over as secretary of the ASCJ Robert Applegarth saw his task as being 'to raise so far as I knew how to do it, the whole tone and character of trade unionism'.[2] Trades councils saw it as their task to 'improve' or 'elevate' the working class, 'morally and socially'. In the 1850s and 1860s trade union meetings moved out of public houses into their own halls and offices or into temperance reading rooms. Daniel Guile of the Ironfounders and Charles Coulson of the Bricklayers both told the Royal Commission that trade unionism had rescued their members from drunkenness and dissipation. William Allan in his evidence repeated the refrain 'we are averse to strikes', 'the executive council does all it can to prevent strikes', 'the members generally are decidedly opposed to strikes'. George Odger, in a much-quoted statement, declared, 'Strikes are to the social world what wars are to the political world. They become crimes unless they are prompted by absolute necessity.' George Potter, often portrayed as a militant, was no different in his public statements, always keen to get across to the public 'our wish to be moderate in all our demands': 'Trades' Unions, as now organised and conducted, are among the foremost proofs of the improved mental training of the working men, and, at the same time, of their increased power of self-control and self-restraint.'[3] With words like 'self-restraint' and 'self-control', and the emphasis on improvement, the trade union leaders were deliberately tapping into the mid-Victorian self-image. It was both how they wanted to be seen and how they saw themselves. Trade unions were the means for self-improvement in an age that believed passionately in the need for and the possibilities of improvement. It was neither cynical deceit nor self-delusion. The evidence of change and of a new standing for trade unionism was there to be seen.

But no more was it a question of an uncritical swallowing of middle-class propaganda. The need to defend positions against the encroachments of employers was never abandoned. 'We must dispute every inch of the ground with the capitalist and not flinch one iota', Richard Harnott told his Operative Stonemasons' Society.[4] The *Flint Glass Makers' Magazine* declared that 'strikes have been the bane of Trades Unions', but it went on, 'it must not be thought from the above that we have abandoned the idea of strikes in all cases; we know that in some cases they cannot be avoided'.[5] And Applegarth specifically rejected any crude individualism, arguing that the purpose of trade unionism was to apply a 'humanising influence' to society and 'to lift up the less fortunate to a proper position'.[6] Despite the public protestations, there was no shortage of major strikes amongst all kinds of workers in the quarter century after 1850. The tone was different, the tactics were more sophisticated, but the issues which were fought over and the positions which were defended were the same.

The ASE within a year of its formation was into strikes and a lock-out, as it tried to resist the use of men whom the union did not accept as qualified to operate planing and boring machinery. Twenty-six thousand Preston weavers held out for seven months in 1853–4 for the restoration of a ten per cent wage reduction.[7] The Flintglass Makers' Union of the Midlands, which the Webbs regarded as another example of a modern union, battled for six months in 1858–9 against an attempt to get them to accept an employer's right to employ a journeyman at under the agreed rate.[8] The Amalgamated Society of Carpenters and Joiners grew out of the alliances created during the protracted campaign by London building workers for a nine-hour working day in 1859 and 1860. One of the key roles intended for the trades councils which emerged in the late 1850s and 1860s was to provide the means by which assistance for striking workers could be provided effectively and a number of these councils arose out of major strikes: in Sheffield out of a printers' strike, in London out of the building workers' strike, in Wolverhampton in 1865 out of an extended plate-lock makers' dispute and in Birmingham in 1866 out of a bitter strike and lock-out of building trades. Alexander McDonald, the miners' leader, often portrayed as the most moderate and class-collaborative of unionists, told the Royal Commission, 'I am satisfied upon the whole . . . that strikes, although in those periods (of over-production) to which I have referred they have proved disastrous, yet as a whole they have been a gain to the men in wages.' By the 1870s, James Cronin suggests, strikes had 'become the dominant form of workers' collective action'.[9] Whatever was happening in this 'age of equipoise' workers and their unions were not docile.

Some Disputes

It is not surprising that there was no shortage of major industrial disputes in these years. It was, after all, a time of very rapid expansion of British industry, when many firms were enlarging their work-forces quickly and when new machine tools were being introduced. Inevitably, groups of workers felt threatened and unions were basically there to protect the position of specific groups. The major disputes were almost all about issues of managerial control, over how work should be carried out and who could be employed on particular tasks. The danger was from other workers who would be willing to undertake work more cheaply. The need for rapid expansion of the work-force encouraged employers to take on new labour who, even if they could not do all that a time-served craftsman could do, could be quickly trained to do different parts of the job. From early in the century craft unionists, like cabinet-makers, shoe-makers and tailors, had battled, with less and less success, against the division of labour and the growth of what they called the 'dishonourable' sections of their trade. Defining skill as having served an apprenticeship or being able to obtain the standard wage, and associating this with union membership, was the central tactic of unions of craft workers. Added to the threat from numbers was the threat from technological change. Each time new machines were introduced, which in many cases were intended to reduce the demand for some expensive skilled workers, the issue of who should man the new machines came to the forefront.

The policy of the new ASE in 1851 was to restrict the number of apprentices to one for every four journeymen; to resist the introduction of piecework, which they argued was essentially a 'slave-driving' mechanism; to drive out 'illegal men' who had not served their time; and to resist systematic overtime being required by employers. It was those issues which led to a dispute at the textile machine builders, Hibbert and Platt of Oldham, in April 1851. The engineers demanded the end of piecework and overtime and that labourers should not be allowed to operate boring, planing, shaping and slotting machines. They also sought the removal of an aggressive foreman, a regular cause of disputes, since it focused on the fundamental issue of how far workers had autonomy in their work patterns. After initial resistance, Platt conceded that the labourers would be phased out by Christmas. It encouraged action against other large firms in the area and, at the end of 1851, the executive of the ASE, pushed by rank-and-file pressure, agreed to ban all systematic overtime and piecework. The employers responded with the formation of the Central Association of Employers of Operative Engineers, linking firms mainly in the North-West and London. They instituted a lock-out and committed themselves not to employ any members of a trade union which sought to interfere 'with the regulations of any establishment, the hours or terms of labour, the contracts or agreements of employers or employed, or the qualification of terms of service'. Nor would they accept any deputations on any of these issues, but only deal with workmen individually.[10]

In February, the employers demanded that anyone to be re-employed had to sign a document renouncing union membership. It strengthened the determination of the workers to hold out. But the Society's resources were being rapidly swallowed up and they were increasingly dependent upon appeals to other unions. By May defeat had been conceded and over the next 14 years the Society had to be gradually rebuilt and there were few major strikes.

In the cotton industry of Lancashire, the hand-mule spinners had been battling since the 1830s to maintain control of the self-acting machines. The powerloom weavers, who had largely lost the struggle to control entry into the trade, were more directly concerned with maintaining wage levels. A series of strikes, to try to claw back the wage cuts which had been made in 1846, generated further organisation. In response, the employers, usually highly competitive, began to organise. Disputes culminated in a lock-out in Preston which lasted for seven months, with employers and authorities in other parts of the region rallying to the support of the Preston masters. The strike leaders were arrested and charged with 'molesting' and 'obstructing'.

The great strike of Midlands Glass Makers at the end of 1858 stemmed from one of the employers in Stourbridge trying to employ an apprentice as a journeyman at less than the usual rate. At the same time another dispute broke out over the attempt by another employer to take on more apprentices. About 20 of the manufacturers set up a Defence Association and, by the end of the year, trade unionists were being locked out in all the main glass-making areas. Other unions rallied to support. Delegates from the London trades met to organise an appeal and raised some £400. The employers tried to insist on a document to renounce union membership, but this was eventually modified to one declaring 'I will not attempt, by myself or through others, to interfere with your freedom in the management of your works, more especially in reference to the engagement of the men or number of apprentices whom you choose to employ.' Eventually, in March 1859, a settlement was reached which gave the union almost complete victory.[11]

As Richard Price has shown, central to a high proportion of the builders' strikes of the 1850s and early 1860s were the issues of machinery, overtime and piecework and the authority of foremen. These issues remained a concern of the London builders who launched the nine hours' movement in 1859. By focusing on hours and the need for leisure, the unions were conscious of how much more appealing a case could be made to a wider middle-class public. But they also saw the reduction of hours as a way to put an end to cheap labour and generally to create more stability and security for regular workers in the industry. As the employers recognised, the issue was about 'controlling the labour market'.[12] The dispute in July 1859 was triggered by the action of Trollopes, one of the largest firms of London building contractors, to dismiss a member of the deputation who had pressed for a nine-hour day. Tension had been building up for some months and a number of the building firms had been trying to create company unions committed to a no-strike policy. When the Trollopes' men struck, every large builder in London shut out their workers and a Central Master Builders' Association demanded that a 'document' be signed before workers would be readmitted. The immediate effect was to make the issue one which all unions regarded as their concern and a potential threat to their existence. Once again the other London trades rallied to support: £800 came from Glasgow and Manchester, £500 from Liverpool. The London Compositors gave £620 and an astonishing £3100 came from the ASE. Although the nine hours was not achieved, at the end of February the employers agreed to withdraw the 'document'. They did, however, increasingly move to payment by the hour as opposed to the day, a major gain for management. The effect of the dispute was an influx of new members into the building unions and a stimulus to the reorganisation and amalgamation of unions. The battles over hours and job control continued through the 1860s.

Other workers began to push demands for better hours and wages in the improving economic conditions of the 1860s, often pulling their union leadership rather tardily behind them. North-East iron shipbuilding workers in 1863 successfully resisted wage cuts and the introduction of a new scheme for grading workers. They brought out both unionists and non-unionists and provided support for non-unionist strikers. In the following year a strike wave spread from Birkenhead and Liverpool to all the iron shipbuilding areas and, by picking off one employer at a time, gains were made. By the end of 1865, as trade turned down, employers began to pull back the gains. The unions tried to respond to growing unemployment by pressing for a nine-hour day and there were some initial gains, but on the Clyde a new Shipbuilders and Engineers' Employers' Association determined to hold out against concessions. Once again the 'document' was brought into play, not just requiring the renouncing of all unions, but 'that they will neither assist morally nor pecuniarily, directly or indirectly, any workmen who may be locked out, or who may be on strike in opposition to the interests of the employers'. Engineers and Boilermakers and others were locked out. The workers suffered total defeat. In all these disputes the executive of the Boilermakers' Union urged restraint and, on more than one occasion, gave no financial support to strikers. The Clyde defeat led to bitter recrimination and the breakaway of many of the Scottish workers to form a separate Scottish union.[13]

The greatest boom of the nineteenth century got underway at the end of the 1860s and for the first three years of the 1870s demand for labour was such that workers were placed in a unprecedently powerful bargaining position, which they seized. Among many of the skilled workers the focus, once again, was on the nine-hour day. The engineers on Tyneside and Wearside led the way with a demand for a reduction in the basic working week from 59 hours to 54. A well-known local activist, Andrew Gourley, led both union and non-union engineers, blacksmiths, iron moulders, boilermakers, brass founders, pattern-makers, coppersmiths and plumbers in Sunderland out on strike in April 1871. The Sunderland employers conceded and the focus switched to Newcastle. There a Nine Hours' League led by John Burnett co-ordinated the campaign. After a strike lasting from May until October agreement was reached, which gave the men most of what they demanded. Hours came down to 54 and wages were raised by something like 11.6 per cent. The strike was entirely organised and led by district officials. Allan and the London executive of the ASE were ambivalent in their attitude, to say the least. The initial advice had been to refrain from 'hasty action' and it was not until the strike was well into its second month that the executive put out an appeal for support. John Burnett was to get his reward for his skilful leadership of the campaign by being elected as Allan's successor as general secretary in 1874.[14]

The success on Tyneside was followed by movements elsewhere. The Clydeside shipbuilders were able to push their hours down to 51, again mainly through unofficial action. The sharp end to the boom after 1873 meant that the second half of the 1870s was largely a vain struggle to resist the counter-offensive of the employers. Burnett's strategy was to defend the nine hours even if it meant accepting wage cuts. The employers, united in the Iron Trades' Employers' Association, were determined to restore ten hours. With unemployment in some areas creeping up to nearly 30 per cent and the ASE's finances creaking under the heavy payment of unemployment benefit, there was little ability to resist. Sidney Smith, the aggressive secretary of the Iron Trades' Employers' Association, argued that 'the time has arrived . . . when the idle hours which have been unprofitably thrown away must be reclaimed to industry and profit by being directed to reproductive work'. In 1878 Clyde workers' hours were pushed up to 54 hours and wages fell by about 20 per cent. None the less, in England the nine-hour day was successfully defended. The ASE spent as much on strikes in 1879 – 'the darkest year in our life' – as they had in the whole of the previous 26 years. Bankruptcy was narrowly avoided, but the employers had not proved able enough nor united enough to break the nine hours' ceiling.[15]

New Attitudes

Clearly, striking was still very much part of the arsenal of trade unionism. It would be wrong, however, to argue, as A. E. Musson tries to do, that there was no change. The leaders of the bigger unions which emerged in the 1850s and 1860s, undoubtedly tried to curb precipitate strike action. Almost all the strikes discussed above started as unofficial rank-and-file movements. The leadership generally favoured centralising decision-making. In national societies the resources, in theory, belonged to all and therefore there should be central approval of strike action. Local activists tended not to see it in these terms. Also, the strike weapon was just one of the tactics which union leaders used. Their approach was becoming much more sophisticated than in the past. In order to be effective, there was a recognition that there had to be continuity; hence the emphasis placed on friendly society benefits. The ASE, whose friendly society side had been inherited from its predecessor unions, was aware that it had survived the major defeat of 1852 because it had a substantial benefits side. There was undoubtedly a big fall in membership and it was five years before it returned to the levels of 1851; but, even so, fewer members baled out of the union than might have been expected when it was not in a position to offer effective industrial protection.

Others learned from the ASE's experience and, although few offered – or had workers well enough off to pay for – such a wide range of benefits as the ASE, few did not try to develop some limited benefit side. But in no way did this turn them into mere friendly societies wary about doing anything which threatened their friendly society funds. Nor, as some suggest, was the development of a trade union bureaucracy itself largely responsible for new, more conciliatory attitudes; in other words, that bureaucracy generates caution. A hostile contemporary was perfectly ready to argue the opposite, that 'smooth spoken secretaries may take credit for their unions for discouraging strikes, while actually ruling a trade by the threat of them'.[16] On more than one occasion Applegarth made it clear, as he did to the Royal Commission, 'that pure and simple ours is a trade society . . . although we have a number of excellent benefits in connection with it'.[17] Friendly benefits attracted membership and retained membership and so increased a union's bargaining strength. There was, however, an understandable concern not to dissipate resources in too many disputes. When the issue presented a clear threat to the position of unionism, such as the use of the 'document' or the 'discharge note' then resources were determinedly used to resist.

Secondly, unions recognised the importance of influencing

public opinion. An expanded and increasingly national press, as a result of Gladstone's removal of the so-called 'taxes on knowledge', with a greater awareness of what was going on in different parts of the country, meant that a localised dispute quickly became known throughout the country. A dispute in Sheffield or Wolverhampton would soon become the subject of an editorial in the London press and influence the perceptions of politicians and opinion-formers. Winning public support was a useful weapon and an increasingly necessary weapon if major disputes were to end in victory. Trade unions were still operating in a hostile environment. Public opinion was necessary to win any modifications of the laws which threatened the position of trade unions. Public opinion was also needed to win battles against employers, many of whom regarded unions as a challenge to their rights, to the mastery of their own business.

Thirdly, to be successful in controlling entry into the trade, in maintaining apprenticeship restrictions, and in retaining control of new machinery, unions needed recognition by employers. Unions' long-term effectiveness depended upon their being accepted as spokesmen for the workers and on the employers being willing to negotiate with them. In many ways this was the achievement of the mid-century decades. By the end of the 1860s there were signs that increasing numbers of employers were prepared to deal with unions. There was a recognition by some that trade unions could facilitate the process of change. A number of the employer witnesses at the Royal Commission recognised that union officials were better informed than the ordinary worker. They were readier to compromise. Thomas Brassay, the great railway contractor, claimed in 1873 that employers had reason to be grateful to 'the executive council of the unions' for 'accepting the use of machinery'.[18] The South Wales colliery owners found the union leaders in the 1870s ready to persuade their members to accept a shift system. In textiles, the need to negotiate on a myriad of cloth weights, patterns and widths to settle piece rates made an effective system of negotiating essential if endless stoppages were to be avoided. The Lancashire weavers' unions developed a group of highly skilled professional negotiators from the 1850s for that reason.[19] The first fully comprehensive agreement on mule-spinning rates came in 1869 with the Oldham list, by which it was agreed that any dispute should be tackled first by the secretaries of the employers' association and of the union, and, failing that, by a joint meeting of the two committees. Henry Broadhurst, president of the Stone-masons' Society, saw his union's central committee as 'an outside body, exempt from local prejudices' acting as a 'go-between'.[20]

Other employers faced with militant rank-and-file movements which could embrace both unionists and non-unionists, as many of the disputes of the 1860s had been, saw unions as a means of helping them impose labour discipline. More could be achieved by negotiation than by confrontation. Elsewhere, many large employers welcomed the stability which standard wage rates gave to their industry, confident that their efficiency would allow them to compete successfully rather than being undercut by some wage-cutting small employer. As Brassay again pointed out, 'the disposition to be liberal towards workmen is developed, as a general rule, in proportion to the business and capital of the employer'. Samuel Morley, with his 5000 hosiery workers, argued that as a result of unions having managed to achieve standardisation of wage rates, he could build up stocks – 'before I could not do that, because I was always afraid of some unscrupulous employer cutting me with lower prices'. Such attitudes were not just driven by short-term economic interests but by cultural perceptions on the part of employers who were concerned with wider goals of maintaining class harmony. As Patrick Joyce and Alan Fox have argued, it is part of the same process which had 'Captains of Industry' (itself a significant phrase) building churches, schools, literary institutes, and libraries in their communities, what they call a 'new paternalism'.[21] It was particularly strong in the Lancashire cotton industry, but also in the booming heavy engineering industries of the North-East. It involved recognising that the 'self-government' of unionism fitted with concepts of Liberal progress and was not necessarily in conflict with goals of class harmony. The Amalgamated Society of Railway Servants is one example of a union which was actually formed largely due to the efforts of middle-class philanthropists. Michael Bass poured time and money into it and for 20 years it had middle-class presidents. It saw its task to reduce hours and generally to improve conditions, but without strikes.[22]

Skilled workers gained most from these changes and most unions were unions of skilled workers. Many employers recognised unions as providing a service in identifying and even finding the best craftsmen. Skills were in short supply in a period of unprecedented growth, with unemployment (as far as can be estimated) at probably below 2 per cent of the working population, and so the wages of the skilled rose. It has been calculated that real wages rose by about a third between 1850 and 1875 with the gap between skilled and unskilled earnings widening. The skilled were also the ones who appeared to be developing those qualities of 'respectability' which were seen as essential to social harmony. They were the ones to whom the community efforts were directed. Hence the arguments that what was going on was the creation of an 'aristocracy of labour' which, in Hobsbawm's words, was 'better paid, better treated and generally regarded as more respectable than the mass of the proletariat'.[23] The presumption of a great deal of writing on the labour aristocracy was that, without the deliberate dividing of the working class by the tactics of Liberal employers and their political spokesmen in making concessions to a section of the working class, the Marxist predictions of the gradual development of a revolutionary consciousness among the working class (the roots of which were apparent in Chartism, it was assumed) would have come about. Instead, the better-off section of the working class, the natural leaders, was bought off, creating what Raymond Postgate 80 years ago labelled 'the servile generation'.[24]

The concept has increasingly come under attack, largely because of the difficulties of definition. While the cruder presentations of it in terms of almost conspiratorial manipulation to maintain social control are rightly abandoned, it would be premature to throw it out entirely as an explanatory tool. There is no doubt that many contemporary commentators saw a section of the working class which they wished to court and influence and they saw union membership as one feature of this section. Politicians like Gladstone and John Bright distinguished between the 'the respectable and the rough', the 'aristocracy of labour' and the 'residuum'. Social reformers like the Christian Socialists and the Positivists all saw trade unionism as providing the natural leaders of the working class they wanted to reform. And even the political economists – always much more sophisticated than their popularisers allowed – found a place for trade unionism.[25]

A fundamental flaw in linking the labour aristocracy and social harmony, as Henry Pelling pointed out, is that higher wages, improved living standards and an expanding economy provide opportunities to push forward working-class demands to a much greater extent than do periods of economic downturn. In the third quarter of the nineteenth century the bargaining position of skilled workers was stronger than it had ever been or was to be again for another three-quarters of a century. They were able to squeeze concessions from employers and government with strikes if necessary, but also, because of the strength of their bargaining position, without sustained strikes. Employers needed to make concessions and could afford to make concessions.

Conciliation and Arbitration

Of course, these are generalisations to which one can find many exceptions. There were numerous employers who had neither the means nor the psychology to give way to worker pressure. The statements of many employers display a deep-seated hostility to trade unionism as an affront to managerial authority. But the extent to which an orderly system of industrial relations began to develop in these years is pretty apparent. Numerous procedures came into existence to allow negotiation between employers and unions and, if necessary, conciliation and arbitration. Some predated 1850. In the Staffordshire potteries, for example, since 1836 all disputes were supposed to be referred to a committee of three employers and three workers with power to call in an arbitrator if they were unable to come to a decision. By the early 1850s, the silk weavers of Macclesfield, the carpet weavers of Scotland and the North of England, and the shipwrights of the Wear were all groups which had well-established mechanisms involving negotiation.

It was the need to settle an eleven-week strike in the Nottingham hosiery industry in 1860, at a time of high demand, that led to the setting up of the Nottingham Board of Arbitration for the Hosiery Industry with six members chosen by the employers' association and six workers' delegates chosen by a general vote organised by the union. It was particularly significant because it brought industrial peace to an industry which had been notoriously strike-prone and also because of the publicity given to it by A. J. Mundella, later a Liberal politician and minister. Mundella believed that union involvement was essential because only the unions had the means of ensuring that their members accepted the decisions and because he recognised that union leaders were generally a moderating influence, creating 'the greatest barrier we have between the ignorant workmen and ourselves', as he told the Royal Commission. Thanks to the work and publicity of Mundella and others, the arguments for the establishment of formal negotiating procedures rapidly gained ground in the late 1860s and early 1870s. Miners' leaders like Thomas Halliday and Alexander McDonald campaigned to get the TUC to commit itself to the principle of arbitration. It was due to their efforts that boards were established to cover most coalfields. John Kane, the secretary of the Ironworkers' Union, sought their help in 1869 and they persuaded David Dale of the Consett Iron Company to take the lead in persuading his fellow employers to establish a Board of Arbitration to cover the Teesside iron industry. The South Staffordshire iron trade followed in 1872. Other industries took it up: the boot and shoe industry of Leicestershire and the developing chemical industry of Northumberland and Durham both set up permanent bodies in 1875 and there were numerous *ad hoc* arrangements.

Although on occasion outside arbiters like Mundella or Dale or Thomas Hughes were called in, mostly differences had to be settled by members within the industry. It was almost impossible for an outsider to get to grips with the technical complexities of piece rates. It was always difficult to get agreement on the general level of wages, but the great hope behind trade union support for collective bargaining was that it would eradicate both variations in wages between firms and excessive fluctuations over time. What was wanted was the eradication of wage differences as a factor in competition between companies. Indeed, some like Alexander McDonald, had an even wider vision which foresaw a situation in which collaboration between employers and workers would eradicate competition and replace it with a producers' co-operative commonwealth.[26] However, employers steadfastly refused to allow profitability to be a factor in settling wage rates. They argued that price was what mattered and they generally pressed for a sliding scale by which wages were linked to selling price. Unions did on occasion argue that wages had to provide 'a reasonable level of comfort',[27] and union negotiators regularly brought in factors such as the state of the labour market, the level of wages in other industries, the cost of living and the quality of management to back up claims. But, with prices rising, most unions were willing enough to go along with rates linked to prices and during the 1870s a sliding scale was introduced in most of the iron and coal areas.

The gains for both sides were fairly obvious. The employers got order and stability and a reasonable prospect of unbroken production, all things for which they were prepared to sacrifice an element of managerial power. The unions got recognition and a clear place in the system; union officials gained status. But unions, too, had an interest in a stable system, which reduced the need for strikes – always a threat to a union. It can be argued that such was their bargaining position in the 1860s and 1870s that workers could have achieved more by a more aggressive policy, but there seems little doubt that that would merely have encouraged hostile legislation. By the mid-1870s, as profits began a long period of squeeze, there were signs that some employers felt that too many gains were being made by the workers. Even some of the best-known conciliation boards met less frequently. In April 1873 a National Federation of Associated Employers, consisting of some of the leading names in British industry, was formed as a political pressure group, initially to counter unionist pressure for repeal of the Criminal Law Amendment Act and the Master and Servant legislation. Through its journal *Capital and Labour*, it tried to rally employers to resist further concessions. 'The way to industrial peace is to prepare for war,' it declared. 'Preparation for "industrial war" will be a new guarantee of industrial peace.'[28] Employers were well-represented in the Liberal Party which held office until 1874, but a number were beginning to look to the Conservatives as better defenders of their interests.

It is a measure of the extent to which the unions had won the battle for public opinion that the Federation proved powerless to halt the progress of legislative reform. Although its witnesses won the argument before the Royal Commission on the Labour Laws, which the new Conservative Government had set up and which made limited recommendations, Disraeli's Home Secretary soon swept away the criminal sections of trade union legislation. The term 'Master and Servant' gave way to 'Employer and Workman' in the 1875 Act, equal before the law. Nine hours' factory legislation, the extension of regulation to workshops, further mines' regulation and employers' compensation for industrial accidents were all brought in over the next few years. The Federation's journal fell into the hands of ideologues who saw themselves as defenders of *laissez-faire* against encroaching collectivism and turned to the wider agenda of the Liberty and Property Defence League. Employers, generally more pragmatic in their attitudes, drifted away and by the early 1880s the Federation had collapsed.

In thirty years the position of trade unions in British society had undoubtedly been transformed. They had grown spectacularly in membership. They had achieved a stability as never before. They had lost the stigma of illegality. They had gained recognition from most substantial employers in the staple industries. The changes had come about through the combination of a whole series of factors. Economic prosperity gave workers the space to organise and to make gains; it also gave the employers the manœuvrability to make concessions. The conditions of skills shortages also forced concessions. The concern, in the aftermath of the tensions of the 1830s and 1840s, to achieve some measure of social harmony, helped to create a cultural atmosphere where compromise was demanded. Liberal optimism that 'improvement' was possible through the application of reason to social organisation drove forward the search for conciliatory mechanisms.

But there were growing signs that in the less favourable conditions of the second half of the 1870s attitudes were changing. Employers' organisations were breaking up as shrinking markets caused firms to look to themselves and at ways of undercutting their competitors. Union leaders were finding it more difficult to control their members. Boards of conciliation were not providing the hoped-for protection of wages. The ground was being laid for a new period of militancy.

4 Revival and Confrontation, 1880–98

Following the Webbs, most historians have continued to see the emergence of what they called 'new unionism' at the end of the 1880s as evidence of new directions in industrial relations. Clegg, Fox and Thompson began the multi-volume *History of British Trade Unions* in 1889 and called 'new unionism', 'one of the most colourful and baffling phenomena in British trade union history'. Many other historians, like the Webbs, tend to link it to the re-emergence of socialist movements in the 1880s and suggest that much of the new movement was shaped by socialist sympathisers. As Sidney Pollard has pointed out, all kinds of people had a vested interest in presenting the short sharp expansion of unionism as something distinctive. Older unionists, who had spent decades polishing a public image of moderation and reason, wished to distance themselves from what seemed to be the newer, more aggressive tones of the emerging unions. Many of the early writers on the period were at pains to show that socialists played a key role in organising the unskilled and that the upsurge of unionism was the evidence of a new class consciousness, which inevitably led on to independent labour and the demand for socialist policies. Later historians, in their search for the elusive class consciousness, latched on to this.[1]

Some, with that peculiarly myopic, London vision, see it as a movement which began in London with the dock strike of August 1889 or perhaps with the Bryant & May match-girls' strike of 1888. It is a view that has long been untenable, although highly persistent.[2] In fact, and not really surprisingly, the changes began in the industrial areas of the North well before August 1889 and were well underway before the middle-class socialists of London had met their first trade unionist.

Pollard suggests that the rise begins in 1886, but this is probably still to postdate the process. There has also been a tendency to assume that, despite the setbacks of the 1890s, the developments of the late 1880s and early 1890s were the start of a process which led inevitably to the bitter industrial unrest of the years immediately before 1914. This chapter will argue that a rather different chronology is required and that they were the product of longer term developments rather than the start of something dramatically different.

Signs of tension within trade unionism, including renewed debates over tactics, and within industrial relations, were appearing by the end of the 1870s. The gains of the mid-century had been possible because of the opportunities presented by economic growth. Wages linked to prices in sliding scales had delivered enough to satisfy both sides as long as prices were rising. By the end of the 1870s all of these conditions were less secure. Employers, experiencing falling profits, were railing against the constraints of a system which restricted their ability to cut wages. Increased competitiveness meant that collaboration among employers was difficult to maintain and boards of conciliation and employers' associations were not able to resist price-cutting for competitive advantage by vulnerable employers. The Dumbarton shipbuilder, William Denny, complained in 1877 that employers had more to fear from one another than from their workers: an employer's 'profits are more reduced by their competition than by any amount of strikes and shortening of hours'.[3] Trade unions, with wages tied to sliding scales, had little way of blocking wage cuts. The large unions like the ASE, paying out unemployment benefits, were seriously weakened by the mass unemployment of 1879 and at the same time were losing membership, although they recovered quickly. On the other hand, prices of foodstuffs were falling faster than wages and, for those in regular work, the 1870s and 1880s brought a clear rise in living standards. This in itself was an aid to trade unionism: more workers had additional resources to spend on trade union membership and workers were emboldened to risk strike action.

Trade Union Growth

While the difficult years of the early 1880s affected most unions, the pattern was still one of substantial growth. The ASE grew from 45 000 members in 1880 to 54 000 in 1888; the ASCJ from 18 000 to 25 000 and the Amalgamated Cotton Spinners from 12 000 to 25 000. Most guestimates suggest that something around 10 per cent of the possible work-force which had the potential for organisation were in unions at the end of the 1880s, about three quarters of a million members. It can be little more than a guess. There were a large number of tiny unions who rarely published membership figures. Membership in all unions tended to be either overestimated or underestimated according to circumstance: a desire for additional delegates at some conferences; a desire to reduce per capita payments at others; a desire to exaggerate the significance of a union. Although these tendencies did not disappear entirely, more confidence can be placed in the figures available from 1892 when official surveys by the Labour Department of the Board of Trade can be set against union-provided figures. The most authoritative calculations give a union membership of over 1.5 million in 1892, rising to over 2 million by 1900; a union density (membership: potential union membership) of 11.1 per cent in 1892, falling to just over 10 per cent in 1895 as most of the new unions collapsed, but rising by 1900 to 13.1 per cent.[4]

Membership was overwhelmingly male, with less than 3 per cent of potential women members organised. Such aggregate figures hide massive variations in the level of unionisation in different industries: around 60 per cent of coal miners and dockers in the early 1890s; around 30 per cent of metal and engineering workers and printers; around 25 per cent of cotton textile workers, glass workers, construction workers, seamen and those in footwear manufacture. At the other end, barely registering, were workers in agriculture and forestry and in the distribution industries; 6 per cent of those in food and drink industries; 5 per cent in local government and education. Such density is at least some indication of the industrial clout of unions within different industries, although there are many other factors that define a union's bargaining position.

New Unionism

The other feature of the period, the one to which most attention has been given, is the expansion of unionism to groups of workers hitherto poorly organised. As shown in the previous chapter, many such groups of workers had set up unions in the good years of the early 1870s, although few of the organisations survived for very long. But it is highly likely that elements of organisation did continue to exist and when opportunities presented themselves they re-emerged. Seamen in certain ports, for example, (not at all an easy group to organise, of course) continued to have some organisation.[5] A union existed in South Shields in the early 1880s, a Hull Seamen's Union emerged from a series of major waterfront disputes in 1881 and when Aberdeen seamen organised in 1884 they joined the South Shields' Union. A couple of years later, the Glasgow shipwright, Alexander Wilkie, with the backing of the Glasgow Trades Council, organised an Associated Mariners' Society to provide witnesses to a select committee looking at the possibility of extending employers' liability to cover seamen. Dockers in Hull were organising in the summer of 1881 and, in Aberdeen, shore labourers were on strike in 1883 and formed a union which sent delegates to the local trades council.

Aberdeen was less affected than many other areas by the depression of the 1880s. The port was expanding rapidly with the development of steam-trawling for white fish and a general expansion of trade. This perhaps explains the early re-emergence there of unions of the unskilled. Women organised in a Workwomen's Protective Society in 1884 and a Gas Stokers' Society appeared in the same year. While Aberdeen Trades Council seems to have been particularly active in supporting new unions, there are plenty of examples from elsewhere. Relative boom conditions in the 1880s in the cotton industry led to a cluster of strikes and lock-outs. A Blackburn dispute brought the formation of the Northern Counties Weavers' Association in 1884, the second amalgamation, gradually absorbing the previous union.[6] A Spinners' strike in Oldham in 1885 which put out of work the large number of cardroom workers, three-quarters of whom were women, led to the formation of the first effective Amalgamation of Cardroom and

Blowing-Room Operatives in 1886, with 9000 members, a number which nearly doubled within two years.[7] Women, along with other millworkers in jute, were getting organised in Dundee in 1885. October 1885 saw the first signs of protest among the women workers at Bryant & May's match factory when they struck for a wage rise and some protection against the disfiguring 'phossy-jaw'. In 1886, the Hull Trades Council, which had dockers and seamen's delegates among its members from 1881, was the first to alter its name to the Trades *and Labour* Council, 'to enable it to widen its scope to gather in or assist to form into societies, the vast number of our fellow men who are termed the unskilled labourer' and some others followed.[8] In Birmingham, the flintglass maker, Eli Bloor, and the printer, Alan Granger, formed the main labourers' society, the Amalgamated Gasworkers, Brickmakers and General Labourers. On Tyneside there was a National Labour Federation established in 1886 by some Newcastle members of the ASE[9] and Havelock Wilson of the South Shields' Union launched the National Amalgamated Sailors and Firemen's Union in 1887 which, during 1888, was pushing organisation into Glasgow and Liverpool and other ports. In the London docks in July 1887, Ben Tillett embarked on his first attempt at a union with the Tea Operatives and General Labourers' Union. In Glasgow, a dock labourers' society challenged the control of the stevedores in 1888 and a seamen's union appeared.

That same year, thanks to the efforts of Clementina Black of the Women's Trade Union League,[10] Christian Socialists like Revd Stewart Headlam, and other socialists like John Burns of the Social Democratic Federation and Annie Besant, 700 East London match-girls formed the Matchworkers' Union. In Liverpool, a Women's Industrial Council led by Mrs Jeannie Mole formed unions among a number of women workers. The Glasgow Trades Council and Clementina Black established a Council for Women's Trades in 1887 and a Glasgow Union of Women Workers was later formed thanks largely to the efforts of Margaret Irwin. In February 1889, Havelock Wilson of the seamen helped two Glasgow Irishmen, Edward McHugh and Richard McGhee turn their local union into a National Union of Dock Labourers for waterfront workers. A separate Dock Workers and General Labourers' Union recruited rather more widely. In a number of areas tramway workers began to organise.

Among the agricultural workers, Joseph Arch's Agricultural Labourers' Society struggled to survive, although Arch himself gained a higher profile as Liberal MP for North-West Norfolk from 1885–6 and again from 1892 until 1902. But again when opportunities presented themselves there was no want of attempts at organisation. A group of Liberal sympathisers in Aberdeen had tried in 1880 to organise Aberdeenshire farm servants. It did not come off immediately, but in 1885, after an approach to the Aberdeen Trades Council and a great deal of help from the Council president, a union was established which in 1887 became the Scottish Farm Servants' Union.[11]

All these activities gave encouragement to other groups. Dissatisfaction with sliding scales, which in the economic situation of the 1880s led to a steady reduction in wages, resulted in the formation in 1889 of the Miners' Federation of Great Britain (MFGB), yet another attempt to link the various county unions. A Union of Electrical Operatives appeared in London and a Society of Telegraph Construction Men in Lancashire and Yorkshire. In 1890 they united into the Electrical Trades Union. It modelled itself on the ASE, trying, not too successfully, to maintain an apprenticeship system. At its formation there was the kind of debate that was going on across the trade union movement. Should the organisation be confined to the 'skilled' engineers or should it incorporate all those involved in electrical industries? Significantly, it was the London men in the more diverse industrial developments there who favoured the more all-embracing approach. A National Union of Shop Assistants, Warehousemen and Clerks was formed in 1890.

Many years ago, Hugh Clegg questioned the extent to which the picture of the unskilled struggling to form trade unions against the hostility of craft unionists was an accurate one. It was one which grew largely from socialist propaganda at the time and from historians concerned to emphasise the particular role of socialist activists. 'New unions' were already appearing before socialist ideas had made much impact and many depended on assistance from 'old unionists', firmly Lib-Lab in their politics. Frederic Harrison, writing of the London dock strike of 1889 in an article which, probably for the first time, used the term 'new trade unionism', argued that 'The new element is this. The trades have stood by one another as they never did before. The skilled workmen have stood by the unskilled workmen in a wholly new spirit.'

The 'new spirit' developed rather later in London than in most other places. In London there was some truth in the accusations that the established leaders of London unionism were not very active and the initiatives were often left to political activists. Socialists took up the cause of the match-girls and helped them get some of the worst features of Bryant and May's fining system removed. But Bill Steadman of the well-established barge builders' union also gave assistance and the London Trades Council acted as mediator. Eleanor Marx and Edward Aveling of the Socialist League helped Will Thorne get his Gas Workers' Union going in March 1889. By July it had over 60 branches and in August it won an eight-hour working day without a strike. When Ben Tillett sought help from the London Trades Council for his Dock Wharf and Riverside and General Labourers' Union, formed in 1887, at the end of 1888 the secretary of the Council declined and asked for more information. He was very hostile to John Burns, the socialist engineer who took up the dockers' cause for his socialism and to Ben Tillett for what he regarded as unrealistic enthusiasm.[12] But this was not a pattern that was usual elsewhere.

Confrontation

The London Dock Strike of August 1889 certainly caught the public attention. It came after a period of deteriorating conditions for dock workers as cost-conscious employers tried to squeeze down payments and cut back on work gangs. Tillett, who was developing skills of oratory and organisation, was extending what had originally been a tea warehousemen's union into one that could embrace all dock workers. He was assisted by Tom McCarthy of the already organised Stevedores' Union. Encouraged by the success of the Gasworkers' Union in the nearby Beckton gas works and aware that August was always a good time for dock strike action, when Essex farm labourers and potential strike-breakers were busy with the harvest, dockers came out on 14 August against one of the companies and quickly spread the strike to others. Although there were various grievances Tillett focused on three main demands: first, to reduce the casual element of work in the docks by demanding that a half-day should be the minimum work period, with two recruiting times each day; secondly, to widen the difference between day-time and night-time payments to discourage excessive overtime; and thirdly, a minimum rate of 6d (2.5p) per hour. It was this demand for the 'docker's tanner' which caught the public eye, but as John Lovell shows, Tillett was more concerned with the pattern of employment than with a simple wage claim.[13] They held out for a month, long enough to attract financial support from across the country and from Australian unions and a great deal of press attention. In the end, they gained their wage increase and a four-hour minimum work period.

Thanks to John Burns, Tom Mann, H. H. Champion and other socialists, who organised spectacular parades and demonstrations out of the East End, immense publicity was generated. This probably played some part in encouraging further developments, but perhaps not as much as is often suggested, because activities were already well underway outside London. But it is right to talk of an 'explosion' of unionism between 1888 and 1891. It triggered a series of very successful strikes. According to Hobsbawm, only 20 per cent of strikes in 1889 resulted in defeat for the strikers. The rest were either a complete victory or were settled by compromise.[14] On the other hand, most of the victories were relatively short-lived as employers, initially taken off-guard, quickly regained the initiative. By the spring of 1890 the London gas companies, by effective use of strike-breakers and police back-up, were pulling back many of the earlier union gains and resisting attempts to tighten union control. A famous victory at the Leeds Municipal Gasworks, when the local authority was forced to abandon attempts to impose a contract which would have required four months' notice of a strike, needs to be balanced against substantial defeats by other local authorities. There was considerable investment by employers in new technology to replace the relatively skilled stokers, but it took time for the effects of this to be felt.

Since unskilled workers were on the whole easily replaced, many of the strikes involved extensive use of pickets to keep out strike-breakers. Tom Mann, like Burns an engineer and pioneer socialist, had organised these pickets most effectively during the dock strike. Not surprisingly, confrontations with strike-breakers could quickly lead to violence. Ideally, unskilled workers wanted to achieve a situation where only unionists were employed, but the employers particularly resisted efforts to impose a closed shop. Tillett's aim had always been to achieve union control over the hiring of workers. Employers saw that as a recipe for reduced output and over-manning at a time when trade was again on a downturn, and Tillett's union was to all intents smashed by the employers in the London docks by the end of 1890. Under the 1889 settlement, sub-contracting had been abolished and gang representatives, initially unionists, negotiated piece rates. The employers balked at this and pressed for an end to the guaranteed minimum of 2s (10p) per day. By the end of the 1890s the union had lost control over the gangs, membership was on a downward spiral and there was a reversion to sub-contracting. It was a similar pattern among dock workers at other ports.

The most systematic attempt to break any union hold on the labour force came from the shipowners when faced with the attempt by Havelock Wilson's Seamen & Firemen's Union to unionise the officers. The Shipping Federation, formed in September 1890, proceeded to organise a pool of what was called 'free labour' and, over the next few years, strike after strike was broken by the use of such 'free labour' transported from port to port under police protection and housed in 'depot ships'. Union membership of the Seamen & Firemen fell from 78 000 in 1891 to 5000 in 1894. The majority of the new unions were, therefore, ephemeral. They were dealing with employers who had little experience of organised labour and had yet to be convinced that unions had anything to offer them. Only a few, like the Hull shipping firm of Thomas Wilson, Sons & Co, the largest in the port, stood out against this and were prepared to deal with the unions.

Employers of the unskilled were generally dealing with poorly educated, under-employed, insecure workers with few material resources to fall back on in times of strike, who themselves had little experience of union organisation. Most of the new unions were formed to pursue a particular demand. When a union was beaten in a dispute or was not making gains, then there was little to keep workers in the union and members began to melt away. Also an insistence on immediate results often led to conflict between the leadership and the rank and file. Thorne, Tillett, Havelock Wilson and others all came to see the value of a longer-term strategy of achieving recognition from employers and were prepared to negotiate and compromise. On more than one occasion, however, they found that they were unable to restrain their branches from striking. With economic conditions deteriorating in the early 1890s, the bargaining position of many unions was weakening and membership was in decline. Employers were pressing for wage cuts and those in work were urging resistance. On the other hand, the leadership, recognising their vulnerability, generally urged caution.

The significance of winning employer support and a measure of public sympathy was most apparent in Hull where, thanks to the favourable attitudes of the Wilson Shipping Line, dock and seamen's unions had remained well entrenched. However, in 1893, under immense pressure from the other employers in the Shipping Federation, from the adverse trade conditions and from one union demand too far, the Wilson Line hardened its attitudes. The Shipping Federation prepared the ground to break the unions' hold and demagogic tactics by Havelock Wilson provided the excuse in April. This time there was to be no negotiation; hundreds of 'free labourers' were shipped in and the state put on a massive display of power with 200 troops and two gunboats in the Humber. Six weeks later, as a result of public pressure, a negotiated settlement was reached which allowed the unions to claim that defeat was not total. In practice, the effect was the end of a significant union presence in Hull docks for some time to come and Hull, for long after, became a prime source of 'free labour'.[15] Havelock Wilson's Amalgamated Union of Sailors and Firemen collapsed, although he immediately reorganised in a National Sailors' and Firemen's Union.

A number of the unions which emerged in the late 1880s and early 1890s presented themselves as general unions open to workers from any kind of work. It was an ideological position which many of the socialist activists favoured, in contrast to what they saw as the exclusiveness of the skilled craft unions. In many cases it was a necessary tactic to organise the different groups of casual, unskilled workers who readily moved from job to job in search of employment. But, as E. J. Hobsbawm pointed out, most of those unions which did survive had a foothold in a specific group of workers with an element of skill which gave them some bargaining clout. Despite their names apparently indicating an all-embracing belief in general unionism, most were usually about defending one particular group of workers against the constant threat from outsiders. A feature of the newer unions was the often intense inter-union rivalry even to the extent of strike-breaking and refusing to work alongside members of rival unions. The new unions, just as much as the old, were about achieving security. John Lovell found in the London docks, where, although dockers were casually employed, there was a core of regular workers, that 'expansive gospels of general unionism carried little weight on the waterfront'.[16] Elsewhere, what Eric Taplin calls 'a finger-hold of recognition' allowed remnants to survive. The National Union of Dock Labourers just managed to cling on for 20 lean years in Birkenhead and Liverpool in spite of the deep hostility of the transatlantic shipping companies.[17]

New Attitudes

Of even more significance than the organisation of the unskilled were the changes taking place among workers who had been organised for many years.

Most of the county miners' unions, with the exception of the Northumberland and Durham, South Wales and Fife, had come together in the Miners' Federation of Great Britain in 1889 thanks largely to the efforts of Yorkshire and Lancashire leaders. Unionisation among different mining areas was never easy to achieve or to maintain, since they were producing for a diversity of markets and in many different conditions of work, organisational structure and tradition. None the less, the Federation, linking mainly those areas producing for the home market, was a new powerful voice. It pushed for wage increases to match the increases in the prices being received by the coal owners at a time of rapidly rising demand and Ben Pickard, the Yorkshire president of the MFGB, called for 'spirit and aggressiveness' in pursuing claims. In 1890 he launched a campaign for a statutory eight-hour working day. In March 1892 the federated unions declared a 'stop week' to reduce the coal supply and keep up prices (and so wages). That and a falling demand for coal produced a hardening of employers' attitudes and a series of localised disputes against wage reductions. The miners' leaders resisted reductions on the grounds that, irrespective of the price of coal, miners still required a 'living wage', a concept which was to become increasingly important. The disputes culminated in a 16-week lock-out of 300 000 federated miners in the summer of 1893. By far the largest industrial dispute yet experienced, this dispute unleashed a new depth of bitterness in local communities culminating in occasional riots. The use of troops and the shooting to death of two miners at Featherstone was merely the clearest manifestation of the widespread bitterness. The Liberal Government took the unprecedented step of intervening in the dispute and appointing the Foreign Secretary, Lord Rosebery, to head a conciliation conference. He charmed both sides and lunched them well. The cuts were temporarily postponed, now that coal prices were again rising because of the prolonged stoppage, and the Federation was able to claim a victory and to consolidate its support in the mining communities.[18]

The late 1880s, amid economically booming conditions, also brought an increase in the number of disputes among the relatively well-organised cotton textile workers of Lancashire. The spinners' leader, James Mawdsley, claimed 95 per cent membership of the Amalgamated Spinners' Union in 1891. The employers responded by tightening and extending their associations. By the end of 1891 the Federation of Master Cotton Spinners' Associations covered more than half the industry. In the spring of 1892, the boom years being over, the Federation imposed a lock-out to try to bring to an end a long-drawn-out strike in a Stalybridge mill. It was over the rates being paid for working difficult, poor-quality cotton, which was increasingly being used in an attempt to cut costs. The imposition of a wage reduction at the end of that year ended in a further strike and lock-out of 7000 spinners, which in turn affected another 40 000 cotton mill workers. Strike-breakers organised by the Masters' Federation were widely used. Not until March was the dispute finally resolved in a far-reaching settlement at the Brooklands Hotel near Manchester, which involved concession by both sides and set up procedures for dealing with future disputes which were to last for twenty years.

In contrast to Lancashire, the woollen workers of Yorkshire were notoriously poorly organised. The work-force was highly sectionalised and contained a very high proportion of young workers and women workers. The weakness came out in the Manningham Mills strike of the winter of 1890–1 when 4000 workers struck against the largest employer in Bradford, Samuel Cunliffe Lister. They were ununionised but their four months' strike developed into a highly emotional and symbolic struggle by local socialists against a leading Liberal employer, which stimulated independent labour politics rather than trade unionism. Two years later, the Independent Labour Party was formed at a conference initiated by Bradford socialists.

Engineering and shipbuilding employers in the late 1870s and 1880s had been trying to reduce costs by extending the use of piecework, introducing new work organisation and, where possible, hiving off tasks to less skilled workers using semi-automated machinery. New, more sophisticated lathes and drills could do much of the work that had formerly required the skills of an all-round craftsman. The variety of tasks once undertaken by the multi-skilled fitters and turners were increasingly being subdivided into specialisms in which some of the workers began to organise their own unions. The changes meant intensification of work for some, but also that fewer highly skilled workers were required. Those who *were* employed, on the other hand, had greater supervisory responsibilities. Skilled workers, boilermakers, plumbers, pattern-makers, shipwrights, joiners, brass workers as well as the fitters and turners, all organised in separate unions, battled for control of the new processes. The result was recurring demarcation disputes. Feeling threatened on a number of fronts, the initial response of the fitters' and turners' union was to ban its members from operating the new machinery, thus leaving the new machines to non-ASE and often to non-unionised workers. In many disputes in the late 1880s and early 1890s ASE members refused support to striking semi-skilled machine workers, or refused to admit any who accepted piece rates. The ASE also tried to resist with struggles over apprenticeship regulation, piecework and overtime. But, since the pattern of change varied greatly between different areas, it was difficult to achieve a uniform and coherent response. The platers and riveters of the Boilermakers' Society were not so very different, refusing, for example, to admit the smiths to their union. They did, in 1882, agree to the admission of their holders-up, but only on condition that they remained holders-up and did not see union membership as a step to becoming skilled boilermakers, and they were not entitled to full benefit.

There was some collaboration between craft unions such as the Boilermakers, the Iron Moulders and the Shipwrights, in the engineering industry, with joint committees to maintain the nine-hour day. But demarcation disputes left long-lasting scars which the ASE members tended to nurse. They backed away from the Federation of Engineering and Shipbuilding Trades, which Robert Knight of the Boilermakers was largely responsible for creating in 1891 with 13 unions affiliated. He saw it as a way of both resisting employer pressure and settling demarcation disputes. As well as providing mutual support in disputes, it was 'to use every legitimate means to abolish the character note system; to promote arbitration or conciliation in trade disputes; and the elevations of labour in general'.[19] The ASE, however, could not be persuaded to join an organisation which contained the small specialist unions, like the pattern-makers and steam engine-makers, which it saw as challenging its monopoly. As the historian of the ASE comments,

> the failure of the ASE to participate in this move, like the failure to develop the unity of all sections of the engineering workers within the framework of the Society, was a reflection of a policy and structure which no longer corresponded with the changing conditions in the industry and the new spirit

in the country. The harvest of these mistakes was to be reaped in the following ten years.[20]

There were those within engineering who were pressing for more confrontational policies with employers and for alternative tactics other than the stubborn defence of the craft élite. In 1886, the socialist engineer, Tom Mann, launched his campaign to persuade unions to demand an eight-hour day, not only as a traditional demand for more leisure, but as a way of reducing the supply of labour. It had been achieved in most government establishments and with some of the bigger employers by 1894. It was more difficult in smaller private firms and the engineering works of the North-East saw a number of disputes in the 1890s to reduce hours and limit overtime. Thanks to the work of Mann and George Barnes, a so-called 'forward' movement developed within the union for the broadening of membership to include all grades of skill. Mann stood for the general secretaryship of the Society in 1891 after a two-year campaign and narrowly missed being elected. The reformers faced deeply entrenched resistance, but the futility of the exclusive approach became increasingly apparent and, in 1892, membership was substantially broadened, although still leaving many machine operatives in engineering workshops outside the union. The administrative structure was modernised with an executive of full-time officials appointed, as well as six full-time district organisers. The changes gave further momentum to those who wanted general support for militant tactics and in 1896 George Barnes, with Mann's support, was elected as general secretary on a programme advocating a militant campaign for the eight-hour day.

The onset of depression in 1895 brought a hardening of employer resistance. A new Employers' Federation of Engineering Associations came into being in 1896, linking Clydeside, Belfast, Barrow and the North-East of England and committed to asserting the rights of employers to restructure work practices, to introduce machinery as they wished and to employ on the machines whomsoever they wished, without reference to the ASE or any other union. They particularly resented *local* union committees making decisions on such matters. It encompassed firms from as far apart as Aberdeen and Bristol. Early in 1897 after a nine-month strike against a shipbuilding firm in Hull, the ASE had succeeded in forcing recognition of the principle that machines which supplanted hand-skilled labour should be operated only by ASE, time-served men. This success encouraged demands in Belfast and on the Clyde and there were constant threats of strikes and lock-outs. Barnes's election came amidst rising tension between local activists and the moderate leadership about both tactics and the perpetual issue of control by the executive over the districts. It was amid an atmosphere of rising tempers that the London engineers struck for an eight-hour day. The Employers' Federation retaliated with a national lock-out and, despite the fact that this was a period of rising trade, held together for six months. Although ostensibly about hours, the central issue was in fact about the way in which engineering work practices were to develop in the future. The union went down to comprehensive defeat.

The dispute brought out the fundamental weakness of the union as a result of its failure to organise those who were working the new semi-automatic machine tools. There had also been no attempt to consult with other related unions in engineering before embarking on the eight-hour campaign. Its aloofness from other unions meant that it was not able to draw on much support and had to depend largely on its own resources. A six months' dispute at a cost of £658 000 drove it to near bankruptcy and left employers the opportunity to impose a draconian settlement under which they were free to employ whom they liked, to employ as many apprentices as they wanted, to move workers between machines, to impose piecework and overtime as required. It also left a legacy of bitter ill-will between unions in the engineering industry, which was to take many years to overcome. Significantly, the employers showed no desire to break the union completely; they were happy for their most skilled workers, whom they still needed as trainers and supervisors of the less skilled and as problem-solvers on tricky jobs, to be organised. They insisted, however, that the union leadership keep control of its local officials, by agreeing that no strike could take place without central approval and after an attempt at settlement between the

ASE executive and the Employers' Federation. It was, as Burgess points out, in the 1890s rather than the 1860s that centralisation of industrial policy was really achieved in the ASE.[21]

The Eight-hour Day

One of the issues that has generally been taken as dividing old and new unionists is the demand for the eight-hour day by legislation. As George Howell explained, there was nothing new in the demand for eight hours as such:

> At anniversary dinners, beanfeasts and drinking bouts, when they so far forget themselves as to indulge in the latter, there is one toast which is at all times enthusiastically responded to, namely: 'The four eights; eight hours' work, eight hours' play, eight hours' sleep and eight shillings a day' . . . through all the vicissitudes of the labour struggles, this aspiration has survived . . . Where differences did arise was on how it was to be achieved.

It was the London socialist cabinet-maker, Adam Weiler, who first tried to reopen the issue at the 1878 TUC in a paper drawn up with the help of Karl Marx. But, as Howell said, there was a deeply entrenched hostility within the trade union movement to legislation for specific social classes. As Henry Pelling argued, the working class 'knew Whitehall and Westminster and the courts as mainly enemies' and the trade union case had always been against special legislation. Nothing much came of Weiler's initiative, but it reappeared in the mid-1880s with rising unemployment. The presidential address at the 1885 TUC saw trade union action to achieve eight hours as the first step to getting out of the depression. In 1886 Tom Mann issued a pamphlet entitled 'What an Eight Hour Working Day means to the Workers' in which he protested at the inactivity of trade unions on the issue. It became a big issue at the Congress of 1887 and caused the first of many rows between Keir Hardie of the Ayrshire Miners and Henry Broadhurst. George Shipton, long-time secretary of the London Trades Council, spoke for the Parliamentary Committee in 1889 against pressing for legislation, when he declared that 'the evils of general state interference would be so great as to outweigh any possible advantage to be gained'. Within a year all this had changed and the London Trades Council joined the May Day demonstration of 1890 for the eight-hour day.

In fact London was a late conversion. If one looks at Scotland, a conference of Scottish unions held in 1887 reviewed the issue and voted for an eight-hour day, but against legislation, except in the case of the miners. However, within a year, the Glasgow Trades Council had come round to supporting the motion at the TUC for an eight-hour bill. Aberdeen Trades Council had come out in favour of an bill even earlier, in 1887, and Dundee too was an early convert. It was certainly socialists at the TUC who kept the issue to the forefront and undoubtedly many of the Parliamentary Committee remained hostile. But there is little doubt that there was a change of attitude on the part of craft unionists before there was a substantial influx of new unionists or socialists. As Clegg and his associates have argued 'there was no clear-cut division between new socialists and an "old gang" hopelessly bound to the doctrines of non-interference'. It is difficult to generalise about what made some unionists support legislation while others held out against it. Some of those on piecework, like the shoemakers, held out longer against it than most. Seasonal workers, like plumbers and painters, had strong reservations, but others in the building trades were enthusiastic. Engineers came round to a prominent role in favour of state intervention. The cotton unions were converted by 1892 when trade conditions markedly worsened and they saw shorter hours as a way of reducing output. But the debate was within the unions not between them and it was part of a wider change in attitude, part of a new militancy in the post-depression years.

Causes and Consequences

It does not seem to be especially useful to look for specific characteristics of the new unions and to see them as somehow different from the more established ones. Nor is it particularly useful to see the 'new unionism' as a product of exceptional circumstances at the end of the 1880s. The spurt in economic activity in many industries, and hence levels of employment that had not existed since the beginning of the 1870s, after a period of dull trade and unemployment certainly created ideal circumstances for a push by trade unions, but the roots of the changes were apparent earlier.[22] Hobsbawm, looking at the emergence of the Gasworkers' Union, pointed to the demands for greater productivity as retorts got bigger and the effort required from stokers increased. There were numerous other complaints from groups of workers about the speeding up of processes as employers struggled in increasingly competitive markets.

The new unions of unskilled workers had low entrance fees and subscriptions compared with most of the older craft unions, but this reflected realistic assessments of what casual and unskilled workers could afford to pay, rather than a policy of trying to make the unions more widely accessible. Those which survived beyond the middle years of the decade were those which had a core specialism to rely upon – stokers in gas, dyers in textiles, shipyard helpers, certain groups of chemical workers. They survived because they had skills which were important to employers who could not afford to antagonise them indefinitely. Also, many were in industries which were expanding – the chemical industry, the gas industry (despite the competition from electricity) – and the expertise was scarce. Most of the unskilled unions did not initially offer friendly society benefits, but in this they were not very different from many of the smaller unions and a large number of Scottish unions. There was no principled opposition to offering friendly benefits and, indeed, a number of the new unions soon introduced them as a way of trying to hold their membership. But sickness benefit in particular was often a heavy drain on union funds, especially among unskilled workers, and necessitated high dues. Sickness benefit was also notoriously difficult to police and generally a complication which struggling new unions could do without. While the idea of general unionism was certainly one that attracted a few socialist activists, it often came about as a response to a particular strike situation rather than by the pursuit of a specific policy. It also reflected the fact that many casual workers moved from job to job, in the docks, in the gasworks, on building sites.

The apparently greater militancy and greater propensity to strike action by the new unions reflected the stage of union development. In order to attract and hold members a new union had to show quick results. There were no procedures for negotiation to which they could turn, and they were faced with employers who found the new challenge to their authority unacceptable and who could draw on a pool of casual and unemployed labour to replace strikers, and did so ruthlessly. No union leader wanted strikes if they could achieve their ends through negotiation. In 1891 the Gasworkers included in their rules the statement that all labour disputes should be settled by amicable agreement or arbitration wherever possible. By 1893, Thorne was telling his members that 'Strikes, through whatever cause, should be avoided wherever possible.'

What has to be explained about these years is not why the unskilled organised, but why there were signs of greater confrontation across the face of British industry. Growth after depression is not enough itself, although it is obviously important. But the profits squeeze of the later 1870s and 1880s and the increased competition from abroad which many industries were facing had undoubtedly made many employers much more cost-conscious. These attitudes did not disappear during what was a relatively short-lived upturn at the end of the 1880s. The emergence of employers' organisations and the extension of these in the 1890s was partly about eliminating some of the effects of price-cutting domestic competition between firms. They were not just a response to union power. They were also at their strongest in those industries going through the greatest changes, particularly technological changes. These inevitably created tensions in the work-place. New machine tools in engineering, linotypers in printing, ring-spindles in textiles, conveyors at the docks, 'the iron man' retort charger at gasworks and electrical power in factories, are just a few of the kinds of advances that were changing relations in the work-place. Many skilled workers were less secure than they had been. Those in work had, rightly or wrongly, a sense of being required to work more intensively. At the same time, they were better-educated, better-organised and probably better-off financially than ever before and, therefore, better prepared to resist.

All these explanations play down the significance of socialism as a factor in the new unions. For every Mann, Champion and Tillett there were half a dozen local Lib-Lab unionists helping organise the unskilled. There was no *a priori* reason why the unskilled should have been more attracted by state intervention than the skilled. Both, in fact, were deeply suspicious of any forms of state activity. Any state intervention, whether it be compulsory education, compulsory slum clearance or compulsory licensing legislation, was rarely seen as a unmitigated good by the working class.[23] The unskilled, probably even more than the skilled, had learned to be wary of middle-class 'do-gooders' interfering in their lives and most early socialists fell into that category.

But one must be wary of casting out all past interpretations. Socialism did matter. Many of the young trade union activists (Keir Hardie among the miners in Scotland, J. R. Clynes among the Oldham piecers, James MacDonald among the London tailors and many others) were inspired by socialist aspirations. Richard Price has asserted that 'socialist sentiment developed most strongly in those trades where the struggle for control over the labour process was sharpest'[24] but this must be almost impossible to prove. Also, socialist analysis of the economic system was perhaps finding a response in a society where class divisions were becoming more pronounced. Residential segregation was dividing most cities between a wealthy west end and a poor east end. Housing shortages and slum clearance programmes were often undermining status division in housing between the 'respectable' and the 'unrespectable'. The social distinctions between eating and drinking places, between places of entertainment and between leisure activities generally, whether it was sport or holidays, were becoming more pronounced. These cultural changes had major implications for employment relationships. The language of social relationships became more confrontational. J. E. Cronin talks of the creation of 'a physical space for the development of a strong and distinctive working-class culture sustained by, and itself helping to sustain, a broad array of social and political institutions'.[25] All these things probably made it easier for skilled workers to think that bit more readily in class terms rather than sectional terms. Conversely, it no doubt helped to harden the tones and attitudes of employers. In some areas too, family firms were giving way to larger, public companies with little of the paternalism which Patrick Joyce and others have argued was a feature of the earlier decades. James Mawdsley, the far from militant cotton spinners' leader, Conservative in his politics, blamed much of the tension in the industry in 1893 on 'a new class of capitalists', the managers of the limited companies which had come to dominate Oldham spinning 'who justify their entrance into middle-class rank by jumping on the men whose labour has placed them where they are'.[26]

All recent work emphasises the uneven nature of British industrial growth. Alongside large, modern, highly mechanised firms bringing in the latest techniques, usually from the United States, there were umpteen small-scale, unmechanised, paternalistic ones where older patterns of production, which left skilled workers with a great deal of control, persisted. This inevitably had major implications for trade unionism and requires any generalisations to be treated with considerable care.

Union Amongst the Unions

Another sign of changing attitudes was to be found in the further spread of trades councils. Collaborative action between trade unions had existed from early in the nineteenth century, but it was at the end of the 1850s and during the 1860s that permanent organisations of delegates from local trade unions and branches appeared, meeting on a regular basis and publicising their activities in the local press. Birmingham, Bolton, Leeds, Leicester, London, Maidstone, Manchester and Salford, Oldham, Preston, Sheffield, Aberdeen, Edinburgh and Glasgow all had well-established councils. A number of new ones had been formed in the union growth in the early 1870s, but only a few of these survived, principally Barrow, Bradford, Bristol, Rochdale, Southport and Swansea. But as unionism revived in the 1880s so trades councils were re-formed and new ones established. Dundee, Huddersfield and Ipswich in 1885; Long Eaton and Norwich in 1886; Oxford, Portsmouth and Stalybridge in 1887; Accrington and Kettering in 1888. It was, however, in 1889 that the explosion in trade unionism was paralleled by an expansion in the number of trades councils. Thirteen were established, mainly in the second half of 1889, and the expansion continued for the next three years, with 25 new ones in 1890, 23 in 1891 and 16 in 1892. Even in the more difficult years of 1893 and 1894, 17 new councils appeared. By 1900 there were 182 of them. Lancashire and Cheshire had the largest number (44), followed by 31 in the North and West Midlands, 24 in Yorkshire, 22 in London in the South-East and 18 in Scotland.

The established councils had all experienced a spectacular rise in affiliations from the end of the 1880s. London Trades Council, for example, grew from 64 affiliates in 1889 to 299 in 1892; Glasgow grew from 54 to 104; Birmingham from 34 to 62. After 1892 many of the new affiliates fell away, but councils gradually began picking up support again in the early 1900s. It was rare, outside a few ports, for the unskilled to take the initiative in forming trades councils although some of them resulted from local disputes. Exeter, Brighton and Richmond, for example, all resulted from disputes in the building trades. A few, such as Carlisle, Plymouth and some of the West Riding Councils, were established by socialists. Most socialists, however, quickly grasped the importance of trades councils as a focus for debate and as one of the few trade union forums where political issues could regularly be discussed. Tom Mann came into London Trades Council soon after the dock strike as delegate for the Battersea branch of the ASE. Mann saw the importance of the Trades Council as 'the body above all others capable of initiating effective action by means of the organised trades of London'. He sought to win it over to the new unionism and to make it more representative:

> The time is rapidly approaching when a Union not affiliated to the Trades Council will be looked upon by other unions as a kind of 'blackleg' society which neglects to carry out one of the fundamental principles of trade unionism – viz. a willingness and readiness at all times to work with other Unionists for the extension of union principles wherever

> and whenever opportunity affords. It is necessary for the sectional organisations to be in continual working touch with each other as it is for an individual to be a member of his union.[27]

There were tensions with the older members, particularly with the secretary George Shipton, but even he succumbed to the new spirit and at the end of 1890 declared his conversion to the legal eight hours' day movement. It was in trades councils that much of the debate over the eight-hour day and over socialism was fought out.

Trades Union Congress

Since 1872 it had been the practice when the TUC held its annual meeting in a particular town for the chair of the local trades council, where one existed, or the most distinguished local trade unionist, to act as president of the session and to deliver an opening address. Most of them could be pretty bland, but one can detect a new sharpness when the Congress met in Southport in 1885 and T. R. Threlfall used his speech to urge a new and more aggressive approach:

> They [trade unions] must either lead or follow . . . the time has arrived for the trades of the Kingdom to take action in securing the eight hours' working day . . . our duty is to organise the masses . . . They must form the nucleus of the labour party of the future . . . From first to last Parliament has always taken the standpoint of the capitalist in all industrial questions.

Over the following years, others took up similar themes. William Bevan told the Swansea Congress of 1887, 'Socialism has lost its terrors for us. We recognise our most serious evils in the unrestrained, unscrupulous, and remorseless forces of capital.' He called for no diffusion of effort:

> If the labour movement is divided into hostile camps, skilled labour on the one side and unskilled on the other, then assuredly the labour cause is irreparably damaged.

Trades councils were also a means by which a number of socialists could get themselves selected as delegates to Congress when they could not get selected by their own unions. Also, as the socialists sought to bring pressure to bear on Congress, the position of the chair was one of increasing importance, since he was responsible for calling the speakers. Since in many cases neither miners nor cotton spinners were on trades councils, they could rarely get their nominees as chair. At the same time the problem of discipline at Congress was becoming more important. As a result there was increasing competition for the job between rival unions and rival factions.

A struggle between Lib–Labs and socialists went on alongside the struggle of the larger unions to increase their influence at Congress in proportion to their size. There was concern on the part of the Lib–Lab Parliamentary Committee that the 1890 Liverpool Congress, the last that Henry Broadhurst attended as general secretary, had carried a resolution advocating a general eight-hour day by legislation, against the advice of the Parliamentary Committee. In addition, a number of the old guard were ousted from the Committee to the extent that John Burns, with some exaggeration, could claim it as a victory for 'us socialists'. Up until 1890 voting was by a show of hands, with each delegate having one vote and there being no limit other than cost to the number of delegates who could be sent by an affiliated body. As a result, an attempt was made to revise standing orders so that voting was on the basis of numbers paid for, at the rate of £1 per thousand members. This was rejected, mainly as a result of protests from trades councils. But the pressure for change continued and in 1894 a sub-committee of the Parliamentary Committee brought out a scheme which gave unions a block of votes on the basis of their affiliated membership. It also excluded trades councils altogether and also excluded anyone who was not an officer of a trade society or actually working at the trade.[28] Finally, the Parliamentary Committee was to be allowed to compress resolutions into what could become sometimes self-contradictory composite motions for consideration and the retiring chair of the Parliamentary Committee was in future to preside over Congress. The new standing orders were arbitrarily imposed at the 1895 Congress despite the protests of trades councils and smaller unions up and down the country. Power at Congress shifted very firmly to the big battalions of miners and cotton workers.

The Parliamentary Committee of the TUC still saw its principal task as being to lobby ministers and Parliament on issues of interest. But it increasingly found itself involved in other issues, such as settling inter-union disputes, taking up fair wages cases and pressing for union recognition by government departments.[29] There was a steady accretion of power to the Committee. Members of it took upon themselves the role of introducing major debates at Congress. Unlike in the past, when deputations to ministers could include as many as 200 union representatives, the 13 members of the Parliamentary Committee increasingly took on the task themselves and with it the authority to speak for Congress. More and more it took initiatives without consulting the wider trade union constituency.

There was talk by various trades councils of setting up a rival congress, but only in Scotland did this happen. Purely Scottish trade unions were disappearing fast in the 1890s, as they became absorbed into all-British organisations. There were now few national headquarters of unions in Scotland. Trade unionism there was generally weak compared with England and therefore trades councils were relatively more important and attracted some able unionists. The loss of representation produced a fierce outcry in Scotland. There had also been for some time talk of the need for a meeting which would discuss specifically Scottish issues. The result was a decision in 1896 to hold a Scottish conference which would include trades councils as well as trade unions and the first meeting of the Scottish Trades Union Congress (STUC) was held in March 1897.

5 The Intervening State, 1893–1914

Gladstone's decision to dispatch Lord Rosebery to try to settle the 1893 mining dispute was a new departure. Neither employers nor unions were enthusiastic about state involvement in industrial relations. Arbitration Acts from previous decades had proved to be largely dead letters. In 1886, however, the Board of Trade began to collect statistics on aspects of labour[1] and in 1893 a Labour Department of the Board was formed. Its main task was still the collection of statistics and it added information on unions, strikes and lock-outs to what it already had on wages and hours. In addition it immediately became interventionist and unofficially mediated in major disputes. The Royal Commission on Labour, by far the biggest inquiry into trade unions and industrial relations yet carried out, reporting in 1894, gave every encouragement to the Board to extend this role. It talked of the need for 'partnership', of 'common interests, by employers and workmen' and looked forward to workers' organisations having 'a consultative voice in the division of the proceeds of industry'. The Government's role, according to the Commission, was to encourage strong voluntary organisations of both employers and workers.[2] State intervention in industrial relations was made official by the Conservative Government's Conciliation Act of 1896 ('to make better Provision for the Preventions and Settlement of Trade Disputes'), which rejected what had become increasingly vocal demands for compulsory arbitration, but allowed the Board, in the event of a trade dispute 'if they think fit' to bring the parties together and, if requested, to appoint a conciliator or an arbitrator. That and the Workmen's Compensation Act of 1897, with its acceptance after decades of campaigning of 'no fault' accidents, seemed to herald a new era.

The Legal Challenge

Yet these developments also came at a time when the courts were taking a new look at the position of trade unions. The legislation of the 1870s had seemed to give trade unions full protection from legal action. They were not legal corporations and therefore could not be sued in their corporate capacity. Picketing was legal and a number of cases had held that intimidation under the 1875 Act had to involve violence or the threat of it. In the 1890s, however, there was a change in interpretation. In the case of *Temperton* v. *Russell* in 1893, over an attempt by three Hull unions to stop Temperton delivering to a building company with whom there was a dispute, the court ruled that this broke existing and future contracts and that unions could not lay down the terms on which people could work. It allowed Temperton to claim civil damages against the trade union official, Russell, 'for conspiracy to injure the plaintiff'. It marked an important step in the evolution of a civil law of conspiracy and it launched both a legal and a political debate into the position of trade unions and over the powers of the courts to interpret the law. The Majority Report of the Royal Commission on Labour pointed to the possibility of unions and employers' organisations acquiring a 'fuller legal personality' to allow collective agreements to be made legally binding.

The courts used the *Temperton* v. *Russell* judgment against picketing and against 'blacklisting' of employers. The case of *Trollope* v. *London Building Trades' Federation* made the publishing of lists of non-union employers and of free labourers actionable. In the *Lyons* v. *Wilkins* case (going through the courts between 1896 and 1898), Lord Justice Lindley drew a distinction between picketing 'to obtain or communicate information' and picketing intended to put pressure on people to strike. It is easy to see such cases as examples of right-wing judges merely reflecting the increasingly loud demands from *The Times*, *The Economist* and other Conservative opinion for a curb on trade union power; and, no doubt, some judges merely responded to their class instincts. It was rarely as crude as that, however, and in the 1890s there can be seen an ongoing debate on the relationship between individuals and corporations. The increasing demands for a closed shop by many unionists, and the development of new tactics for exerting pressure on employers, all raised fundamental issues of the relationships with both members and non-members and the extent to which coercion could be allowed. Also the decisions were not all one-way. The courts had allowed unregistered companies to be sued, and not all cases went against the unions. In *Allen* v. *Flood* in 1898 the unions could claim a victory in a case which stemmed from a demarcation dispute between the shipwrights and the boilermakers. Allen, the London district officer of the Boilermakers' Society, had threatened strike action unless two shipwrights, accused of doing boilermakers' work, were dismissed. The employers duly complied and the shipwrights sued Allen, the Executive of the Union and Robert Knight, the general secretary. The case against Knight and the Executive was dismissed, but damages were awarded against Allen. This was upheld on appeal, but the Law Lords threw out the case by a majority and appeared to uphold the right of workers 'to decide with whom they should work' and reaffirmed that broadly the courts should not interfere in industrial disputes.

The spate of cases culminated in the final Taff Vale judgment and in the *Quinn* v. *Leathem* case of 1901. During a strike on the Taff Vale railway in August 1900 the company had used blacklegs from the National Free Labour Association. The general secretary of the Amalgamated Society of Railway Servants had authorised the use of pickets. Ammon Beasley, the general manager of the company, who had always refused to deal with the union, won an injunction against the union officials *and* the union as a body. Although the strike was settled by mediation after 11 days, the case continued through to the House of Lords (where the composition of the Law Lords had altered over the previous couple of years), which ruled that Parliament could not have intended to allow 'numerous bodies of men, capable of owning great wealth and acting by agents' to have no responsibility for the damage done to others by their agents. A trade union, therefore, was a legal entity, trade union funds were vulnerable for damages inflicted by its officials and the ASRS was required to pay the damages of £23 000 plus costs of around £7000.[3]

Within a fortnight of the Lords' judgment on Taff Vale came *Quinn* v. *Leathem*. In this case the Belfast Journeymen Butchers' Association had tried to persuade Leathem to sack non-unionists. He refused, but he did offer to pay their union dues. The union refused the offer and exerted pressure, threatening a strike on one of Leathem's best customers unless he stopped buying meat from him. Leathem then sued the union and others for damages as a result of a conspiracy against him. The Law Lords ruled that such a strike or boycott – or the threat of either – could, in certain circumstances, be regarded as a conspiracy to injure and, once again, trade union funds were liable for the damages. The judgment appeared to be based on the argument that there was malice against the plaintiff and the union was not merely pursuing its own interests.

These last two judgments, coming on top of the earlier ones, and taken as precedents in a number of later cases, stimulated the unions to action. The implications for unions were immense. Just as the threat to trade union funds in the 1860s, after the *Hornby* v. *Close* case had driven trade unions to get involved in politics and to support the campaign for parliamentary reform, so these judgments drove them into affiliation with the new Labour Representation Committee. Many unions who to date had had no great enthusiasm for independent labour politics now recognised the need to have a voice in Parliament and to have the means of applying pressure to the other political parties to have their funds protected. By 1903–4 well over half the affiliates of the TUC were in the Labour Representation Committee.[4]

The judgments also triggered a debate. Not all trade union leaders or their sympathisers saw the direction which the courts were taking as completely bad. Richard Bell, the secretary of the union against whom the Taff Vale judgment had been made, believed that unions were paying the price for abusing their earlier position. Thomas Burt, former Northumberland miners' leader and the oldest serving Lib–Lab MP, wanted trade unions to accept legal responsibility for their actions. Some, like Sidney Webb, saw the judgments as a useful way of ensuring that union officials kept a tighter curb on their membership. But the gradual realisation of the financial implications of the judgment, and the decision of the Conservative Government to delay any action until a Royal Commission on Trade Disputes and Trade Combinations, set up in 1903, had reported, firmed up attitudes. With remarkable insensitivity to the changing political atmosphere (not untypical of Prime Minister Balfour), the Government refused to appoint any trade unionist to the Commission. Sidney Webb, who was a commissioner, was not perceived as particularly sympathetic to the unions on this issue and at least one other member, the engineer and coal owner, Sir William Lewis,[5] was seen as an arch opponent of unionism. As a result, the unions boycotted the Commission and demanded the complete reversal of the Taff Vale decision. Webb and two lawyer members of the five-man Commission produced a majority report, which did not accept that the Taff Vale judgment involved some great new principle and argued instead that there was 'no more reason that [trade unions] should be beyond the reach of the law than any other individual, partnership or institution'. It proposed that only a union's benefit funds should be protected from liability.

The new Liberal Government, which came into power at the end of 1905, initially proposed legislation roughly on these lines. But the unions pressed for complete immunity for their funds and were confident that in a free vote in the Commons this view would be carried. Thanks to the Prime Minister Campbell-Bannerman's intervention, immunity was conceded, against most legal advice, and the unions gained most of what they wanted in the Trade Disputes Act of 1906. The concept of civil conspiracy in trade disputes was overthrown, thus reversing the *Quinn* v. *Leathem* decision, and unions could not be sued, either directly or by representative action, for damages carried out by their members in the course of a trade dispute, thus reversing the Taff Vale decision. An act carried out by a union during a trade dispute was not illegal because it induced a breach of contract, or interfered with another's business or prevented someone working. It gave unprecedented and unique protection to trade unions, making, as A. V. Dicey wrote, 'a trade union a privileged body exempted from the ordinary law of the land. No such privileged body has ever before been deliberately created by an English Parliament.'[6]

Although in Campbell-Bannerman's view trade unions had now got enough and although he refused to go along with Labour Party demands for a Right-to-Work Bill, which would have made the state responsible for providing work for the unemployed, the Government remained relatively sympathetic to trade union pressures. A trade union campaign for old-age pensions played its part in the introduction of pensions in 1908. The activities of Sir Charles Dilke, Mary MacArthur of the Women's Trade Union League, the Cadbury Brothers and others in drawing public attention to the condition of women working in the sweated industries, form the background to Churchill's Trade Boards Act of 1909. Boards of employers, workers and impartial figures were to fix minimum wages for some of the sweated trades, like the chain-makers, lace and net-finishing, box-making and ready-made tailoring.

The year 1909 brought another court judgment – the Osborne judgment – against trade unions, which particularly affected the Labour Party, as the Labour Representation Committee had now become. In this, the House of Lords, by a majority, upheld an injunction which had been granted to W. V. Osborne against his union, the Amalgamated Society of Railway Servants. The injunction restrained the union from spending its funds for political purposes. The Chief Registrar of Friendly Societies, with whom many unions registered, had already sent some warnings that political action was not covered in the definition of lawful trade union activity under the 1876 Trade Union Act. Osborne's objection was not to using union funds for general political purposes but to using them only to fund the Labour Party, which, he argued, was not necessarily in the interest of trade unions.

The unions' concern was that the decision seemed to allow a minority a veto over the declared wishes of the majority of members. Some unions tried to get around the judgment by asking those who objected to opt out of payment, but this too was declared illegal. Eventually, in 1913, the Trade Union Act gave unions the right to engage in political activities if a ballot of members supported them, with individual members being free to contract out of the political levy.[7]

Industrial Relations

It is an over-simplification to imply, as some writing does, that in these years trade unions were having to operate in an environment of hostile employers, hostile governments and a hostile judiciary, all reflecting a class hostility to the trade unions as representative of the working class. The state's role was not unambiguously on the side of capitalist interests, as some older Marxist writing implied. The state's main concern was generally to achieve social stability and this often meant strengthening the bargaining power of labour. The Labour Department of the Board of Trade was openly critical of employers who refused to recognise trade unions, believing that such tactics would only strengthen the influence of more militant elements from among the rank and file. The Department's strategy was to find ways of reinforcing moderate trade union leaders against those whom they saw as extremist. They openly condemned people like Lord Penryhn and the Taff Vale Company for their labour policies. According to Roger Davidson, they saw the developments in trade union legislation in the early 1900s as resting 'to an unacceptable degree upon the social and economic prejudices of judges and juries who were drawn predominantly from the middle and upper classes'.[8]

That said, there are undoubtedly plenty of signs of a hardening of class divisions. One can quote numerous examples of a deep hostility to trade unionism in the newspapers and journals of the right. Bodies such as the Liberty and Property Defence League were highly vocal in their denunciations, but this was because they saw collectivism, which included an acceptance of trade unionism, as gaining ground. The great battles in 1896–8 and again in 1900 when the North Wales Quarrymen's Union confronted the unbending anti-unionism of George Pennant-Douglas, the 2nd Lord Penrhyn, who rejected all attempts at mediation and any outside interference in what he described as 'my private affairs', brought out a very clear polarisation of opinion.

But Penryhn was in no way typical and Clegg, Fox and Thompson had no doubt that,

> had British employers wished to be rid of trade unions, the depression years of 1902–5, with the Taff Vale precedent valid in every court, were as favourable an opportunity as ever presented itself. There are, however, relatively few instances of organised employers taking advantage of it to attempt to weaken or destroy the unions. . . . But the experience of the first five years of the twentieth century suggests that, despite Taff Vale, the majority of organised employers preferred to make a serious attempt to work with unions.[9]

Most significant employers had come round to accepting that trying to exclude unions was counter-productive and disruptive and were prepared to deal with them, at least through their employers' organisations. The exceptions were the shipping industry and the railways who argued that the effective running of their organisation required something like military discipline and where unregenerate attitudes still prevailed.[10] Ben Tillett talked of a 'growing confidence of employers in Trades Unionism, the more practical seeing the need for closer association and discussion with the workers' representatives'.[11] Because of this, it is important to move the perspective away from strikes to emphasise the more normal patterns of industrial relations.

As much a feature of the 1890s as new unionism were the attempts to establish boards of conciliation, often inspired by what was happening at the same time in Belgium, Germany, France and New Zealand, where formal systems of conciliation and arbitration were being devised. In many cases the initiatives came from local chambers of commerce, but in other cases the local trades council made the first move. In the first few years of the 1890s some 300 local boards of conciliation were set up in such places as Aberdeen, Bristol, Derby, Dudley, Halifax, Leeds, Liverpool, Manchester and Bradford. Usually they were made up of representatives from the trades council and the chamber of commerce, but sometimes representation was wider.[12] The success of such general boards was fairly limited since both trade unions and employers were wary about people outside the industry playing a part. But they encouraged the further development of collective bargaining. If nothing else they brought employers into contact with the leading trade unionists of their town. The Royal Commission on Labour of 1894 upheld the value of a system based upon collective bargaining:

> Powerful unions on the one side and powerful associations on the other have been the means of bringing together in conference the representatives of both classes, enabling each to appreciate the position of the other, and to understand the conditions subject to which their joint undertaking might be conducted.

Many employers also continued to see the central role which the unions could play in maintaining a level playing field in competition. A striking example was among the West Riding textile dyers where union and employers in 1894 agreed to work together to eliminate competition. A joint board of the industry fixed both wages and selling prices. The unions in their turn were granted a closed shop and were expected to strike against any firms which reneged on the agreement.[13] Something similar developed among the metal-bedstead makers when W. J. Davis, secretary of the Brassworkers' Union, collaborated with bigger employers to squeeze out the smaller, undercutting, back-alley firms. He helped to extend the strategy to a number of other Birmingham trades.[14] This kind of attitude – essentially a conspiracy against the consumer – was prevalent elsewhere. As John Hodge, secretary of the Steel Smelters' Union bluntly put it in his memoirs, he persuaded his members to collaborate with employers and to accept technical change 'provided we got a fair share of the plunder'.[15] The Lancashire cotton spinners, their wages' position regulated by the Brooklands Agreement, happily collaborated with employers on wider issues affecting their industry. The gradual spread of dispute procedures was taking place in many industries, largely on the employers' initiatives.

The early twentieth century brought a period of remarkable industrial tranquillity in many industries with the number of disputes in 1903, 1904 and 1905 falling to half what they had been in 1899. Part of the explanation was yet another downturn in the trade cycle, weakening the unions' bargaining power. The beginning of a sustained fall in real wages made many workers wary about taking on the cost of disputes.

Also, frightened by the implications of the court cases, union leaderships were putting a curb on striking.

The defeat of the ASE in 1897–8, not surprisingly, brought for a time a sharp falling off in the number of disputes in the engineering industry. The main gain for the employers had been the establishment of national bargaining procedures which were intended to remove power from local workers and to allow a restructuring of work patterns. In practice, as Jonathan Zeitlin has argued, there were strict limits as to what could be achieved. Much recent writing has been influenced by the influential American work, *Labor and Monopoly Capitalism. The Degradation of Work in the Twentieth Century*.[16] In this Harry Braverman painted a picture of workers building the machines which effectively deskilled them. Research has concentrated on the many and varied changes which were taking place in the labour process and directly linked these to the spread of unionism and the levels of militancy. As Richard Price has shown, new machinery often involved a substantial disruption to established relationships within the work-place, relationships between different groups of workers, and (perhaps more importantly) between workers and management. New techniques and inter-related processes meant more supervision, more timing of tasks, reallocation of duties and different payment methods as well as the usual debate over how far the gains of new technology should be shared between workers and employers.[17] The tensions of the 1880s and 1890s were often about demarcating the 'frontiers of control' between workers on the one side and the employers and their managers on the other. But there was always a limit to how far the employers could afford to dispense with their core of skilled workers and few technical innovations could entirely replace old skills.

Most British firms still remained relatively small and lacked the capital for a complete restructuring of their plant. They were a long way from assembly-line production. There was not the standardised mass market such as was developing in the United States and many firms were still dependent for markets on overseas customers looking for very specific, custom-designed items. Machines could not yet produce to these specifications and the skills of the all-round fitter and turner were still required. Also, even when new workers and new machinery were coming in there was still a need for people to train and supervise the new workers. Even if they may have wanted to avoid reliance on key groups of skilled workers, most employers were not in a position to do so. The reorganisation of the work-place and the deskilling of workers was something which took place only over a lengthy period of time and was a long way from being achieved before 1914. None the less, the desire to reorganise and the small but often significant changes being gradually brought in with new technology added to work-place irritation.

There is no doubt that the defeat of such a powerful union as the ASE had an immense effect on all groups of workers. One result was to strengthen calls for greater co-ordination between unions, resulting in the creation of the General Federation of Trade Unions in 1899. It never lived up to the high hopes of its founders, which included securing 'the power to determine the economic and social conditions under which they shall work and live', and to secure unity of action amongst all societies forming the Federation, but none the less it attracted some of the large unions, including the ASE.[18] A second result was moves within the engineering industry to try to create some unity among craft, semi-skilled and unskilled workers. Tom Mann ran with the idea, calling for a general union of engineering workers. The outcome was the Workers' Union, but it did no more than barely survive for the next decade. The official leadership of the ASE, anxious about the implications of unofficial action, was determined to assert control of its membership. The rank and file of the ASE rejected a revised version of the 1898 settlement at their 1901 conference but the ASE executive fairly ruthlessly imposed control. An unofficial strike in the Newcastle District in December 1902 was brought to an end by the executive stopping benefits. A similar dispute on the Clyde a month later, over a refusal to accept a reduction of wages in line with the rest of the country, resulted in the District Committee being suspended for having paid out benefits and in demands for repayment of those benefits already paid out.[19] The executive's comment was that as well as preventing 'a useless squandering of the Society's money.... A much needed lesson in trade union discipline has been taught.'

Relations in engineering were being further strained by the introduction in some areas of a system of payment by results, the 'premium bonus system'. It was a product of the American enthusiasm for systematic or scientific management, often known as Taylorism after its populariser, F. W. Taylor. It started from the belief that 'the natural instinct and tendency of men is to take it easy'.[20] One of the problems for management with the existing piecework systems was that with improved mechanisation and improved production methods workers would gain. Therefore, piece rates would be cut, causing tension in the work-place. To avoid their being cut too much workers would reduce output, thus defeating the point of piece rates.[21] The premium bonus system gave a worker a guaranteed fixed time rate, but offered a bonus if the job was carried out in less time. The time rate was based on past records and 'guestimates' of norms. There were, however, strict limits to what a worker was allowed to earn under the system and if the bonus rate appeared too high then the guaranteed time would be reduced. As it developed in Britain with what was known as the Rowan system, the usual formula was

$$\frac{\text{time saved}}{\text{time allowed}} \times \text{time taken}$$

so that the maximum bonus could never exceed double time.[22] It also gave employers the power to identify and if necessary, weed out slower workers. Despite opposition amongst the membership, the ASE accepted the system in the Carlisle Agreement with the Engineering Employers' Federation in 1902. Indeed, the union collaborated with employers to ensure that the rival, sectional unions like the Amalgamated Patternmakers were brought into line. The system spread to expanding areas such as the cycle, motor vehicle, locomotive and electrical industries and to the government factories and dockyards. It was accompanied by other changes. There was a tightening of supervision of workers. One of the things that the Engineering Employers' Federation had done in the aftermath of the 1897 lock-out was to set out deliberately to detach foremen from the union, by establishing a Foremen's Mutual Benefit Society from which trade unionists would be banned. Joe Melling has written of the emergence of foremen as the 'non-commissioned officers of industry', being firmly brought on to the side of management in the years before 1914. But at the same time, in some cases, the power of foremen was also being reduced and decisions on hiring and firing were increasingly being passed to white-collar managers who had no ambivalence about their position. There were growing complaints about constant timing, about 'policemen in various shapes and under different names' in the shipyards, about being 'watched and dogged by a whole army of non-producers', about work-hustling.[23] Skilled men had a sense of losing the remains of their autonomy.

Despite these developments, however, and the expectations of employers in the 1898 Settlement that they would be able to marginalise the craft workers and free themselves in the work-place, in practice this did not prove possible. New automotive machinery came in apace, but the ASE was effective in established firms in keeping control of the new machines for its members. Jonathan Zeitlin points out that 60 per cent of the work-force in firms covered by the Engineering Employers' Federation in 1914 were still classified as 'skilled'.[24] Most engineering firms remained relatively small and were wary about challenging worker power. Only 10 per cent of engineering workers, for example, were operating under the premium bonus system in 1909 and it was not until the war years that it was introduced into a major engineering centre like Sheffield.

In shipbuilding, the Shipbuilding Employers' Federation, formed in 1899, used its bargaining strength in the depression to curb the power of the Boilermakers' Society, to resist the well-used tactic of playing off one district against another in a system of wage leapfrogging and to impose a uniform wage-bargaining procedure.[25] But in heavy engineering and shipbuilding, because so many of the products were still one-off designs to meet a specific customer's requirements there were always opportunities for negotiations outside national procedures. Most recent work suggests that Taylorism was not very important in Britain before 1914. Craig Littler concludes that 'the majority of firms were unaffected, and even in the firms that were affected, the currents of change only represented the first stirrings of systematic management'.[26]

Workers' Response

Developments in industrial relations were bringing with them changes in union government, with more power being concentrated in the hands of full-time officials and executives becoming more properly representative. Some unions, like the cotton amalgamations and the MFGB had had representative executive committees from an early date. But many of the craft societies still made use of some local committee, usually from the town where the often movable headquarters was based. From the 1890s, however, that pattern rapidly fell into disuse.[27] To Richard Price, what was happening in these years was an attempt at deliberately strengthening central union control in order to reduce the extent of worker control within the work-place. He writes,

> There was no contradiction, for example, between the introduction of the premium bonus system on the very day that the engineering lock-out of 1898 was ended and the general strengthening of union authority that resulted from the Terms of Settlement.[28]

His study of building workers shows the same processes taking place in many builders' unions. More formal systems of industrial relations required a shift of authority to the negotiating body which increasingly was not in the locality, but at the centre. It required the executive to have the authority to override, if necessary, the wishes of the rank and file. In a union like the Boilermakers, where Robert Knight had built up immense autocratic power, central control had been maintained through district delegates who dealt directly with employers and were answerable to Knight. Elsewhere, such patterns gradually developed from the 1890s. In the building unions Price shows how the role of 'organiser' began to develop from the 1890s with the job not just of expanding membership but of intervening in local disputes.[29] There was generally rank-and-file resistance to handing over too much control to the centre and to officials, and elected executives were not always entirely malleable in the hands of the full-time officials. George Barnes, the secretary of the ASE, which in 1892 had established a fully representative executive, was driven to resign in 1908 by the persistent refusal of districts to accept executive rulings.

Growing Unrest

It was the attempts in many industries, in the face of increasing competition, to restructure their work-force and to alter patterns of work that, as much as anything, contributed to the unrest which began to reappear from about 1908. But there were also other factors. Once again economic improvement provided opportunities. There had been, for the first time since the years after Waterloo, a sustained period of declining or stagnating real wages, a product of the most extensive rise in prices since the 1820s. In industries such as coal mining the fall was probably as much as 10 per cent. After a relatively long period from the 1870s to the 1890s, when most of those in work were probably conscious of a rise in their standard of living, the setbacks of the early 1900s produced a sense of relative deprivation.

Although the period of labour unrest is usually taken as 1910 to 1913 when union membership begins to rise sharply, the signs of it and most of its features were there as soon as the economy began to move out of the depression of 1907–8. Industrial unrest predated union growth. The three main railways unions, the Associated Society of Locomotive Engineers and Firemen, the footplate men, the Amalgamated Society of Railway Servants, which had some footplate workers, and the General Railway Workers' Union, which organised the unskilled grades, launched a joint demand for an eight-hour day for drivers and firemen and a ten-hour day for the rest, together with improved overtime payments. The 40-odd railway companies were notorious for their refusal to deal with unions and Lord Claud Hamilton, chairman of the Great Eastern Company and chief spokesman for the companies, was an active opponent of unionism in principle and, on the additional ground, that military-like discipline was required in the railways, which trade unions would undermine. Also, the railway companies' room for manoeuvre was circumscribed by the fact that freight rates were controlled by law and any wage increase without an adjustment of rates would cut into profits. A ballot of members for strike produced an overwhelming vote in favour. The President of the Board of Trade, David Lloyd George, was an instinctive interventionist and he bullied the companies and the union into accepting the establishment of conciliation boards for each company. There was still no formal recognition of the unions, but it was agreed that worker representatives on the board need not be company employees. To Hamilton and his associates, however, the scheme was an alternative to union recognition and they went out of their way to try to keep unionists off the conciliation boards and to sabotage the working of the conciliation scheme. Lloyd George's hope that the experience of working with union officials would make the companies more amenable proved to be a vain one.

There were signs of growing unrest among engineering workers against what they saw as an excessively conciliatory policy on the part of the union leadership which had prevailed since the Settlement of 1898. There was a particular dislike of the readiness of the leadership to accept the introduction of the premium bonus system. Despite subsequent votes for strike action against the system the executive would give no lead on the matter.[30] North-East engineers in 1908 refused to accept a local conciliation settlement and only with great difficulty agreed to accept a union ruling that work should be resumed. Reform Committees began to appear to challenge the leadership. Within the shipbuilding unions there were signs of rank-and-file frustration at union complacency in the face of employers' efforts to weaken craft control and union power, by the renewed use of such techniques as the discharge note.

On the other side of the country, in the cotton industry, the traditional family-owned firm was giving way to the limited liability company. The paternalist world which Patrick Joyce has described as being common from the 1860s through to the 1890s was giving way to the harsh search for efficiency by managers answerable to shareholders. Despite a depressed period in the cotton industry, the predominantly female Cardroom Amalgamation broke with the more moderate

Spinners in 1908, rejected initial mediation and struck for five weeks against a wage reduction, bringing out 120 000 workers. Churchill tried to intervene by setting up a conference of the Employers' Federation and unions to look at ways in which some scheme for 'future automatic regulation of wages' might be devised, but it failed. In the following year, a further demand for a 5 per cent wage cut was withdrawn in return for a five years' wage freeze agreement by the Spinners' Amalgamation.[31]

Miners

Government action on the railways was a foretaste of further intervention in industrial relations' matters. In 1908 the Government gave coal miners a statutory eight hours' day. Although miners had been pressing for this for more than a decade, it added to the mounting problems of the industry. There had already been a marked decline in productivity over the previous 20 years, as pits became deeper and, in many areas, the geological conditions became more tricky. Output increased, but only by increasing the labour force, which in itself produced tensions both underground and in the already bad housing conditions of many pit villages. Coal prices were falling, leaving some of the smaller coal companies struggling, but profits were rising overall. In a labour-intensive industry with many small companies the response to these problems was a downward pressure on earnings and growing bitterness. Miners' earnings had risen sharply in the last half of the 1890s, but from 1901 the trend was firmly downward by some 20 per cent between 1900 and 1905. They picked up after 1905 but in 1909 were falling again and in 1913 had only just got back to where they had been in 1900. Roy Church concludes that miners had no real justification for feeling that there was a deterioration in their position, but that nevertheless the evidence is that some of them did.[32] He identifies two key factors in the level of unrest among miners. First is the increase in union membership from just over 40 per cent of miners in the 1890s to 81 per cent in 1913; secondly, he identifies the increased number of young lads being taken into the industry and the fact that many of the strikes were not of the experienced hewers at the coal face, but of the young lads on the surface. Given the high proportion of strikes which were mining strikes, it is clear that any attempt to identify the unrest of 1910–13 as a unique phenomenon needs to be treated with considerable caution.

The eight-hour day legislation created as many problems as it solved. In the Northumberland and Durham coalfield and in Fife, the legislation disrupted a pattern of working and actually lengthened the working day from pit-head to pit-head. In January 1910, 115 000 North-East miners struck against the new arrangements and particularly the proposal to initiate a three- instead of a two-shift system. The union leadership, which had pressed for the Act, could hardly support a fight against its application and the Durham and Northumberland men were left to battle on their own. It took more than three months before they conceded defeat.

Shorter hours in other coalfields also meant there was increased concern about working geologically difficult seams, so-called abnormal places, where maintaining output was difficult. This generated demands for the introduction of a minimum wage, particularly from South Wales where conditions were most difficult and where there was a refusal to move from a single- to a two-shift system in order to increase productivity. The fact that the two-shift system was resisted hardened the attitudes against any wage concessions on the part of the South Wales owners, who were moving into coal combines and were determined to make the industry profitable.[33] This came to a head in, first, the dispute with the Cambrian Coal Company over the need for a minimum wage in difficult or 'abnormal' places, which ran through the winter of 1910–11, and then in the Rhondda dispute at the end of 1910 which shut the pits for nearly nine months.

There were signs of a new bitterness in many of the disputes. The Rhondda miners, for example, 11 000 of them spread over four collieries, tried to bring out the safety men who normally remained to stop the pits flooding. They organised mass pickets to which the authorities responded by bringing in police reinforcements and eventually the military, although, contrary to legend, the military did not fire on the Tonypandy rioters. There were also bitter attacks from younger militants on what was seen as the excessively cautious leadership of the South Wales Miners' Federation, 'the creeping crawling, cowardly set who pose as leaders but do not lead'.[34]

As the problems continued and as relative earnings began to go down again, tensions increased. Attempts at district negotiation came to little and, in January 1912, there was a national ballot which came out three to one for a strike, but with a quarter of the members not voting and with considerable opposition in the important Durham area. Negotiations failed and, on 1 March, the miners across the nation struck for a minimum of 5s (25p) a shift. It was the first national strike of the MFGB. After a fortnight, the Government agreed to legislate for a minimum fixed by district. A new ballot in which fewer than half the members voted gave a narrow majority in favour of continuing the strike until a *national* minimum was written into the bill. But it was clear that neither owners nor government were going to make any further concessions. The militant South Wales area, where mining families had to cope with two strikes within 18 months and had few resources to continue, had voted two to one for acceptance. The union leadership called off the dispute.

Widening Unrest

The bitterness was real enough in these and other disputes, intensified by the fact that many of the strikes were longer than normal and involved many more workers; so that although there were only about half as many disputes in 1908 than there had been on average in the second half of the 1890s, the working days lost reached levels not seen since the exceptional years of 1897 and 1898. It also brought a renewed surge of organisation among those unskilled workers who had been at the forefront of the 1889–93 new unionism, but this time the scale of organisation was very much larger.

Havelock Wilson's Seamen's Union revived, taking advantage of rising freight rates and increased tonnage as demand expanded, to take on the Shipping Federation and push for a wage increase. In the summer of 1911 strikes spread among seamen in ports around the country. Dockers and carters came out in sympathy with the seamen. The shipowners quickly broke ranks and made individual settlements and the Federation was unable to use its usual strike-breaking tactics at so many different ports. Its hold over seamen was broken and the settlement in Cardiff even gave specific recognition to the union.[35] Just as at the end of the 1880s, strikes among seamen encouraged action among the port workers. Thanks largely to the efforts of Ben Tillett and Tom Mann, both revitalised by a spell in the industrial battlefields of Australia and refreshed with new ideas, a National Transport Workers' Federation was formed early in 1911 to bring together seamen, dockers and carters and to instil a belief in workers' solidarity. It worked, and by the end of August, with few strike-breakers available, concessions had been made after dockers' strikes in London, Liverpool and the Humber. The Federation could claim that hardly any dock workers were not organised. Seamen and dockers now had the highest level of unionisation of any industrial groups in the country.[36] At the same time, the timing was fortuitous. There was a growing demand for shipping space and few companies were willing to miss out on the potential profits. Employers agreed to local standardisation of wage rates and the seamen's union gained a measure of recognition.

A feature of almost all the seamen's and dockers' strikes was that they began as unofficial action. Many of the workers were new to unionism, which in their areas had been largely non-existent since the mid 1890s. There was little acceptance of the importance of organisation other than for immediate results. Mann and Tillett, neither of whom was a particularly painstaking administrator, found themselves having to accept strike decisions even if strategically they did not make a great deal of sense, and they struggled to maintain some kind of control over the situation as trouble flared in one port after another. In various places attempts to break the strike led to rioting and looting. Mann rushed around from port to port and was inevitably accused of stirring up the dispute when in fact he was generally a moderating influence, seeking settlements and perfectly prepared to work out deals with the owners and with G. R. Askwith, the main Board of Trade conciliator, who had an equally hectic time.

That same summer of 1911 also brought a national rail strike as railwaymen reacted to the frustrations produced by the tactics of many of the companies to circumvent the intentions of the 1907 conciliation scheme. Again, unofficial action stung the leadership into action. The Government was particularly anxious at disruption of a key transport area during a war scare with Germany in the aftermath of the arrival of the German gunboat *Panther* at Agadir. Lloyd George used the prospect of war to force the employers finally to sit down with union officials, while offering a Royal Commission to look at the conciliation scheme and at the issue of freight rates. More significantly, the strike seems to have generated a new enthusiasm for union. Membership of the ASRS and of the other rail unions grew so that by 1914 they were the third biggest group after miners and cotton workers. Secondly, the united action of all the rail unions in the 1911 strike gave encouragement to those who had been working for a single union to cover the whole industry. In 1913 the National Union of Railwaymen amalgamated the ASRS, the General Railway Workers' Union and the United Signalmen and Pointsmen Society. Only ASLEF and the Railway Clerks' Association stayed out. Although falling short of the aspirations for a single industrial union, it was the most spectacular success of the move towards industrial unionism and it grew fast.

A feature of many of the disputes of the period was frustration at the slowness of existing procedures. The Brooklands Agreement established in cotton spinning in 1892 broke down in 1913 because of its inability to deal fast enough with problems over bad material, which affected piecework earnings. There were regular disputes on building sites where *ad hoc* decisions had to be made about rates and where elaborate procedural structures were incapable of dealing with such issues. Similar problems in engineering were dealt with by the growth of workshop bargaining. The continuing need for rapid decisions for the variety of engineering tasks had pushed managers into negotiations with the one union representative on the spot, the shop steward. The very fact that the 1898 settlement had tried to confine the union's role to agreeing general time rates with piece rates negotiated at the shop floor had, paradoxically, enhanced the power of these unpaid local activists.

Elsewhere there were few union victories in 1912. A strike of lightermen on the Thames against an attempt to break their traditional closed shop spread to a port-wide stoppage. An attempt to bring out other ports in sympathy proved hopeless and the port employers would make no concessions. Tillett's demagogic rhetoric could keep the strikers going only so long and they gradually drifted back. Liverpool and London dockers also lost, although in Liverpool there was not the kind of overthrowing of earlier agreements which happened in London. With trade continuing to improve, some advances were won during 1913. London taxi-cab drivers, Yorkshire dyers, Lancashire cotton spinners, groups of municipal workers, shop assistants, London printers, Lancashire agricultural labourers, and High Wycombe furniture workers all won concessions after strikes. In the very different circumstances of Dublin there was a sustained counter-attack against union advance when, in August, the Dublin employer, W. M. Murphy, deliberately decided to confront the Irish Transport and General Workers' Union, the creation of James Connolly and James Larkin, which since 1908 had been sweeping up members in many different industries. It began as a tramwaymen's strike, but quickly spread to the ports and, when Larkin was sentenced to seven months' imprisonment for urging a general strike in support, Dublin degenerated into days of rioting and Larkin was rapidly released. Despite considerable financial support from Britain, although not the general strike that Robert Smillie and some others called for, near starvation among many strikers' families led to a drift back to work at the beginning of 1914. Before it ended five workers had been killed, thousands injured and hundreds arrested.

Some historians have seen the unrest peaking in 1912 and the tide of strikes waning. There seems much evidence against this. There were more strikes in 1913 and 1914 than ever before and although the number of working days lost was fewer than in 1912 at just under 10 million in each year, the levels were still exceptionally high. A recent study of the Scottish strike record in 1913–14 finds a change of tactics, but no loss of militancy. Strikes were more likely to be unofficial, shorter and involving the unskilled rather than the skilled. It also finds that the number of strikes was considerably underestimated in the Board of Trade statistics.[37]

One of the most significant developments was the spread of organisation amongst new engineering workers in new industries and here the crucial organisation was the Workers' Union. It had developed since 1898 as a catch-all for various groups of workers in different parts of the country, often being organised for the first time by local socialists. A major breakthrough came in 1904 when it succeeded in recruiting machinists at the British Small Arms factory where the modern techniques of mass production were being applied. From there it began to spread to other factories in the expanding new industries of the Midlands: cycles, cars and electrical goods. It was on these foundations that the Union was able to build spectacularly in the years after 1910. In 1911 membership rose from 5000 to 18 000 and, by the summer of 1914, had reached 143 000. The main gains were among those engineering machine operatives which the ASE was still declining to recruit. By 1914, 40 per cent of the Union members were in the Midlands. A dispute at the BSA works in October 1911 had brought an influx of new members. A year later disputes throughout Birmingham and the Black Country to win minimum wage rates stimulated a new membership drive and success brought further support. Support for women's claims and the appointment of a women's organiser tapped into the steadily growing numbers of women in engineering, a group quite beyond the horizon of the skilled members of the ASE. The Workers' Union, with its relatively low subscriptions and its open policy, was the best place to react speedily to a demand for support and organisation from workers appreciating the importance of organisation for the first time. Success – and even just action – bred success, and in 1914 the Union was employing six full-time organisers in Birmingham and the Black Country. In Coventry too, where the cycle trade was rapidly being transformed into the motor vehicle industry, inroads were being made. The all-embracing nature of the union, and the flexible structures of its organisation, made it ideally suited, not to defend customary patterns, which was the role of the ASE in old-established firms, but to carve out new terms and conditions in newer plants where the techniques of mass production were beginning to be applied.

The period also brought the increased involvement of women workers in disputes, often bringing a new joviality and exhilaration to strike action, as dancing and singing and a general carnival atmosphere accompanied the subverting of male authority – whether managers, foremen or strike-breakers – by ridicule and sexual innuendo.[38] Women workers initiated a major strike at the Singer Sewing Machine plant at Clydebank where the introduction of 'modern' management methods involved deskilling, hustling and increased supervision and timing, together with a host of 'petty tyrannies'. It involved many who were active in the Socialist Labour Party and other of the plethora of socialist organisations which were emerging in the West of Scotland. The union, as befitted an American-owned works, was a section of the Industrial Workers of the World. The strike in March and April 1911 was responded to with mass sacking and victimisation, scattering the activists to other firms all over the West of Scotland. The longest strike also involved Scottish women workers, mainly relatively young girls, curtain-net workers in Ayrshire, who held out for six months in 1913. Since neither of these were areas where women were competing with men for work, the women were able to attract support from men's unions. Support was not always forthcoming if the right of women to undertake certain jobs was in question.

Explanations

It is important to keep the scale of industrial unrest in the period 1910–14 in perspective. It is easy to be carried away by the seductive thesis of George Dangerfield that the industrial unrest was merely one manifestation, along with militant suffragettes and rebellious Irish, of a wider social malaise that marked the end of 'Liberal England'. As Table 1 shows, the number of disputes and the days lost certainly rose from 1910 onwards.

Year	*Stoppages*	*Days lost (thousands)*
1909	422	2687
1910	521	9867
1911	872	10155
1912	834	40890
1913	1459	9804
1914	972	9878

Table 1

On the surface the figures look clear enough, but work by Roy Church has pointed to the defective nature of the figures, both of numbers of strikes and days lost: lock-outs, for example, *are* included but many small strikes are not. Church has also drawn attention to the fact that none of the crude strike data takes account of the changing size of the work-force. Even with the existing figures, there were many more disputes in the years 1894, 1896 and 1897 than there were in 1912. Only 1913 and 1914 were worse than any year of the 1890s. The average number between 1895 and 1900 was 753; between 1908 and 1913 it was 750. Secondly, in the six years between 1895 and 1900 the average number of working days lost through strikes was 6 740 160; between 1908 and 1913 the average was 14 031 333. This would seem to indicate a spectacular rise, but the number of working days lost in 1911, 1913 and 1914 fell well short of the levels reached in 1893, 1897 and 1898. Only the nearly 41 million days lost in 1912 surpassed the 30 million of 1893 and inflated the average. Only in 1911 and 1912 was the number of workers involved in disputes higher than in 1893. The average number of workers directly involved was 163 500 in the 1890s; 554 333 in the 1908–13 period. Taking into account the increase in the size of the labour force, Church finds that for all workers the average number of strikes per thousand of workers was 0.023 in the 1890s and 0.052 in 1908–13; working days lost per employee per year were 1.0 in the 1890s and 1.4 between 1908 and 1913. The greatest rises in working days lost per employee were in textiles and transport (a fourfold increase in the latter). In metal, engineering and shipbuilding the average *fell* from 1.3 in the 1890s to 1.2; in building and construction the fall was even more spectacular: 0.7 in the 1890s to 0.2 in the 1908–13 period. In mining the figure remained at 6.5 working days per employee in both periods.[39]

There were, then, some national strikes on a bigger scale than before and they certainly added to widespread anxieties that the nation was in crisis, but, 1912 excepted, these years were less abnormal than is often suggested. Hugh Clegg has identified 14 strikes which between them account for 51 million out of 70 million working days lost in strikes between 1911 and 1914. More than 36 million days are accounted for by coal mining, particularly the national strike of February to April 1912.[40] It is true that there was a sharp rise in the number of trade unionists, a 61 per cent increase between 1910 and 1914, more than two and half times the increase of the previous decade, but at least some of that increase after 1912 was due to the recognition of trade unions as approved societies under the national insurance legislation rather than evidence of a new enthusiasm for industrial action. In terms of union density the most spectacular rises were in cotton textiles and in local government and education.

Nor was there much evidence that the disputes of these years were the rising of a class. Two out of three working men were not in unions and fewer than one women in twelve. There was little evidence of greater solidarity among different groups of workers than there had ever been. The efforts towards industry-wide amalgamations generally were not a success. The formation of the NUR was an important step in that direction, but the better-off footplate men and railway clerks stayed out. The different building unions showed little interest in the schemes for amalgamation proposed in 1912. The small engineering craft unions continued to set their face against absorption by the ASE and continued to battle for control of jobs in the work-place. The General Federation of Trade Unions formed in 1898 and which some socialists had hoped would become the greater co-ordinating force for industrial action, struggled to survive. One success was the so-called 'Triple Alliance' of Miners, Transport Workers and Railwaymen's Unions in April 1914. The idea which had emerged from the miners' conference was that they would make all their agreements end at the same time and would help each other in disputes. As the miners' president, Robert Smillie, explained,[41]

> Sympathetic action . . . is no longer to be left to the uncontrolled emotions of a strike period, but is to be the calculated result of mature consideration and careful planning. The predominant idea of the alliance is that each of these great fighting organisations, before embarking upon any big movement, either defensive or aggressive, should formulate its programme, submit it to others, and that upon joint proposals joint action should then be taken.

The miners' leaders, unfortunately, were to be the first to forget the second sentence.

Although there were syndicalists who saw the Alliance as creating a potential for the great general strike which would bring down the industrial and political system, this was hardly the motivation of the leaders of the unions who enthusiastically endorsed the proposals. Rather they saw it as a means of giving them massive bargaining clout, thus probably reducing the need for strike action. It would also, they hoped, eradicate the unofficial sympathy strikes which were a feature of the transport industries. The mechanisms for bringing the Alliance into operation were highly elaborate and did not remove power from the individual union executives. It was never to succeed in getting concerted programmes and had always to respond to sectional demands.

Nor was it a question of employers necessarily seeking confrontation. Some clearly did. The class conflict tones of Lord Claud Hamilton of the North-East Railway or of Lord Davenport of the Port of London Authority aggravated delicate situations. But there were equally endless efforts to cool the temperature. Askwith and his Board of Trade associates worked tirelessly as conciliators and never lost the belief that the voluntary system could work. It was at the suggestion of Sir Charles Macara, president of the Cotton Spinners' Federation, that an Industrial Council was established in 1911 and in a report of 1913 it reiterated the belief in voluntary collective agreements. Also, there was a government in power which was broadly sympathetic to the need to accept trade unionism and used its clout to get recalcitrant employers to negotiate. The rise of the rail union membership is a clear example of the effect which that could have. In a whole variety of ways government was keen to create a new consensus which would bring social harmony and revitalise economic efficiency and saw trade union officials as crucial figures in achieving such a consensus.

What then of the causes of the unrest? There clearly is a need to look beyond single causes. There were many different things happening in different industries and parts of industry. A whole variety of factors came together, not all affecting all workers. Once again economic conditions were right for many of the poorly organised workers to revitalise their organisations. Labour demand was high. Secondly, there had been a sustained period of falling living standards for many workers, particularly in coal-mining and textiles and of sharp bouts of unemployment for many skilled workers. Changes in the work-place, pressure from employers who themselves were feeling the pressure of increased competition, demands for new work practices, continuing technological change were all creating tensions. This is Richard Price's argument: that 'The labour militancy grew out of the historical struggle for work control'; that many different groups of workers had a sense that they were losing control of the labour process as a result of employers' advances, more centralised trade union control and the whole process of laying down collective bargaining procedures and that this was producing revolt.

The unrest also stimulated discussion of alternatives to the existing economic system. Out of the debates and discussions surrounding the 1911 Rhondda mining dispute came *The Miners' Next Step*, published by the Unofficial Reform Committee, but mainly the work of a Maerdy checkweighman, Noel Ablett. It rejected what it saw as the increased bureaucratisation of trade unions, which removed effective democratic control, and the accompanying incorporation of them into capitalist structures. Instead, it called for more radical policies where leadership responded to rank-and-file demands. It called ultimately for workers to have control of their own industry. This was not nationalisation, which merely handed power to the state, but a call for an alternative, more democratic structure: 'To have a vote in determining who shall be your foreman, manager, inspector, etc., is to have a vote in determining the conditions which shall rule your working life.'

Certainly there were those who had picked up the ideas of Daniel de Leon and the Industrial Workers of the World that trade unions could become the focus for the creation of a revolutionary working class and that capitalism could eventually be overthrown by the great general strike of the workers united in industrial unions. There were also key figures around who believed that industrial action could be the most effective means of bringing about political change. The often-inflated hopes in what the new Labour Party would achieve had gone by 1910 and a certain disenchantment with politics was apparent even among relatively moderate trade union leaders. The kind of people who were attracted by these exciting ideas were precisely the kind who would undertake the often soul-grinding work of organising. Not surprisingly they feature in disputes. The indefatigable Tom Mann, his fervour refreshed by these ideas which he picked up in Australia, gave a particularly English pragmatic touch to them by seeing industrial unionism as the necessary response to the new unity among employers. In the shipbuilding industry, he argued, employers 'take care to act concertedly over the whole – and this covers some twenty different trades, organised into some twenty-four different unions. These twenty-four unions have never been able to take combined action against the capitalists. Hence this weakness!'[42] Unlike the American syndicalists he did not believe that dual unionism, alternative revolutionary unions to the existing ones, was likely to be successful, but rather that the existing unions could be changed from within. He shuttled to and fro between disputes, organising, coaxing and arguing for changes, but the success in breaking down sectional barriers other than for brief moments was decidedly limited.

Bob Holton, J. E. Cronin and Richard Price have all argued that the influence of syndicalist ideas in explaining the emergence of growing demands for direct action coming from the rank and file has been excessively underplayed by most historians.[43] Certainly, there were perhaps more opportunities for a younger, more militant, generation to emerge into positions of influence. That younger generation, who had come into unionism in the 1880s and 1890s, were now coming to the end of their careers and were losing their fervour for a fight. Some, like Tillett, could still produce the demagogic rhetoric when occasion required, while regarding most of their members with considerable contempt. A few, like Thorne, were now respectable parliamentarians conscious of reputation.[44] But there was also the additional factor that there were more opportunities than ever for trade union officials to move into new careers. *The Times* commented on the sight of many officials moving into the new government jobs created by labour exchanges, trade boards, old-age pensions, national insurance, and extended factory inspection (all of them products of a concern to modify social tensions, improve industrial efficiency and encourage labour discipline). As an older generation moved out of their unions, new, younger activists were moving into positions of influence, with credentials for action yet to be won from their members. There is no evidence that committed syndicalists, with the possible exception of Larkin and the Socialist Labour Party activists at the Singer factory, were able to generate a dispute. Rather, they would throw their energies into the field once disputes had broken out.

It is important to try to get behind the rhetoric and the propaganda which the disputes of these years generated. There were blatant exaggerations from syndicalists and socialists about what was happening. There were equal exaggerations from the political right, who saw doom beckoning the nation at so many turns – a declining economic condition, a declining military position, government-led class war against the wealthy, and open rebellion in Ireland. Industrial unrest created by revolutionary socialist agitators was part of this doom-driven scenario. In fact, in sharp contrast to employers in most European countries and in the United States, most British employers continued to accept the value of trade unions and to work with them. Secondly, there was a limit on the extent of deskilling that was being carried out. Employers need skilled workers and continued to cosset them and to permit the continuation of a high level of job control by workers.

The early years of the twentieth century had seen a remarkable advance in the position of labour. Foundations were laid which were to survive until the 1980s. Churchill's Trade Boards Act of 1909 had brought direct government intervention into a range of industries essentially on the side of the workers and had inaugurated minimum wage legislation. The Labour Department of the Board of Trade, particularly when Lloyd George was in charge, had greatly extended the practice of intervention to try to settle disputes. Old-age pensions and both health and unemployment insurance had provided new levels of social security. The Trade Disputes Act had reaffirmed the right of workers to organise and to strike, the Trade Union Act of 1913 had confirmed their right to back their own political party. Despite the great stoppages, the years before 1914 saw collective bargaining agreements spreading, with procedures being developed for associations of employers and federations of unions to meet together.

6 Workers, War and the State, 1914–21

Few historians have doubts about the size of the impact of the First World War on British society and therefore on British industrial relations. In these, as in other areas, it can be debated how far the war actually created new conditions and how far it merely speeded up developing trends. But its effect was massive. Government needed the support of the trade unions to get the necessary increase in the production of war materials. Therefore, trade union leaders were called into consultation with government in a way they had never been before. The pressure from government on employers, to ensure that production was not disrupted, intensified and unions gained recognition in areas where they had never done so before. Government itself was directly involved in manufacturing. Not only were government departments providing the bulk of the contracts to private industry, but they controlled the railways, took a measure of control over coal mining and in munitions established 'national factories' to expand the production of war equipment. By the end of the war five million workers were employed in state-controlled establishments. But to achieve the necessary war production required changes in the work-place, and the war accelerated many of the technological and managerial developments which had been proceeding relatively slowly before 1914. In engineering areas, the process of the marginalising of the highly skilled and their replacement by semi-skilled machine operatives was speeded up. This was to involve the increased use of new workers, including women workers, moving into areas formerly controlled by skilled, time-served workmen. At the same time, as Chris Wrigley has argued, with two-fifths of the labour force in the services, the bargaining position of those left in the work-place increased immensely. Union membership continued to grow, although less fast than in the previous four years. By the end of the war it stood at over 6.5 million and covered something like 36 per cent of the potential membership. Growth continued for another two years until in 1920 it peaked with over 8 million members and, for the first time, more than half the potential *male* membership had been recruited.

Mining

The coal exporting areas were immediately hit by the disruption to markets caused by the outbreak of war. Output fell and with it the demand for labour. In Northumberland and Durham the fall in employment was some 30 per cent in the first year of the war. Large numbers of miners volunteered for the forces. About 13 per cent of the labour force left in the first six months of the war. Many of those who remained got caught up in industrial unrest. During 1915 some 1.5 million working days were lost through strikes in the industry and levels of absenteeism were high. By the end of 1915 surpluses of coal had turned to shortages, but miners refused to give up the hard-won eight-hour day. Loss of manpower continued until July 1916 when recruitment of miners into the armed forces was forbidden.

In March 1915 the South Wales Miners' Federation put in a demand for a rise and for adjustments to back-shift and night-shift pay. When the owners refused, the Fed. (as it was popularly known) gave notice of the end of the existing agreement. Political mediation failed and, in July, a delegate conference called for a strike. The government's activating of the recently passed Munitions of War Act to declare the strike illegal aggravated the situation and the men came out in defiance. Twenty thousand went on strike and ships were held up because of lack of coal. But it was not possible to arrest 20 000 miners and the Government pressed the employers for further concessions which were duly made. It was a learning experience for government that little could be done through direct confrontation.

Dilution of Labour

The leaders of the trade union movement showed themselves anxious to co-operate with the Government in the war effort and a voluntary industrial truce was declared. As hopes of the war being over by Christmas receded and it turned into a grinding slog on the Western Front, and as prices and rents rocketed, patriotic fervour gave way to more practical considerations and there were recurring disputes, particularly in the important Clyde area. The need for a rapid expansion of the labour force in the munitions industries became apparent, but there was rank-and-file resistance to working with non-unionists or to outsiders being brought into firms.

It is a measure of how far older patterns of craft control were still the norm, and how limited had been management success in taking control of the workshop, that the central problem which had to be tackled was to get the lifting of customary work practices to allow other than time-served workers to undertake certain tasks. The engineering employers tried to get the constraints on machine manning, on flexible use of labour and on overtime lifted as early as the end of 1914, but with little success. The ever-growing demand for munitions brought government intervention, with the Treasury Agreement thrashed out with Lloyd George in March 1915. It followed a wages' dispute on the Clyde where 10 000 engineering workers, faced with rising food prices and soaring rent rises in an area of massive housing shortages, came out on strike for an unprecedented 2d an hour rise. The dispute was unofficial, coordinated by a group of shop stewards in a body calling itself the Central Labour Withholding Committee. At this Treasury meeting it was agreed that trade unions should take the lead in trying to persuade their members to relax rules governing work practices which involved restriction on who could be employed at particular tasks; semi-skilled or female workers would be admitted. As a *quid pro quo,* profits in munitions firms were to be limited. In addition, the unions agreed that there would be no stoppage of work on munitions and disputes would, if necessary, be settled by arbitration.

While the unions discussed the implications of this and conspicuously failed to persuade their members to act on the basis of the Agreement, the war situation deteriorated rapidly. In June 1915 Lloyd George became the all-powerful Minister of Munitions and he proceeded to incorporate the Treasury Agreement into legislation – the Munitions of War Act. It made strikes or lock-outs at munitions works illegal, with the power to extend the Act to other establishments if necessary. The Act also now *required* that at such establishments restrictive practices affecting production or the employment of workers had to be suspended for the duration of the conflict. But it also limited employer power. Disputes over which work practices reduced output had to be referred for adjudication to the Committee on Production under Askwith. Alan Fox points out that this was the real measure of how union bargaining power had been transformed by the war situation because here was government actually recognising the existence of and the right to exist of restrictive practices.[1]

Part of the Act's purpose was to stop skilled workers taking advantage of the growing shortages to push up their earnings and bonuses, and to stop firms poaching skilled workers from one another. It required workers to get 'leaving certificates' from their employers, something which unionists rightly recognised would quickly develop into character notes, a subject of grievances for decades. It was the leaving certificate or discharge note, which remained in existence until 1917, which caused the greatest bitterness among skilled workers. They talked of the 'slave clauses' of the Act.[2] Its introduction reflected concern among Labour Department officials that discipline was breaking down. Llewellyn Smith talked of economic control over workers having weakened and 'to a very considerable extent men are out of control of both the employers and of their own leaders'. But it also lent itself to abuse by employers who could temporarily lay off workers without pay but still refuse to let them move firms. The Munitions Act meant that there was no longer a voluntary agreement, but a requirement on workers to obey foremen's instructions, to accept changes in work practices and to allow the imposition of piece rates. For this reason Joseph Melling sees it as tipping the balance at the 'frontiers of control in firms firmly towards management and away from skilled workers'. Hamfisted handling of disputes (perhaps even deliberate provocation on the part of some firms) resulted in workers being fined or imprisoned.[3]

The changes taking place also gave an enhanced role to workshop representatives, the shop stewards. These had been around in some unions since the late nineteenth century as collectors of subscriptions, checkers of union cards and generally taking responsibility for keeping an eye on piece rates. They had existed in the Boilermakers' Society since 1874 and had been officially appointed in the ASE from 1892. Not surprisingly, they developed into repositories for complaints and work-floor representatives on delegations to employers. But the rapid changes in work patterns made their role even more vital and committees of the different shop stewards in a factory and then in different factories began to appear. The fact that so many changes taking place in the workshops were job specific meant that, all the time, employers were having to negotiate with groups of workers about how jobs were to be tackled and who was to do them. Shop stewards increasingly developed a role as shop-floor negotiators. Rather unwillingly, both employers and unions came to accept that shop stewards had to carry out this function. With the industrial truce and a plethora of bureaucratic committees into which full-time trade union officials were drawn, the role of the shop steward within the union became ever more significant.

Clydeside

The Munitions Act was intended as a prelude to the introduction of untrained workers into the war industries, including female workers. When the process began in a firm near Glasgow in the late summer of 1915 there was immediate resistance. The ASE had agreed to dilution on condition that women workers were paid the full craft rate for the job, expecting that this in itself would exclude them. The firm refused on the grounds that they were only doing part of a craft job. When attempts were made to bring in dilution in some of the main Glasgow munitions' plants resistance intensified and was co-ordinated by the unofficial shop stewards' committee, now calling itself the Clyde Workers' Committee.

Most of the leaders of the CWC were articulate political activists influenced by Glasgow's diverse socialist scene in the years before the war. A few had been associated with the extreme 'impossiblist' Socialist Labour Party, others with the British Socialist Party, as the Social Democratic Federation had become. Lloyd George's attempt, on a Christmas Day visit, to woo the workers to acceptance of dilution was heckled by the shop stewards. The Munitions of War Act was duly amended to require dilutees to be paid at craft rates and to modify the leaving certificates if workers were out of work for more than two days. The result was that dilution proceeded with reasonable rapidity, with visiting commissioners working out arrangements with management and unions. Only a very few women gained access to skilled work and most were confined to labouring or unskilled jobs with semi-skilled *men* being moved up to the skilled ones. With renewed confidence, the Government then acted against what they saw as subversive figures among the shop stewards and their allies. Some were jailed and others received the ultimate punishment of exile to Edinburgh. Although there were some small protest strikes little came of them. Engineering and shipbuilding earnings were on the whole keeping up with price increases and employers were prepared to make unofficial wage concessions rather than face a dispute.[4]

A great deal of the literature on war-time events has focused on Clydeside, an important munitions and shipbuilding centre. Indeed, no other area of Scottish labour history has been studied in such detail as the period 1914 to 1922 and come to such diverse conclusions. Earlier accounts, shaped by the memoirs of participants, presented a heroic picture of socialist workers challenging the government over house rents and over dilution, leading on to an anti-war campaign. James Hinton's study emphasised the role of engineering shop stewards representing the skilled craftsmen who were threatened by new technology, the introduction of which was speeded up, and by the loss of their craft privileges due to dilution of labour. The initial response, he argued, was a traditional defence of craft privileges but, thanks to the influence of a range of Marxist ideas on many of the shop stewards who had formed the Clyde Workers' Committee, these defensive tactics broadened into a campaign for workers' control and a class confrontation with government and employers and in defiance of the official union position. The 'revolt of the Clyde' was only crushed by the full might of the state being applied and the arrest and exile of the leaders.[5]

Ian McLean, Christopher Harvie and others have forcefully challenged what they see as the 'Legend of Red Clydeside' and have concentrated on the essentially conservative and sectional nature of much of the activity, as the skilled sections of the work-force battled to defend their craft positions.[6] Alistair Reid, concentrating on the shipbuilding yards, finds that dilution there was much less significant than in the engineering shops and the Boilermakers successfully defended craft positions and resisted the introduction of unskilled female labour. Others have argued that far from having to battle against a hostile state, skilled workers in these years, because of the strength of their bargaining position, found the state ready to make concessions in order to maintain industrial peace and to increase output. Far from there being an alliance of the state and the employers, Board of Trade and later Ministry of Labour officials continued as before the war to try to strike a balance between capital and labour and always to encourage negotiation with unions.[7] At various times there was a debate within government about how far workers could be coerced into collaboration in the war effort and how far they needed to be coaxed with concessions. On the whole, it was the latter argument which prevailed.

A great number of disputes took place along the Clyde because a very high proportion of the work-force in the area – substantially higher than any other region – were involved in shipbuilding, engineering, metal-working, chemicals and coal mining, all industries very much affected by war-time conditions. But there were other factors. During the nineteenth century, Scottish employers had had to deal with relatively weak unions, many of them specifically Scottish, and with a relatively low-paid work-force, perhaps as much as 10 per cent lower than in English firms. That had gradually changed in the years before 1914 as unionism spread and Scottish unions were absorbed into British-wide ones. Wages began to rise faster than in other areas and employers faced challenges which they had never before experienced. The shipbuilding boom of the immediate pre-war years had allowed employers to accept further union gains, but there was still a deeply entrenched employer hostility among many of the Clydeside employers towards unionism. John Foster has argued that Clydeside managers had little experience of real collective bargaining and relied largely on the 'autocratic power of undermanagers, foremen and chargehands and the ultimate sanction of dismissal'.[8] A vibrant socialist movement in all its various manifestations – itself a product of the fact that trade unionism was relatively weak – was also present and that, coupled with appalling housing conditions, produced a potentially explosive mixture. It was, however, a localised phenomenon and one which the government handled with particular skill, conceding control of rents and combining concession and coercion in industrial policy. By the end of 1916 many of the 'exiles' were back in Glasgow. By the summer of 1917 Beardmore's Mile End shell factory was employing two of them as shop stewards and another as a foreman. They helped push up both output and bonuses.[9] Elsewhere the process of dilution and the suspension of restrictive practices proceeded relatively smoothly.[10]

Gains and Losses

The introduction of conscription in 1916 meant further problems of 'dilution' as more women were brought in to areas other than munitions. Textiles, shoe-making, printing, pottery and transport were the areas most affected and one has the piquantly ironical situation of unions demanding equal pay for women. The ASE rejected any suggestion that women should be admitted to the union, although unskilled labourers had been admitted since 1912. But, anxious to keep women's wages under trade union control, and to keep women from joining the Workers' Union, the ASE encouraged the National Federation of Women Workers to organise them, but only on condition that the Federation would agree to the withdrawal of women from craft occupations when the war had ended. There was little success and little effort made in pushing up the wages of women munitions workers, with some earning less than a pound a week.[11] It took until nearly the end of the war before women workers began to see some real improvement in their earnings. The Spinners' Unions, despite a shortage of piecers, resisted the introduction of more women and pressed instead for a relaxation of the rules on child labour.

Inquiries into the reasons for persistent industrial unrest pointed to various other issues. There was a perception that the burden of war was not being equally shared and that many companies were making excessive profits, having taken the opportunity to push up prices. The Government had failed to carry out earlier pledges to curb such profits. There were also problems created by the fact that substantial differences in earnings began to emerge between skilled workers in cognate industries and in a narrowing of the differentials between skilled and semi-skilled workers. Skilled engineers on time rates found that pieceworkers like boilermakers could sometimes earn three or four times more. There was evidence of mounting grievances over how the system was operating in all the main munitions centres. The issues themselves became much more shop-floor issues involving rapid changes in method or organisation. New products being brought in required local decisions. As Richard Hyman points out, the war produced the paradox of collective bargaining being pushed from district to national level, while the struggle for job control was pushed down to the work-place.[12] But it is worth remembering that for much of the war years it worked. Despite the potential for tension, the number of strikes fell back during the first three years of war to the kind of level that had existed in the late 1890s and the working days lost down to pre-1908 low levels. Not until the final year of the war did they begin to pick up again.

Although most attention has focused on disputes in the war industries, there were recurring problems in other areas. Relations broke down in the cotton industry, badly affected by the closing of export markets, and resulted in a strike and lock-out in the spring of 1915, before the government intervened and agreed a war bonus. In 1917 a Cotton Control Board was established and this encouraged, for the first time, industry-wide collective bargaining in cotton. Miners' earnings rose more than those of any other group of workers as naval demand for coal grew. The miners' bargaining position was immensely strong because so many had volunteered and joined the army, while others had moved to more lucrative jobs in munitions. There was no army of surplus labour to replace strikers. A new demand for 15 per cent was countered by an owner's suggestion that what was needed was a reduction. In November 1916 the Board of Trade took control of the South Wales' mines under the Defence of the Realm Act, regulating most aspects of the industry, but leaving day-to-day control in the hands of the owners. The levels of industrial unrest fell, but so too did output.

Government intervention in industrial relations during the war years had major implications for the future. The various bodies generally insisted on union recognition; the Dilution Commissioners required works committees to be established to settle disputes. The Committee on Production, originally intended to find ways of increasing production, but converted into a mandatory arbitration body, brought a major step towards standardisation of wages between different districts in many industries. Overall there were substantial pay rises, although these probably still fell short of the rise in the cost of living. On the other hand, for at least some groups of workers (mainly those on piece rates) earnings rose substantially. Unskilled workers probably gained more than any from the war years. Bonuses, plus opportunities for reasonably paid work for women raised the households of many unskilled out of dire poverty for the first time.

There were other gains. As part of his deal to get Labour support for his coalition government in December 1916, Lloyd George established a Ministry of Labour, something for which the TUC had been pressing for a few years. John Hodge of the Steel Smelters' Union was the first minister, but he found it difficult to carve out an effective role for the new body. The new Ministry pushed forward schemes for national wage bargaining in engineering, coal mining, chemicals, shipping and wool.[13] The national wages' agreement in engineering in 1917, in which the Engineering Employers' Federation, pushed by fears of leapfrogging wage claims, gave formal recognition to

47 unions at national level, allowed a quarterly review of wage movements. It was the war years which, at long last, saw the spread of unionisation among the mainly women workers of the woollen textile industry, for long notorious for its lack of unionisation. Membership of the General Union of Textile Workers, which was less than 13 000 in 1914, increased nearly fivefold during the war years.

But it was not all gain. Employers seized the opportunity to alter work patterns, sub-dividing and simplifying processes and speeding up tasks. The relaxation of factory and workshop legislation allowed the unscrupulous to exploit and endanger their workers and the new women workers in many industries were particular vulnerable.[14]

Total War

The coming of conscription, in contradiction to many assurances given by Liberal leaders, created problems about who should be exempted. Initially it was up to employers to decide which workers were 'unnecessary'. This led to a crisis in the autumn of 1916 when a previously exempt worker at Vickers' Sheffield works, Leonard Hargreaves, was called up. A strike resulted, organised by the shop stewards but backed by the ASE District Committee and almost all the skilled engineering workers in Sheffield. A deal was worked out with the ASE that the union could provide exemption cards to key workers whom it regarded as necessary for the war effort. But it also created embittering anomalies as dilutees, doing the work of skilled men but not in the ASE, found themselves conscripted. Little wonder the song went,

> Don't send me in the army, George – I am in the ASE
> Take all the bloody labourers, but for God's sake, don't take me.

In preparation for the Sheffield strike a national conference of engineering shop stewards was held in Manchester. They talked of united action but this proved difficult to achieve. A strike in Barrow was left to collapse on its own. The most serious war-time strikes in engineering spread from Lancashire to Sheffield and London in May 1917 and resulted in eight of the strike leaders being arrested. They were triggered by the decision to abolish the trade card scheme and to extend the dilution of labour beyond government-regulated firms to private work.[15] The ASE resisted all efforts to equalise protection and forced the Government to accept that no skilled men or apprentices would be called up until all male dilutees in the particular munitions area had been withdrawn. These struggles reflected inter-union battles. The craft exclusiveness of the ASE had provided opportunities for the Workers' Union to recruit among the new workers and there was bitter resentment at this by the ASE officials. In the May strike the Government refused to negotiate with the shop stewards, but the size of the strike persuaded them to try to get agreement with the ASE leadership. The executive was willing to accept a modified measure of dilution in private work, but the compromise was overwhelmingly rejected in a ballot of members and the Government backed away. It also finally withdrew the hated leaving certificate.

The readiness with which the Government worked with the union leadership caused internal problems. Officials were excluded from organising industrial action and, not surprisingly, often condemned precipitate unofficial action. As a result, the influence of the shop stewards and other rank-and-file activists in the work-place increased. Many trade union leaders were co-opted on to government committees and, therefore, were increasingly perceived as part of the state machine. There was a sense, easily generated by anti-war elements, that they were no longer protecting their members' interests. Clegg effectively argues that there is little justification for this. The ASE officials doggedly resisted erosion of members' rights. On the other hand, attempts by some of the shop stewards to create some kind of national movement and alternative leadership were never really successful. There had long been carping criticism of the conservatism of trade union bureaucracy, and activists liked to see themselves as representing a homogeneous rank and file. They claimed, like the Clyde Workers' Committee, 'to represent the true feelings of the workers'. But the majority of shop stewards probably did not see themselves in these terms and regarded themselves certainly as spokesmen for the rank and file but not as alternative leaders to the union officials.

In November 1917, 50 000 Coventry workers were out because a firm refused to deal with shop stewards and there was a danger of a national strike until the employers conceded recognition. But here the skilled craft workers were a minority amid the semi-skilled who had been recruited to the car and truck factories and rank-and-file pressure was contained within the union organisation. Altogether nearly three million working days were lost in engineering in 1917. Given that the rank and file had specific and limited and variable industrial aims, however, co-ordination was difficult. Anti-war shop stewards in all industries found little workshop response to demands for strikes to end the war. Formerly left-wing leaders of some of the general unions threw themselves into patriotic pro-war activities, but received little criticism from their members. Since gains were being made by the unions organising the semi-skilled and unskilled, there were few reasons for discontent.

Looking to Peace

Although the outcome of the war was still far from certain, the unions and the Government were, as early as 1916, looking to the world after war. Harry Gosling, secretary of the Watermen and Lightermen's Union, presiding at the 1916 TUC, indicated some of the demands when he declared that something more was required than 'a mere avoidance of unemployment and strikes'. He urged employers to consider letting workers have some share 'not in profits but in control':

> We do not seek to sit on the board of directors, or to interfere in the buying of materials, or with the selling of the product. But the daily management of the employment in which we spend our working lives, in the atmosphere and under the conditions in which we work, in the hours of beginning and ending work, in the conditions of remuneration, and even in the manner and practices of the foreman

> with whom we have to be in contact, in all these matters we feel that we, as workmen, have a right to a voice – even to an equal voice – with the management itself. Believe me, we shall never get any lasting industrial peace except on the lines of democracy.[16]

The Government, prompted by the Labour Department of the Board of Trade, appointed a committee of officials from employers' associations and trade unions, plus some academics under the Deputy Speaker J. H. Whitley, to make proposals 'for securing a permanent improvement in relations between employers and workmen and to recommend ways of systematically reviewing industrial relations in the future'. Like all other reports into industrial relations, Whitley reaffirmed a commitment to the voluntary system and rejected any great expansion of the Government's role, stressing instead 'the advisability of a continuance, as far as possible, of the present system whereby industries make their own agreements and settle their differences themselves'. Its five reports proposed major innovations. In its first report, in the summer of 1917, it recommended three levels of joint machinery in the main, well-organised industries, joint industrial councils at national level, joint district councils and works committees. In a second report they proposed an extension of the system of trade boards, which Winston Churchill had introduced in 1909, where there was little or no existing organisation, and a system of joint councils with some government assistance in poorly organised industries. Finally they proposed an Arbitration Council to which, as a last resort, disputes could be referred, although rejecting any system of compulsory arbitration. In addition, the Minister of Labour could authorise a court of inquiry into disputes.

The big unions largely chose to ignore the recommendations. Coal, engineering, shipbuilding, iron and steel and textiles all rejected them. But in the less organised and newer industries the opportunities presented were seized with some alacrity. National Councils were set up by the end of the war in baking, furniture-making, hosiery, pottery, rubber, vehicle-making among others and negotiations were in hand in the boot and shoe trade, commercial road transport, electrical contracting and power supply, newspapers, printing, tramways, the tin plate industry, the gas industry and in the civil service. A number of unions, particularly white-collar ones which had spread fast during the war, seized the opportunity which Joint Industrial Councils (JICs) gave them to achieve formal recognition by employers.[17] The National Union of Journalists, for example, thanks to Northcliffe's support, received recognition from the various newspaper groups between 1917 and 1921 and the EEF came round to recognising the Clerical Workers' Union (CAWU) and the Draughtsmen and Allied Technicians (DATA). Although the original intention was that the industrial councils would cover private industry, in fact public servants were major gainers. Local government officers in NALGO and other municipal employees in the National Amalgamated Workers' Union and in the National Union of Clerks all gained recognition for the first time on joint industrial councils. They were also of great importance for many areas of both service and manufacturing industry. At the beginning of 1920, Ernest Bevin of the Dock Workers sat on some fourteen JICs.[18] Altogether some 74 joint councils were established in the three years after 1918.

Whitleyism was a recognition of the changes which the war had brought about, in that it involved a clear acceptance by government that unionism and collective bargaining were normal and fundamental to relations in the work-place. Most of the established employers' associations had little enthusiasm for the idea of works' committees which they believed impinged too directly on management prerogatives. But union officials too disliked anything which might bypass their roles. None the less there were general hopes in 1917–18 that the post-war world would bring more orderly and more co-operative industrial relations. An employers' Federation of British Industry formed in 1916 committed itself to joint discussion of wages and work practices. It saw future industrial development taking place on a tripartite basis of co-operation between employers, unions and government. However, even before the war ended there were signs of renewed militancy among unions. Part of it no doubt stemmed from a general war weariness and from discontent over food shortages and high prices. But another factor was the fresh impetus given to the left by the Russian Revolution. In many ways, the timing of the Whitley proposals was unfortunate because the boom conditions in the immediate aftermath of war were encouraging the bigger unions to push for all they could get, with some activists on the left convinced that it was only a matter of time before a socialist revolution could be achieved. They showed little interest in developing new procedures or in schemes which fell short of workers' control.

The final year of the war had seen union membership leap by over a million to just under eight million members compared with the 4 million at the outbreak of war. By 1919 there was a union density of 43.1 per cent and for the first time more than 50 per cent of the male potential membership was organised. The growth continued during the next year when a further 400 000 members were added. Many workers were unionised for the first time and women unionists became a significant factor. The Workers' Union, which had 5000 women members in 1914 had, thanks largely to the work of Julia Varley, their women's organiser, 80 000 by 1918, a quarter of its membership. The National Federation of Women Workers could claim 76 000 and the National Union of General Workers another 60 000. The United Garment Workers recruited 20 000 women members during the war. Despite this, two-thirds of women munitions workers had not been unionised and only one woman worker in five was in a union. The world of unions continued to be predominantly a male one and there was only one woman on the executive committee of any major union.[19] Government did little to help. The Ministry of Reconstruction in a report concluded that 'the employment of married women outside the home is not to be encouraged'. Most unions insisted that 'women must go' and the TUC equivocated.[20]

It is clear also that there were signs of pent-up frustrations and demands. Nineteen eighteen saw the highest number of stoppages of any previous recorded year, with the exception of 1913, and the number rose for the next two years. The number of working days lost in 1918 was twice what it had been in any of the other war years and 1919 surpassed any previous year with the exception of 1912. Yet Lloyd George seemed genuinely to have believed that the post-war world could find some better way of dealing with industrial relations. An Industrial

Conference of employers' organisations and unions was called in February 1918, which it was hoped would produce a permanent council and ideas for peacefully settling differences.

Post-war Boom

From the unions' point of view the main, initial post-war concern was the threat of unemployment when 4 million members of the forces returned. For some dilutees there were immediate problems, as many of them got their notice on the day war ended. But, at least there was an unemployment 'donation' for 13 weeks even for those who were not covered by the insurance scheme. Legislation ensured that there was no sudden reduction of wages, which had to be maintained for at least six months. The Minister of Labour could also extend the 1909 Trade Boards Act to any trade which it considered necessary and, by the end of 1919, 1.5 million workers were covered. The right to strike was restored and compulsory arbitration ceased.

Both sides of industry were pressing for an end to war-time controls. A central issue was the restoration of pre-war practices. In order to smooth the process of dilution the Government had promised that all changes in working practices in engineering workshops would be reversed after the armistice. The ASE were determined to ensure that this was carried out and that the rights of craft engineers were not confused with other issues. They refused to discuss the procedure for achieving this with any other unions and insisted on direct negotiation with government. Once again the bargaining strength of the ASE is apparent in that the reversion to pre-war patterns seems to have proceeded reasonably smoothly, with recalcitrant areas swept up by the Restoration of Pre-war Practices Act of August 1919.[21] British engineering workshops, according to the TUC, were 'badly laid out, often badly lighted, inadequately equipped, and, many of them wastefully managed'. But hopes that the war-time changes would become permanent, and bring greater efficiency in an engineering industry which was recognised as deeply inefficient compared with Britain's competitors, came to nothing.[22]

For most unions the main means of preventing excessive unemployment appeared to be the reduction of the working day. The expectation that Britain would ratify the Washington Convention, establishing the International Labour Organisation and making the eight-hour day legally binding, persuaded some employers to concede it right away. The cotton textile unions, collaborating as never before, won a 48-hour week after a strike, compared with their previous 55.5 hours.[23] The ASE and the other members of the Federation of Engineering and Shipbuilding Trades had managed to negotiate a reduction in the working week from 54 to 47 hours, but this was rejected by the Clyde District Committee which was now dominated by a revived Clyde Workers' Committee, who were suggesting that the agitation should be for a 30-hour week. In January 1919 the Glasgow district of the ASE struck for a 40-hour week and, according to Iain McLean, for a restoration of the traditional 9.15 breakfast break.[24]

The strike seems quickly to have become of major symbolic importance, with other workers believing that a victory for the engineering workers would have spin-off for others. The STUC and local trades councils all declared their support for an eight-hour day, five-day week. There were sympathy strikes among electrical supply workers, miners and iron moulders in the surrounding areas and enthusiasm, but not strikes, among the leaders of some of the unions of the unskilled. But it was mainly an engineering strike and mass picketing ensured that it spread to most shipbuilding yards and engineering workshops. According to John Foster, unemployed, discharged servicemen also played a significant part. On 31 January 1919, a mass demonstration ended in riot, police baton charges and the arrest of various bloodied shop stewards. Troops and tanks were deployed in the streets. In Lanarkshire, miners led by a British Socialist Party-inspired Miners' Reform Committee seized the union offices reputedly at gunpoint and forced the officials to declare a sympathetic strike.[25] Five of the leading organisers were found guilty of incitement to riot and of rioting and the two future Members of Parliament, Emanuel Shinwell and William Gallacher were sentenced to five months' and three months' imprisonment respectively.

Whether it was the revolutionary moment lost has continued to be much debated. There were particular circumstances in the West of Scotland such as employer attitudes, dreadful housing conditions and socialist networks which made the situation particularly fraught and, within three years, the Independent Labour Party candidates were to win 10 of the city's 15 seats. But the link between the demand for shorter hours and the wider discontents and disenchantment with Liberalism which produced the 1922 vote is tenuous.[26]

A similar near-general strike in Belfast had already begun pressing for 44 hours and there was an attempt by some London engineering stewards to generate a general strike. The ASE's executive demanded an immediate return to work and suspended the district committees in both Glasgow and Belfast. Other areas of Scotland were highly critical of the irregular manner in which the strike had been brought about and clearly saw the riot in George Square and the subsequent trials as having damaged the shorter hours' movement. The Glasgow men went back on 11 February and the Belfast ones a week later. Despite this failure, more than 6 million workers had their hours reduced in 1919 and the 47- or 48-hour week became common. Miners, railwaymen and transport workers had all seen their leisure time extended by the end of 1919.

Government was less keen to see its war-time powers of regulation altogether abandoned. In line with the Whitley recommendations a permanent Industrial Court was established to which, with mutual agreement, disputes could be referred. Failing consent of the conflicting parties, the Minister of Labour could order a court of inquiry which would report to Parliament. Also in line with Whitley, industrial councils, which had started to be established before the end of the war, continued to spread – again particularly in the newer industries.

In the three industries in which government had been directly involved, railways, coal mining, and other transport, the government was unwilling to relax its influence. Lloyd George, no doubt mindful of his earlier experiences with the rail companies, was determined that there should be no return to the pre-war situation and the Government forced amalgamation into four companies. The unions liked the situation since they found the Government amenable to pressure, such as for an eight-hour day, introduced early in 1919, but there was tension created by the fact that the war years had seen a narrowing of the differential between footplate men and the unskilled porters and others.

The MFGB in January 1919 launched a demand for a 30 per cent increase in wages, a six-hour day and public ownership with 'democratic control'. They argued that wages during the war had failed to keep up with the cost of living while profits had trebled. The mine-owners themselves were not peculiarly brutal but they were faced with great problems, only some of which were of their own making. Coal seams in many regions were getting more difficult, costs were rising and profits were falling. The structure of the industry, despite some pre-war combines, was still relatively primitive with most companies consisting of only two or three pits. British coal was less able to compete in the post-war export markets than it had ever been.

The Triple Alliance supported the Miners' Federation with strike threats and the Government quickly succumbed and agreed to a Commission of Inquiry on which the MFGB would nominate or approve of half the members. It was regarded as a major victory for the Labour movement. The Commission under Mr Justice Sankey reflected all the difficulties and the prejudices of the industry. The employers had reason for some anxiety since an interim report by the four government nominees declared that 'Even upon the evidence already given, the present system of ownership and working in the coal industry stands condemned, and some other system must be substituted for it, either nationalisation or a method of unification by national purchase and/or joint control.' The tone was set by the aggressive questioning of the aristocratic owners of mining royalties, and by Robert Smillie, the president of the MFGB. The one thing the whole Commission could unite on was support for the nationalisation of mining royalties. Interim reports recommended a seven hours' day and a 20 per cent increase, which the miners and owners eventually accepted. In the final stages, the Commission generated four separate sets of recommendations from the various parties in the membership. The union representatives and their sympathisers on the Commission and Sankey himself recommended nationalisation of the mines: Sankey on the grounds that it was the only way to achieve the necessary efficiency and economies of scale, the lack of which had bedevilled capital investment in the industry; the union representatives on the grounds that only nationalisation would bring just and adequate working conditions.

Nationalisation was a policy which had been floated by socialists at the 1892 TUC, but it had only been supported by the MFGB since just before the war. Some saw nationalisation as a step to workers' control of the industry, but most of the leadership clearly envisaged some kind of partnership between union and government. It was not an idea which had any chance of getting through a Parliament with a huge Conservative majority. The employers and two of the Government representatives categorically opposed nationalisation, although one of the Government people proposed some form of district unification. On the other hand, the employers had no desire to get the mines back while wages were at the inflatedly high position which abnormal war-time conditions had produced. The Government rejected nationalisation but accepted only the idea of some district grouping of companies and, in the end, little in the structure changed.

Disputes in the railways and in the mines in these years were, therefore, disputes against government. The Railwaymen, too, looked to the Triple Alliance. In March 1919 they were able to use the threat of a strike backed by the Alliance to squeeze concessions from government. At the end of the year an attempt by the NUR to have war-time additional payments incorporated into the standard rate, as the footplatemen in ASLEF had just managed to achieve, led to a nine-day rail strike, with ASLEF, for once, coming out in sympathy. The Triple Alliance threatened to widen the action and Lloyd George and J. H. Thomas, general secretary of the NUR, helped by Ernest Bevin of the Transport Workers' Federation (TWF), negotiated a compromise settlement. It proved more difficult to co-ordinate support for a wider, political 'hands off Russia' industrial movement in 1919 and 1920, when there seemed the possibility of an extension of direct intervention in the new Soviet Union, although a number of trades councils tried to galvanise support.

The end of 1919 also brought the establishment of a court of inquiry under Lord Shaw into the dockers' grievances. It was here that the Bristol dockers' leader, Ernest Bevin, enhanced his reputation as the 'Dockers' QC'. In an 11 hours' speech, which ranged over the dockers' experience over the previous 30 years, he set out to show that dockers' wages had fallen behind the cost of living, despite the high profits which had been and were continuing to be made by the port employers. Bevin also took the opportunity to argue the case for a system which would end the casual nature of dock labour, an issue which had arisen at various times in the past and was to continue to be debated in the industry. There already existed voluntary registration schemes which were not working very effectively. In supporting decasualisation, however, Bevin came up against opposition from many of the dockers themselves. They objected to the loss of freedom which this might involve for them, tying them to weekly, as opposed to daily, wages and perhaps even to particular employers. The result of the inquiry was a considerable triumph for Bevin. Shaw endorsed a nation-wide rate of 16s (80p) a day, supported a registration scheme and a Joint Industrial Council was established. The Report declared,

> The system of casualisation must, if possible, be torn up by the roots. It is wrong. And the one issue is as to what practical means can be adopted to readily provide labour, while avoiding cruel and unsocial conditions.[27]

In fact, after an initial flurry of enthusiasm, little came of it. By the end of the 1920s dock wages were down to 10s (50p) a day and did not reach Shaw's 16s level again until the Second World War. Some desultory attempts at registration came to little.

Meanwhile, the MFGB was determined to push ahead with its campaign for nationalisation and to get Triple Alliance support for a strike to back the campaign. The TUC promoted the 'Mines for the Nation' campaign, but, by a vote of four to one, a special congress rejected calls for a general strike and the campaign fizzled out. In July 1920, when the Government rejected claims for a second wage increase in a year, the miners balloted for strike. Lloyd George offered arbitration, but this was refused and they once again turned to the Triple Alliance for assistance. But J. H. Thomas of the NUR insisted that, if the Triple Alliance were to be involved, then the MFGB had to accept that the running of the dispute had to be placed in the hands of the Alliance. This the Miners' Federation would never accept and so neither the railwaymen nor the TWF would support strike action. Smillie urged the miners to give into the Alliance demands to maintain the unity which had been so painstakingly built up, but his advice was rejected and in October 1920 the miners' strike began.

The Government brought in the Emergency Powers Act which allowed it to declare a State of Emergency if there was a threat to deprive the community of 'the means of life', by cutting food, fuel, light, or of the 'means of locomotion'. It looked set for confrontation and there were many unionists who were prepared to accept the challenge. The railwaymen's conference delegates insisted that the NUR executive reconsider its earlier refusal to help and threatened to take strike action if the miners' case was not settled. Negotiations were resumed and Lloyd George came up with a temporary six months' wage increase. It gave a false view of trade union strength. For many, influenced by the new Communist Party of Great Britain, which had emerged out of the old British Socialist Party, and some of the shop stewards, here was evidence that even the *threat* of 'direct action' by unions could force concessions from government.

Trade unions had emerged from the war greatly strengthened. Numbers were up and still rising. Their leaders were accustomed to dealing with government ministers; some indeed were government ministers in the coalition governments. They were recognised as spokesmen for workers to an extent they had never achieved before. They were at the heart of national bargaining procedures. They had successfully defended their right, despite dilution, to control who could work in certain crafts and had been guaranteed a return to pre-war patterns. Both sides of industry had accepted negotiation, conciliation and arbitration as the means of doing things. Unlike in many European countries the state backed away from imposing its authority on industrial relations. Compulsory arbitration was quickly abandoned in favour of a voluntary industrial relations court which had hundreds of cases referred to it. Nothing could come to that court until all the existing mechanisms for settling a dispute within an industry had been exhausted. There was no attempt to make collective agreements legally binding or to require co-operation between management and union representatives. The Whitley Committee's ideas were no more than recommendations of good practice and achieved no force of law. This suited the views of the trade unions who had persistently resisted state intervention in industrial relations. Most of the big unions would have nothing to do with a National Industrial Council, which Lloyd George had instituted, and it achieved little in its brief two-year existence.

While a great deal had changed, much had not. The structure of most of the older industries and, indeed, the structure of society, had not fundamentally altered. Most of the same problems and attitudes remained and the hopes of 1917 and 1918 soon disappeared. The industrial strife of the four years after the war was worse than in the immediate pre-war years. There were more working days lost in 1921 (nearly 86 million) than in the whole period from 1910 until the outbreak of war. The immediate post-war demand for labour allowed many of the craft unions to reintroduce quickly most of their pre-war restrictive practices. It had also produced a new atmosphere, among the miners in particular. They were determined not to lose the substantial gains which had been made during the war and miners' earnings continued to rise in the two years after the armistice to nearly three times the level they had been at in 1914. They had developed a perception that they were a special group which required exceptional treatment and a belief that they were the vanguard of the entire labour movement. They also had a confidence that with pressure the Government would move from control to eventual nationalisation of the mines.

7 The Industrial Relations of Depression, 1921–33

By the winter of 1920 there were clear signs of an economic depression setting in. Unemployment took a sharp leap in December and short-time working began to spread. By March 1921, unemployment had reached over 10 per cent by one measure – 15 per cent of insured workers. The miners' lock-out from April pushed the figure up to over 20 per cent of insured workers. Union membership which peaked at 8.3 million in 1920 fell by 1.7 million in a year. By 1926 three million members had been lost and not until 1935 was the downward slide to be halted. A union density of 45.2 per cent in 1920 had become 22.6 per cent in 1933. It was a period of disastrous decline and often misdirected effort and one in which workers lost out badly, both in terms of wages and in struggles over the 'frontiers of control' in the work-place.

Black Friday

The miners were negotiating in conditions rapidly deteriorating to their disadvantage as coal stocks rose and coal export prices plummeted. Union membership was in decline. The 1920 Coal Mines Act provided for state control to continue until August 1921, but in February the Government, faced with growing losses (in South Wales these ran at 6s (30p) in every ton), announced its intention to bring forward the date for decontrol to the end of March. The mine owners, who without government subsidy had now to bear the losses of the industry, were determined to abandon any idea of a pooling of profits and insisted on district settlements. They posted the new rates involving wage reductions of 30–40 per cent in the exporting areas of Durham and South Wales. The MFGB, while willing to accept an across-the-board-cut, was determined to resist the reimposition of district negotiations. The owners announced that the miners would be locked out unless they were prepared to accept the new rates. The union responded by calling out the safety men and enforcing this with mass picketing. The Railwaymen and the Transport Workers' Federation both committed themselves to assist. The TUC gave backing and ASLEF and the Electricians' Union promised support. The rhetoric talked of an 'attack on a living wage' and on the principle of national wage agreements. Activists in the NUR and elsewhere saw it as merely the first step of an attempt 'to reduce the Working Class to conditions worse than pre-war':

> They have attacked the Miners first – believing that the Miners hold the weakest sector of the working-class front. If they break the line they will easily defeat the rest of the Workers.[1]

The Government continued negotiations while calling up army reservists and taking regular troops home from abroad. As usual, the miners were not keen for any others to be involved in the negotiations, arguing that they had no right to be consulted until they were actually on strike. But the leaders of the Transport Workers and the Railwaymen met with Lloyd George, who indicated that there was room for manoeuvre on wages, but not on the issue of district rates. The night before the Railwaymen and Transport Workers were due to come out on strike, Frank Hodges, who had succeeded Smillie as president of the MFGB, speaking to some back-bench MPs, was reputed to have hinted that there was room on the part of the miners for moves towards some acceptance of district wages. Latching on to this, Lloyd George offered further talks. The Railwaymen and the NTWF seized the opportunity to call off their strikes. Bevin declared, 'joint Action and autonomy are impossible', while Lloyd George commented privately, 'I have complete confidence in [J. H.] Thomas's selfishness'.[2]

It was the end of the Triple Alliance. To many it was 'Black Friday' and a powerful myth of betrayal of the miners by the leadership of the NUR and the Transport Workers' Federation was engendered which was to shape attitudes and prevent realistic flexibility when roughly parallel circumstances arose in 1926. The miners had expected their allies to rally to their support, without any attempt to discuss the issues with them. For the less well-paid, less unionised, more replaceable transport workers a long-drawn out strike was a much riskier affair than for the miners. Also there was little likelihood that the NUR and the Transport Workers would be able to bring out their members on the issue of pooling profits, which the MFGB were insisting upon. With unemployment rising fast, there was not likely to be enthusiasm for supporting workers whose wages rates were substantially higher than those of most other workers. There were already signs that the NTWF was breaking up under employer pressure.

The Government continued to try to achieve a negotiated settlement by offering a temporary subsidy of wages as long as the demand for national rates was abandoned. The MFGB overwhelmingly rejected this and the strike and lock-out continued until July. Industrial chaos did not ensue however. Unemployment and short-time working had gone up, but the miners had failed to halt industry and had only succeeded in squandering much public sympathy. Demoralised and with few resources left the miners could do little to prevent continuing wage reductions, and average earnings fell by almost a half between the end of 1920 and the end of 1922.[3] The terms of settlement which ended the strike involved a basic wage plus a district percentage based on district profit levels. In some districts the union was bitterly split between a Communist Party-inspired Minority Movement and the official union. Fife and Lanarkshire both became areas of vicious conflict. In Fife, differences became focused on voting procedures and whether all branches, big or small, should have the same vote. Militants tended to be concentrated in the large branches which were often voted down by the more moderate small village branches. The outcome, in 1923, was the setting up of a Mineworkers' Reform Movement in opposition to the Fife, Kinross and Clackmannan Miners' Association.[4]

The recriminations which 'Black Friday' generated, the demoralisation of the miners' defeat and the continuing high levels of unemployment all took their toll on the trade union movement. Wage cuts were imposed in the shipyards, engineering, building, on seamen, cotton workers and agricultural workers, often in excess of the fall in the cost of living. Arthur McIvor notes a distinct hardening of attitude on the part of cotton employers and a determination to assert managerial authority, through fines and dismissals. There was a readiness to threaten industry-wide lock-outs to see off union demands.[5] In the building industry employers repudiated an earlier agreement for a 44-hour working week and slashed wages, again using the threat of a lock-out. Hopes of a new era in industrial relations to which the Whitley Committee had pointed were shattered and symbolically ended with the dissolution of the National Industrial Conference in July 1921. There seems little doubt that some employers welcomed the opportunity for revenge for what they regarded as union recalcitrance in previous years and the opportunity to claw back concessions made in a time of weakness.

Organisational Reform

These challenges to the advances of the previous decade gave increased urgency to the calls for organisational reform. There had long been dissatisfaction with the Parliamentary Committee of the TUC, originally formed to keep an eye on any parliamentary developments affecting trade unions. It had previously consisted of 12 members plus the secretary but was increased to 16 in 1906, elected by ballot at Congress using a single transferable vote system. It could result, thanks to wheeling and dealing behind the scenes bartering votes, in a situation where powerful voices were excluded. In 1920, for example, no miners' representative was elected. There were demands for a central co-ordinating body which could provide leadership and guidance on policy and 'become the central co-ordinating body of all future Trade Union activities'.[6] There was concern that the employers were now organising more effectively and a perception of the Federation of British Industries as a rather sinister presence shaping employers' policies on a national scale.[7] A committee was appointed which recommended the replacement of the Parliamentary Committee with a body which would represent the main areas of industry. The 1921 TUC approved a scheme, drafted by the socialist historian, G. D. H. Cole, for a General Council of 32 members from 17 industrial groups, plus a women's group, elected by the whole Congress. It was accepted because the other rival co-ordinating groups were no longer of significance. The General Federation of Trade Unions had failed to make an impact, the Triple Alliance had crumbled and the trade union group on the National Industrial Conference was no more.

Among the General Council's tasks were 'to keep a watch on all industrial movements and, where possible, co-ordinate industrial action'. The idea was that unions would inform the General Council of impending major disputes; when negotiation had broken down, the Council could try to promote a settlement; and in the last resort, the Council would organise support for the union involved. On the other hand, thanks largely to pressure for the miners, limits were placed on how far it could in any way impinge on the autonomy of individual unions. There was to be no diminution of the sovereignty of individual unions. As a result the General Council was never to become the co-ordinator of industrial action which some of the advocates of reform had hoped for. Indeed, some argued that it was little more than a larger version of the Parliamentary Committee. However, the first full-time general secretary was appointed, Fred Bramley of the Furnishing Trades' Association, in 1923 and two years later, Walter Citrine of the ETU, who over the next 20 years was to do more than any other to shape the TUC's role.

Amalgamations

The crisis of the early 1920s also gave a further boost to amalgamation proposals. While the steel smelters' leader, John Hodge, was no great success as Minister of Labour, he did see through the Trade Union Amalgamation Act of 1917 to simplify the process of union amalgamation. There had been amalgamations in the past, usually when a particular union had difficulty in surviving. Many of the Scottish unions had amalgamated with their larger southern brethren in the 1890s and early twentieth century. But Richard Price argues that while many of the rank and file were keen on amalgamations, as evidenced by the support for industrial unionism in the years immediately before 1914, the officials were much less so. They were more attracted by the idea of looser federations, which allowed unions to maintain their autonomy and the officials to retain their offices, and there were a number of such federations.[8] One area which took advantage of the Act was the building trades which, according to G. D. H. Cole in 1913 was organised by 67 unions and 13 local federations. Attempts just before the war to create an industrial union had won a majority in 11 unions, but not a large enough one to achieve the support of two-thirds of the membership which was the pre-1917 requirement for amalgamation. The old-established societies of Amalgamated Carpenters and Joiners and the Amalgamated Union of Cabinetmakers combined in the Amalgamated Union of Carpenters, Cabinet Makers and Joiners in March 1918 and then with the great rival of the ASCJ, the General Union of Carpenters and Joiners in 1920, in the Amalgamated Society of Woodworkers (ASW). The Stonemasons and the Bricklayers merged in the Amalgamated Union of Building Trade Workers and there were amalgamations of some of the Labourers' Unions. Alongside this there was the National Federation of Building Workers, which co-ordinated industrial activity, and in areas where numbers were small established composite branches of different trades.[9] The Workers' Union had been attracted by the idea of amalgamation before 1914, but war came before much could be achieved. In 1916 talks began with the third largest general union, the National Amalgamated Union of Labour and the Municipal Employees' Association. A joint executive committee was established at the end of 1917 and a year later the National Amalgamated Workers' Union, a federal structure despite its name, came into being. Smaller amalgamations followed among unions of postal and telegraph workers, of blacksmiths and ironworkers, of gasworkers and municipal workers among others.

The most important outcome of the amalgamation process was the creation, as a result of a process begun in 1920, of the Transport and General Workers' Union (TGWU). The largely Liverpool- and Bristol-based National Union of Dock, Riverside and General Workers believed that there needed to be 'uniform direction of policy if progress was to be maintained' and unity to face associations and federations of employers. Tillett had formed the National Transport Workers' Federation in 1910 with the aim of providing mutual help in strikes. There was, however, no concession of autonomy by the different unions and rivalry continued between them. Any attempt at closer amalgamation generally foundered on fears that such an amalgamation would allow general labourers to flock into the docks. The Federation's membership and influence had increased during the war as it was called on to negotiate with the authorities on the plethora of issues which inevitably arose in the ports. The war also brought national negotiations and a revival of interest in amalgamation. A first proposal for the Dockers' to amalgamate with the National Union of General Workers (the old Gasworkers' Union) failed to secure enough votes among the dockers. The dockers were still resistant to the idea lest dock labour be opened up to non-dockers within the general union.

The docks were not the only area of inter-union tension and an attempt to avoid this among bus and tramway drivers led to the short-lived United Vehicle Workers' Union. This union in turn battled with the National Union of Vehicle Workers, working among road haulage workers. Both were facing rapidly falling membership from 1920. Havelock Wilson of the Seamen's Union had long proved an impossible partner within the Transport Workers' Federation and his virulent anti-communism in the atmosphere of 1919–20 merely added to the difficulties of co-operation. The Federation was rapidly disintegrating. Yet there was a recognition that collaboration was essential. The solution, usually attributed to the Bristol organiser, Ernest Bevin, but probably picked up from the American Federation of Labour, was to have a centralised organisation but with distinct trade groups which would retain some of the sense of separate identity. Initial discussions among dock unions were broadened to include various carters and motormen's unions and eventually 19 of them balloted their members and 14 of these agreed to amalgamation.[10] By the time the ballots were completed the process of amalgamation was hastened by the onset of slump, with many of the unions finding their membership tumbling. By the time the TGWU came into existence in January 1922 some of the unions had lost 50 per cent of their members and the new union's membership continued to fall.[11] Another half-dozen unions joined during 1922 and, over the next 18 years, only in 1927, 1931 and 1932 did some further amalgamation with the TGWU not take place.[12]

The new union of around 300 000 members was in some ways a highly centralised organisation, holding all the funds of the former organisations. On the other hand, there were 11 regional divisions and five national trade groups, with each trade group having a place on the executive council. The support of the officials (245 of them) had been bought by guaranteeing their jobs, salaries and pensions. The union survived only because the leadership showed a sensitivity to sectional interests and, from time to time, was prepared to tolerate unconstitutional action. There were persistent threats from sectionalism. Although undoubtedly an authoritarian figure, Bevin, who was elected general secretary, never had dictatorial control over the union. It was against his advice that an annual delegate conference was given supreme power. He was suspicious of union ballots which he believed could easily be manipulated and insisted that officials were appointed not elected. His decisions, particularly his strategy in the 1920s of accepting wage cuts but defending conditions, were frequently challenged by the rank and file and he survived by being responsive to rank-and-file pressure.[13] But he could not always pull it off and, within a few months of the union's formation, groups of London dockers, disgruntled at his acceptance of a wage cut, had pulled out to form a breakaway National Amalgamated Stevedores, Lightermen, Watermen and Dockers' Union. There was still the burden of history. The stevedores had never forgiven Bevin for refusing to accept that there should be a differential between shipboard loading work (the stevedores' role) and shore unloading work (the dockers' role).[14] The entry of the badly weakened Workers' Union into the TGWU in 1929 broadened the coverage of the TGWU into the newer expanding light engineering area and an engineering trade group was established in 1931. It also brought in many textile workers and agricultural workers.

Another important amalgamation had taken place in 1920 when the ASE and nine other craft societies united in the Amalgamated Engineering Union (AEU).[15] It was not easy to achieve, since the ASE had built up much resentment in the war years by its insistence that it should negotiate with government on its own and to the exclusion of other crafts. On the other hand, shop stewards had learned the value of co-operation in the work-place in the war-time joint shop stewards' committees. But they all faced an Engineering Employers' Federation determined to claw back some of the loss of management control, which they believed they had suffered during the war years, and to push ahead with new work organisation. The election of the veteran, Tom Mann, long an advocate of industrial unionism, as general secretary in 1919, assisted the process.

The Engineering Employers' Federation and the Shipbuilding Engineering Federation had agreed to a 47-hour week at the end of the war in return for negotiations on payment by result, but little had resulted from these and there were recurring local disputes over issues of manning, payment systems, number of apprentices and overtime working. At the end of 1921, after, it should be said, nearly a year of negotiations on the issue, the EEF demanded that the AEU accept management's right to decide on what was acceptable overtime and to alter existing work conditions *before* embarking on the extended agreed disputes procedures. Until then the rule had been that the *status quo* should be maintained until all procedures had been exhausted. When the AEU refused, the employers instituted a lock-out, which lasted from March until June 1922, and ended in total victory for the employers. The settlement, which according to Jonathan Zeitlin, was more complete than in 1898, required the AEU and fifty other unions in the industry which were involved to recognise that 'employers have the right to manage their establishments'.[16] Wage cuts quickly followed the defeat.

A third important amalgamation was the National Union of General and Municipal Workers in 1924. There had been various attempts in the past to eradicate inter-union rivalry between the many unskilled unions. The General Federation of Trade Unions had set up the General Labourers' National Council in 1906 to arrange the recognition of one another's union cards. Attempts to co-ordinate bargaining came to fruition in 1917 with the formation of the National Federation of General Workers and, under government pressure, national negotiations developed in a number of areas. As a result, there was little involvement of general workers in the unrest of the 1919–20 period and J. R. Clynes and Will Thorne, president and secretary of the National Union of General Workers both steadily losing their socialist fervour, had no sympathy with talk of a general strike. When the Dockers rejected amalgamation in 1920 negotiations started with the National Amalgamated Union of Labour, the Workers' Union and the Municipal Employees' Association.[17] The Workers' Union withdrew from the talks, but in 1924 the National Union of General Workers, the National Association of United Labour and the Municipal Employees formed the National Union of General and Municipal Workers (NUGMW).

There were various pressures towards amalgamations. For a long while there had been concern at union disunity, and unions were conscious of their weakness *vis-à-vis* growing employers' organisations. The pre-war syndicalist pressure for industrial unionism as a way of providing strength had shaped attitudes. Ambitious young union bureaucrats were attracted by size and frustrated by traditional, often petty rivalries. Yet at the same time there were massive barriers of history, local loyalties, craft rivalries, vested interests of officialdom and just general suspicion of change to overcome. The process of amalgamation was never an easy one.

Strains in the System

The downward spiral of prices inevitably brought demands for wage cuts although the impact of these for different groups of workers in the same industry was varied.[18] The result was a strain on national bargaining procedures, as the implications of agreements on different workers varied. Also, employer competition increased and firms not participating in Joint Industrial Councils were free to undercut. It also put a strain on union membership and numbers fell sharply in the more recently organised or weakly organised areas. Unionism in agricultural industries, having reached almost a 25 per cent density by 1921, plummeted to less than 5 per cent over the decade; in pottery, density fell from a half to one in four; in bricks and building materials from 47 per cent to 13.5 per cent in a decade, in the construction industry from nearly 70 per cent density to just over 30 per cent. The areas which held their own or grew were fishing, food and drink, tobacco, clothing, footwear, glass, furniture, some of the newer manufacturing areas and most white-collar areas.

Two of the most badly affected unions were the National Union of Agricultural Workers and the Workers' Union. Government, in a U-turn of breathtaking callousness, had pulled out of farm subsidy and wage-fixing for agricultural workers in the summer of 1921. The conciliation boards largely carried out the farmers' wishes. As a result there was little role for the unions to play and fewer and fewer resources in farm labourers' families for union dues. The story of the Workers' Union, after its remarkable successes during the war and immediately afterwards, is even more traumatic. New members, with little tradition of unionism, were quick to pull out when times were bad. In three years from 1920 membership fell by 72 per cent and although it was halted for a year or two, it again tumbled after the general strike. Generous unemployment benefits introduced to try to attract and stabilise membership decimated funds in the poor economic conditions of the 1920s. With membership and income falling there was little alternative but to reduce the union bureaucracy, which in turn had its effects on recruitment. The areas of engineering in the Midlands, where the union had built up membership, were badly hit in the early 1920s with a 90 per cent loss of membership in Birmingham and Coventry.

Another area of dramatic change was among seamen. As a key group during the war, they had made considerable gains in earnings and in terms of recognition. The Ministry of Shipping had bought off discontent in 1917 with the establishment of a conciliation committee and a joint Shipping Federation and Union committee. One of the big problems was the demand for labour, since many foreign seamen were being employed.

Havelock Wilson's Sailors and Firemen's Union was pressing to be recognised as the sole supplier of labour. The Shipping Federation agreed to a jointly controlled system of registration, the National Maritime Board. Within the Union, Wilson wanted to achieve central control of funds as opposed to the traditional pattern of branch autonomy. As a result there were frequent breakaways, calling for a more confrontational policy towards employers. After the war, Wilson's main strategy was to maintain recognition by the Shipping Federation and for this he was prepared to go along with wage cuts. These resulted in a wave of unrest. A British Seafarers' Union and a Cooks and Stewards' Union[19] amalgamated in 1922 into the Amalgamated Marine Workers' Union and was perceived as presenting a threat to Wilson's control. To see off this threat, Wilson collaborated with the employers in introducing the PC5 system, by which any sailor wishing to obtain employment had to obtain the PC5 card from the Sailors' and Firemen's Union and then get it stamped by the Shipping Federation. In other words, it was a closed shop for Wilson's Union. The Marine Workers' Union survived in companies outside the Federation, but Wilson became obsessed with the need to destroy it. That and his virulent detestation of socialism and his view that the general strike was a sectionalist attempt by communists to bring about a revolution led to his union being expelled from the TUC in 1927, but it survived. Wilson-instigated litigation eventually undermined the Amalgamated Marine Workers, which finally folded in 1927, and even the TGWU, which started to recruit seamen after 1927, found it impossible to break Wilson's hold. But his death in 1928 allowed relations between the National Union of Seamen and the rest of the trade union movement gradually to improve.

The change of government in 1922 and the end of Lloyd George no doubt also had a significant impact. Lloyd George had retained at least some of the pre-war Liberal interventionism, with a general desire to try to improve the condition of the working class. Stanley Baldwin and his associates had no such commitment and were determined that wages and the cut and thrust of industrial relations should be left to market forces. There was no restraining hand on employers, and government, after thirty years of a relatively sympathetic attitude towards unionism, now if anything, threw its weight behind the employers. Attempts to extend trade boards to retailing were abandoned and no new boards to set a minimum wage were established in the 1920s.[20] The short-lived Labour government of 1924 made very little difference. Anxious to prove that they were fit for government, Ramsay MacDonald and his colleagues found the TGWU strikes in the docks and among London tramway workers and a seven weeks' national lock-out of building workers an irritation and embarrassment.

The slight economic recovery which came at the end of 1923 (although unemployment levels still remained over 10 per cent) encouraged a more confrontational policy. Some of the earlier reductions in wages were being clawed back and once again there was widespread talk of a united union movement forcing changed attitudes on government. The miners, railwaymen, transport workers, engineers, boilermakers and others were talking about a new Industrial Alliance jointly to resist wage reductions. But the recovery did not last and, by the time the action was co-ordinated, circumstances had once again turned unfavourable. The post-war enthusiasm for a new era in industrial relations cooled. By 1924, 30 of the Joint Industrial Councils set up under the Whitley recommendations had disappeared and only some 45 survived until the end of the 1930s.[21]

General Strike

In coal mining the French occupation of the Ruhr in 1923 had brought an unexpected rise in prices and, with exports up almost to 1913 levels, wage rises were conceded. However, French withdrawal had, of course, the converse effect and, in 1925, exports, prices and profits were down. The return to the gold standard, with an over-valued pound did nothing to help. Bevin condemned what he saw as the usual action of finance capitalism enriching itself without considering the effects on manufacturing industry, and ridiculed the idea that reducing home consumption would somehow encourage exports. The mine owners demanded wage cuts of around 10 per cent, the abolition of the national minimum wage and the extension of daily working hours to eight. The General Council of the TUC committed itself to support, threatening to call out most unions if necessary. A court of inquiry agreed that the minimum wage should be retained, but without specifying what that wage ought to be. The Cabinet buckled on 'Red Friday' and granted a temporary subsidy for nine months and set up the Samuel Commission. Now it was Baldwin's turn to be accused of betrayal by the right, particularly when the subsidy required turned out to be twice what had been predicted.

The Commission reported in March 1926 and, like Sankey in 1919, supported the nationalisation of royalties. With 73 per cent of coal being produced at a loss, it argued that there had to be a way of reducing the industry's costs. It proposed that small companies among the 1400 separate undertakings be pushed to amalgamate to generate the necessary capital for modernisation. It accepted that a cut in wages was necessary, but rejected the owners' demand for a lengthening of hours which, it pointed out, were already among the longest in Europe. Any lengthening of hours would merely lead to greater absenteeism. Most significantly it argued that the minimum wage had to be abandoned and it accepted that government subsidy of the industry must end.

Baldwin declared that the report would be accepted only if both sides in the dispute agreed. The chances of that were nil. The miners' chant was 'Not a penny off the pay, not a second on the day'; the owners were set on both wage cuts and longer hours. On 30 April the new rates were imposed and the miners struck. Negotiations between the government and the General Council of the TUC continued until the evening of 3 May when the *Daily Mail* printers refused to set a hostile editorial. Baldwin broke off the talks and the General Council called a general sympathetic strike. It called out rail and transport workers, iron and steel workers and printers. The last proved to be tactically unwise since it left government with the monopoly of communications.

The Government had been preparing for such a strike for many months. In the aftermath of 'Red Friday' a semi-official Organisation for the Maintenance of Supplies had been formed, which surreptitiously laid down plans and recruited volunteers ready to act in the event of a strike. They already had the mechanisms in place for keeping essential supplies moving. They could confidently count on being able to keep road haulage going and they ensured that the BBC played down the strikers' case. The unions, on the other hand, had made remarkably little preparation and many of them had used up substantial reserves in earlier disputes. There had been no meetings to try to get some co-ordination between unions in an industrial alliance and it was not until 27 April that a TUC committee was formed to plan strike action. A motion at the 1925 TUC, carried by a vote of two to one, had called on Congress to organise for the overthrow of capitalism and demanded the setting up of workshop committees to lead the struggle. Yet the TUC had also refused to grant the General Council the power to levy unions or to order a stoppage of work. In other words, despite all the calls for unity, most unions were not prepared to sacrifice autonomy, and behind the votes for revolution there remained a movement as conservative as ever. Even the most powerful unions paid very limited strike pay and others were too weak to do very much.

None the less, up and down the country there appeared to be enthusiasm for extending the strike to additional groups of workers. Local committees of action wallowed in the power to humiliate employers, begging to get permits to move their goods, and there was no doubt that many of the union leaders were concerned that control of the situation was slipping from their hands to irregular local activists. Sir Herbert Samuel, on an unofficial basis, worked with members of the General Council to find some formula for compromise, including a continuation of subsidy. But the miners would not concede a wage cut to any grade of mine worker and without a wage cut there could be no basis for agreement. On 12 May, when there were reports of a drift back to work, the General Council called off the general strike. Apparently abandoned by all except the Communist Party, the miners maintained their resistance until nearly the end of the year. As early as June there were the first signs of cracking, particularly in Nottinghamshire, where the mixed communities and the new pits made miners vulnerable to local pressure from non-miners. By August nearly 13 000 had returned in Nottinghamshire and the local leaders accepted that the strike was over. This led to their suspension from the MFGB and George Spencer formed a breakaway Nottingham Miners' Industrial Union. By October and November, however, there was a slow drift back to work elsewhere and pleas, especially from Lancashire and Scotland, for a district settlement. Pressure from the activists in the CPGB and the Minority Movement probably frustrated earlier attempts among the executive to beat a retreat.[22] The miners' conference eventually had to accept that the strike could no longer be sustained and districts were instructed to settle.

The story of the general strike is well-known and there is a myriad of publications looking at local aspects of it. How significant it was in the broader history of trade unionism and industrial relations is debatable. For some, like Clegg and G. A. Phillips, the strike is essentially a miners' strike, coming belatedly at the end of the period of militancy which had had wider significance and support between 1919 and 1921. Certainly, there were signs that a high-point of militancy had been passed. The TUC of 1925 had elected back on to the General Council most of those 'moderates' who had had to resign in 1924 because of their membership of the Labour Government. For others, the general strike was a necessary disaster to bring to an end the idea which had gained such a hold since around 1910 that direct industrial action, properly directed, could be invincible. As those on the left recognised, a general strike had always been regarded as a revolutionary weapon ever since William Benbow had proposed it back in the 1830s. It had been at the centre of the tactics advocated by pre-war syndicalists. Yet there was little sign that most of those who advocated its use had faced up to what it meant, and none seemed to have appreciated fully that it would be resisted. But of course it had an appeal. It seemed to offer an alternative to 40 per cent wage cuts and it offered action. It was, as much as anything, a product of a rhetoric which had lost touch with reality, but in order to combat such appealing verbiage the leadership of many of the unions had had to adopt, often against their better judgment, the language of militancy.

Despite the apparent solidarity with the miners there were many who, like the general secretary of the ETU, felt that the miners were prehistoric in their attitudes, failing to adjust to a changing situation in mining and showing little sympathy for other groups of workers.[23] The defeat helped, as Cronin says, to lower the collective temperature. Alan Fox is probably right to note, however, that it should not be regarded as a complete failure: 'it probably deterred employers in other industries from attacking wages and as an impressive display of labour solidarity and power it can hardly have failed to leave a mark on political as well as on industrial thinking'.[24]

There is no doubt that in the aftermath of the general strike there were some particularly vindictive examples of victimisation, especially in areas like the railways, where there had always been a sour note in industrial relationships. In some cases strikers lost any recognition of previous company service. Many activists paid a heavy price for their role, although some of these had already been squeezed out in the earlier redundancies in the older industries from 1921. Victimisation benefit was another drain on union resources. It weakened all the demands from rank-and-file militants for more vigorous confrontation with employers and strengthened the position of full-time officials within the unions. There was no post-mortem at the TUC, but a quiet satisfaction that the strike had been survived with only limited damage. The criticism was of the miners.[25]

The impact on the miners was catastrophic. They had held out for ten months and, in the end, lost on all issues. Parliament restored the eight-hour day, the minimum wage was reduced and district variations were imposed. The nation lost because the mine owners generally gave up any effort to reduce production costs other than by reducing wages. Some individual miners were never again to find work in their own coalfield and had to move to other areas. The MFGB was without resources and, therefore, relatively powerless. Union branch life crumbled. The unity between coalfields, achieved with such difficulty since before 1889, was broken. The MFGB began to fall apart and differences of opinion at conferences occasionally ended in fisticuffs.[26] The breakaway unions in both Nottinghamshire and Leicester became firmly established. In both areas older work patterns of sub-contracting persisted and the 'little butties', as the sub-contractors who recruited miners' gangs were known, were the core of these unions.[27] But even the fabled solidarity of South Wales was shattered by the appearance of a non-political Miners' Industrial Union based largely on the newer pits. In Scotland, where the strike had helped reunify the two rival Fife unions, there were years of what can only be described as internecine warfare. The Reform Unions of the Minority Movement and the National Union of Scottish Mine Workers used courts, police, propaganda and dirty tricks in their battles with each other. In 1929 the Communist Party created a new United Mineworkers of Scotland, but from a peak of about 4000 members in 1929, its numbers soon dropped.[28] Both old and new unions were drastically weakened to the extent that the coal owners could largely ignore them.[29] Especially in South Wales and in the Midlands, coal owners played a rough game after 1926, vigorously circumscribing union powers, encouraging breakaway unions and, as was apparent to many observers outside the industry, generally creating a great depth of bitterness.

Since many unions participating in the strike had broken collective agreements there were opportunities for other employers to lay down new terms. John Hodge of the Steel Smelters' Union was forced by the Employers' Association to sign a document admitting the guilt of striking. The Scottish newspaper owners declared that trade unionists would no longer be employed. Union membership fell by another million to under five million.

Baldwin had to concede to back-bench pressure with the Trade Disputes and Trade Union Act of 1927, which declared sympathetic strikes 'except within the trade or industry in which the strikers are engaged' and any strike aimed at coercing government illegal. It also was intended to injure the Labour Party by requiring that union members had positively to contract *in* to the political levy of their union. The effect was to reduce Labour Party income by about a third, but also, paradoxically, it probably had the effect of pushing the Party and the unions, whose relations had been strained since 1924, closer. The Act also strengthened the laws on intimidation and banned civil servants from joining unions affiliated to the TUC. Some employers in the National Confederation of Employers' Organisations wanted the immunities of 1906 removed, but other leading employers like Sir Alfred Mond of ICI and leaders of some of the country's larger employers were willing to try to find an alternative to confrontation. Most big employers had no desire to get involved in a war of attrition with their workers. Nor had Baldwin's Government and, as Rodney Lowe has argued, what is significant about the 1927 Act is what is *not* there: no compulsory arbitration; compulsory strike ballots; no extension of the criminal law; no repeal of 1906.[30] On the trade union side the rhetoric of the left for an 'unceasing war against capitalism' sounded increasingly vacuous[31] and Bevin was able to persuade the TUC to look at economic policies which were well short of socialism, but which might have some prospect of influencing government thinking. The General Council was asked to look at the effects of tariffs and cartels and Bevin hoped to persuade them to look at 'a policy having for its object the creation of a European public opinion in favour of Europe becoming an economic unity'.[32]

On the Government's side, there was a desire to try to play a role in achieving some balance between employers and unions. Baldwin was no admirer of the leaders of British industry and, while accepting that, at the end of the day, the employers had to have the upper hand, there was no question of his challenging the legitimacy of trade unions.[33]

Mond–Turner

The Mond–Turner talks also reflected a new centralisation of considerable power in the TUC and in union officials and a confidence to ignore militants. The aim was to find areas for co-operation between employers and unions. There had been some earlier informal contacts between members of the General Council and some employers' leaders which had been scuppered by the bitterness over the Trade Union Act. At the end of 1927, Sir Alfred Mond, the chairman of ICI, and a group of big industrialists, invited Ben Turner, as chair of the General Council, and the TUC leadership to talks. Mond's firm, ICI, had been at the forefront of developing a system of personnel management which worked closely with union representatives, buying industrial harmony by means of good wages, good welfare conditions and good communication.

The talks, which started in 1928, repeated many of the recommendations of the Whitley Committee on what should be the norm in industrial relations: recognition and negotiation with unions, not just on wages and work conditions, but on all aspects of the industry. The employers' group declared unequivocally that 'it was definitely in the interest of all concerned to belong to a *bona fide* union and that negotiations were facilitated by such membership'. The talks called for a National Industrial Council, to examine regularly aspects of industrial relations, with a conciliation committee which could be called on if necessary. Later talks focused on issues such as unemployment and rationalisation.[34] It was the last which was most attacked by critics of the talks. A. J. Cook, communist secretary of the Miners, who, of course, rejected the possibility of good relations under capitalism, argued that all that rationalisation did was to strengthen capitalism at the expense of the workers.[35] Bevin and Citrine, on the other hand, backed by an overwhelming vote at the TUC, wanted to get employers to consult with unions as a matter of course and perhaps even to get agreement between leading manufacturers and leading unions on a common economic policy so that together they might influence government thinking. Some knowledge of what was happening in the United States, where desperate rationalising was creating mass unemployment, made the TUC anxious to mollify the effects in Britain.[36]

Economic and Political Crises

Unfortunately, there was little sense of urgency among most employers in the late 1920s to go along with any drastic changes in their industrial relations. Few unions were in a position to exert much pressure on them. The number of disputes fell to the lowest level for a generation. The National Confederation of Employers' Organisations and the Federation of British Industries rejected the Mond–Turner proposals, although they did not abandon talks with the union leaders. Despite that, the unions were not entirely unhappy about their position. With a Labour Government in power from 1929 to 1931, trade union leaders were in the Cabinet and others, like Bevin and Walter Citrine, the general secretary of the TUC, were on committees and inquiries. Ben Tillett told the 1929 TUC that 'Today the unions are an integral part of the organisation of industry. . . . There is nothing in the organisation of industry that can be regarded as the exclusive concern of the employer.'[37] As Eric Wigham says, 'The great trade-union debates of the early 1930s were not about general strikes . . . but about whether trade-union members of the board of nationalised industries should sit as individuals or as representatives.'[38] There was talk of a 'new direction', which was not about undermining capitalism, but working for improvement within it.

The committee which was involved in the Mond–Turner talks became the economic committee of the TUC and Bevin was able to get Congress to endorse economic policies which he himself formulated, largely under the influence of Maynard Keynes, when both were members of the Macmillan Committee on Finance and Industry. They proved unable to convince a government and particularly Philip Snowden, the Chancellor of the Exchequer, whose ideas had largely been shaped in the pre-war world of Liberal economics, that protecting industry was as important as protecting the City's financial interests. They were unable to persuade a government, intimidated by the scale of the problems coming upon them, that increased state intervention, state planning and state expenditure would point the way out of depression. They were equally unable to convince them to devalue the pound and to look at tariffs.

In August 1931 the Government broke apart and MacDonald went on to form a coalition government which both devalued and brought in tariffs. The ensuing general election was disastrous for the Labour Party which was reduced to only 46 MPs. The effect was to give the trade unions increased influence on the Party, although the leaders were non-unionists, such as the pacifist George Lansbury, and intellectuals, like Stafford Cripps and Clement Attlee. In 1933 the Party went so far as to agree that no future Labour leader would take office as Prime Minister without the approval of a National Joint Council made up of an equal number of representatives from the Party and the General Council. In the euphoria of 1945 this was to be forgotten.

By no means everyone agreed with the search for co-operation with government and industry. The left found it difficult to swallow demands for state intervention which were not seen as steps towards a socialist society but as a way of baling out capitalism from its crisis. Since 1926 the Minority Movement had declined in influence, weakened by the general disillusionment with militancy and the direct onslaught by official union leaders. The General and Municipal Workers had declared Communist Party membership incompatible with union office and the TUC had taken action against communist influence in trades councils. Communist Party strategy up until 1928 had been to work with other forces of the left, but, in line with Soviet policies, this changed and the CPGB was now going through a phase of denouncing moderate leaders as class traitors and encouraging the formation of alternative shop-floor organisations and even breakaway unions. London, as always, proved fruitful ground for such activity. The usual pattern was to start with a defiance of an executive instruction by the local leadership. In 1928 the London organiser of the Garment Workers' Union formed the breakaway United Clothing Workers. There were endless battles within the Electrical Trade Union, with accusations of the leadership selling out. In engineering, cuts in overtime rates from time and a half to time and a quarter, the loss of one of the main gains of the previous 20 years, gave opportunities for rank-and-file committees to emerge. Within the TGWU Ernest Bevin fought hard to discipline communist-influenced sections among London and Glasgow dockers and London busmen.

After the initial drop immediately after the general strike, union membership stabilised, although by 1933 it was only half what it had been in 1920. Industrial relations entered a period of comparative tranquillity. The number of disputes fell to unprecedented low levels for the next decade. With the exception of the 1929–31 period when the Labour Government encouraged hopes of improvement, the number of working days lost through stoppages also fell to levels even lower than those which had been achieved in the early 1900s. None the less, many tensions remained, particularly in those staple industries which were being most affected by the economic slump.

Under pressure of falling markets, cotton employers were driving to reduce costs and curb union power. They tried unsuccessfully to lengthen the working day in 1928, but, with employer collaboration breaking up, the pressures within individual firms remained. In the summer of 1929 the Master Cotton Spinners proposed a further reduction in piece rates. The workers rejected it and the employers would not accept arbitration. At the end of July, 350 000 were locked out. Pressure from the Labour Government eventually brought arbitration and, with a rapidity which produced much criticism, a compromise wage cut of half what the employers had wanted was proposed. The collective bargaining structure in the cotton industry was crumbling as individual firms battled for survival by means of price and wage cuts.

Disputes in the woollen industry, similarly over wage cuts, led to the breakdown of negotiating machinery which had been established during the war. In the hosiery industry and in some other areas the attempts to apply the American Bedaux system of time and motion study, by which each task was timed – the idea being, of course, to increase productivity and reduce the work-force – exacerbated relations. In mining, a new Act in 1930 reduced the miners' working day to seven and a half hours but, thanks to a House of Lords' amendment, with the possibility of the hours varying within a 90-hour fortnight – what was called the 'spreadover'. It was presented as the alternative to a wage cut. The minority Labour Government was not strong enough to overthrow the amendment. The South Wales miners struck against it but could not sustain a strike. Inevitably there was resistance to any wage cuts, but the cost of living was falling much more sharply than were wages in these years and Clegg argues convincingly that there was no great rush by employers to cut wages, especially if it was likely to mean a strike.

In the conditions of high competitiveness in falling markets which existed in the early 1930s, it was almost impossible to maintain co-operation between employers. Membership of employers' federations fell as each pursued their own tactics for survival and these often meant avoiding disputes at all costs. On the other side, unemployment was mounting with frightening rapidity, from 12 per cent at the start of 1930 to

20 per cent by the end of it, and not until the summer of 1933 was the level of unemployment to fall below one in five of the insured population. A TUC campaign for a 40-hour week as a way of spreading employment got nowhere. On the other hand, in some industries, there was a readiness to compromise. Both employers and unions told the Royal Commission on Transport that some regulation of the road transport industry was required and this resulted in Road Traffic Acts in 1930 and 1933, which introduced an elaborate licensing system.

How far the weakness of trade unions in the 1920s and 1930s allowed employers to make major alterations in work organisation and extend the processes of division of labour and deskilling is still being debated. Howard Gospel argues that in engineering they did, in the aftermath of the defeat of the AEU in 1922. Zeitlin, on the other hand, is less convinced and emphasises the failure of engineering employers' organisations to hold together effectively in adverse market conditions. McIvor and others, looking at the cotton industry, finds that the opportunity was taken for a more aggressive assertion of management authority and more direct interference with the organisation of work. But, at the same time, McIvor's work confirms that many of the changes actually wrought were relatively limited.[39]

Scientific management had made very little progress in Britain, but in the years after 1918 Taylorist or scientific management ideas began to take a hold. The ideas of Charles Bedaux, who claimed to have developed a way of scientifically calculating the proportion of work and rest required to undertake tasks, were particularly influential and he and his company made a fortune offering consultancy. The idea was that time and motion studies of different jobs would allow both time and piece rates to be calculated with exactitude. A number of major firms took it up – ICI, Lucas, Jo Lyons, Wolsey Hosiery among others – and, by 1937, Britain was second only to the United States in the number of firms using the Bedaux system – 225 of them, compared with 500 in the USA and only 144 in France.[40] There was considerable resentment at the watching and timing of work which was necessary before the system was introduced, and Littler has argued that, even where the Bedaux system was not brought in, there was an increased bureaucratisation of the work-place going on in these years, with more formal systems of management, and that workers were conscious of increased supervision. As against that, Lewchuk claims that British management was, on the whole, not greatly convinced of the value of the Bedaux system. There was still a great deal of faith in managing labour by traditional means, which he describes as a mixture of paternalism and exhortation plus the continuation of payment by results.[41]

8 Renewal, Regulation and Consolidation, 1933–51

The economic upturn after 1933 gave most unions the opportunity for growth. By 1940 union membership was back to the level which it had reached in 1921, over 6.5 million, including once again over a million women workers. The war years gave membership a further boost to nearly 8 million and a steady rate of growth was to continue through until 1948 when numbers reached 9.4 million. From roughly one in four workers unionised in 1931, 45 per cent had been reached by 1951. Some areas had well over that. Coal mining and the docks had a union density of over 90 per cent; engineering struggled back to the 50 per cent it had achieved in 1921; cotton, post office workers and printing reached 80 per cent; footwear, gas and electricity over 70 per cent. The weak areas remained the financial sector, retailing, food and drink, agriculture and parts of the building industry.

It was a period of relative industrial tranquillity. Despite the spurt in economic activity in 1935–6 there was no strike wave. After 1933 there was not a single national dispute for the next twenty years.[1] The number of disputes until the war years remained comparable to those in the quiet years before 1910. Working days lost in disputes did not cross 2 million until 1944. Now in part this could be ascribed to the inability of unions seriously to challenge employers because unemployment levels remained high. There was much demoralisation among workers to overcome. But industrial peace can also be taken as a sign of some union strength. Although unions were only slowly moving back to their immediate post-war position, they were generally much stronger than they had been. Amalgamations had strengthened their bargaining position. Inter-union rivalry, on which employers in the past had been able to play, was reduced. Many of the leadership had acquired both authority and skills. On the other side, employers were having to compete hard to survive in shrinking markets. Attempts at rationalisation of industries did nothing to encourage collaboration between employers. Also the government went out of its way to continue to encourage collective bargaining. The Ministry of Labour still saw its job as being 'to take every opportunity of stimulating the establishment of joint voluntary machinery or of strengthening that already in existence'.[2]

Losses and Gains

There were still major problems in the old staple industries. In the cotton industry, in the face of fierce competition from the more technologically advanced industries of Japan and elsewhere, employers responded by means of wage cutting and price cutting. As a result there were constant disputes in the early 1930s. Employers tried to push weavers up to minding six rather than the normal four looms, at the same time as reducing piece rates and renouncing their agreement with the unions. The weavers were mainly women workers and, despite unemployment levels of around 38 per cent in Lancashire, they struck. However, it ended with their having to accept the six and even eight looms to mind, although with a rise in payment which greatly reduced the value of converting to six looms. It may be that the union leadership was not altogether averse to six looms on condition that the work was done by adult males rather than by women.[3] Further major disputes took place in 1934 following wage cuts. The Government eventually intervened, supported by the employers and the cotton unions, although not by the TUC, with the Cotton Manufacturing Industry (Temporary Provisions) Act of 1934 which made negotiated rates legally enforceable by means of a ministerial order. But problems remained and the cotton industry gained little from recovery in the second half of the decade. Membership of textile unions fell by 100 000 in the 1930s. Another attempt by government in conjunction with the employers and unions to rationalise the industry in an orderly manner was overtaken by the outbreak of war. Government also tried to bring order into the chaotic and cut-throat road transport system by a system of licensing which required the payment of fair wages. The Road Haulage Wages Act of 1938 brought government intervention to regulate wages, but it also made some drivers question the necessity for union membership if wages were set by some outside body.[4]

The economy generally began to improve in the second half of the 1930s. The gradual acceptance of the need to rearm helped the situation in engineering. Even before then, there was growth in the newer industries concentrated in the Midlands and in the South-East, producing the consumer goods for the new housing estates which were spreading. The completion of the national electrical grid in the 1934 allowed universal electrification. The ETU's membership more than doubled in the six years after 1933. On the other hand, unionism was slow to gain ground in the expanding motor-car industry. But even some of the most poorly paid groups began to make gains with the establishment of some new trade boards. Only coal remained little affected by the revival and it was bedevilled by regular local disputes, often quite drawn out. Seventy per cent of the days lost by disputes in 1935 were in coal mining and in all other years the figure was usually at least 50 per cent.

There were continuing internal tensions in many unions. John Saville talks of union officials in the 1930s lacking 'imagination, inspiration and energy'. They were often more interested in merging and consolidating than in expanding membership. The more vigorous Communist Party, at the forefront of the struggle against fascism, was gaining support and there was a revival of usually communist-led rank-and-file movements. As in the past, such movements were particularly strong in London. Among busmen, for example, there seems to have been a resistance to being part of a wider, national transport grouping and, ever since the Transport and General amalgamation, the London area had demanded a considerable measure of autonomy.[5] Despite being granted that, it proved relatively easy in the 1930s for communist activists to play on sectionalist sentiment. A. F. (Bert) Papworth led the London transport workers' rank-and-file movement and was a thorn in the flesh of Ernest Bevin throughout the 1930s. He had emerged as a key figure in the Busmen's Rank-and-File Committee in 1932 to fight an agreement which Bevin had made with the London General Omnibus Company. The resistance was strong enough to force Bevin to withdraw from the agreement. The high point of such activity was the three-week 'Coronation strike' of May 1937. Negotiations for a seven-hour day had broken down. There was friction between the executive of the TGWU and the Rank-and-File Committee, who had great influence on the strike committee to whom the Union had granted plenary powers. Bevin's tactics were to allow the Rank-and-File Committee to overreach themselves in their demands and then to step in and make an agreement which most busmen were ready to accept. Bevin was able to present the battle as not so much against communism as against unofficial action. Expulsions and attempts at discipline led to the formation of the breakaway National Passenger Workers' Union in 1938 but, as in other instances, breakaways usually had the effect of rallying support for the official organisation.

In the ETU the London District Committee was expelled for unofficial and communist-inspired activities, but communist sympathisers gradually gained control of key positions. Within the AEU also there was an active rank-and-file movement and a CP member was elected in 1933 as president of the union. The CPGB changed its policies in the second half of the 1930s, following the line of the Communist International, and was prepared to co-operate in a united front with those they had formerly regarded as 'social fascists'. One area of regular conflict was in the trades councils, in many of which communist influence was strong. In 1934 the 'black circulars' from the General Council warned that trades councils would not be recognised if they admitted delegates associated with communist or fascist organisations and the STUC followed soon afterwards with the 'wee black circular' which banned co-operation with the CPGB, but not communist delegates.[6] Those trades councils which failed to conform found themselves reformed as the TUC firmly asserted that they *had* to voice TUC policy. Not until 1943 was the ban on communists lifted only to be reimposed ten years later.

Another recurring problem, linked with the trades councils, was their association with the National Unemployed Workers' Movement. Trade unions had always had problems with the unemployed in that they were often seen as a threat to those in work and, once they ceased to pay their dues, then trade unions felt less responsibility for them. Enthusiasm for organising protests of the unemployed had generally come from the left. The Social Democratic Federation had led the way in the great Trafalgar Square demonstrations of 1886 and 1887. It was a tradition which the CPGB inherited and the leadership of the National Unemployed Workers' Movement was from the start in 1921 dominated by communists. It quickly got into conflict with the TUC General Council, and the hunger marches which it organised were without official trade union support. Even the 1936 Jarrow March, which was not communist-led, received only lukewarm backing from official union leaders. Many trades councils, on the other hand, actively involved themselves in the movement, giving help on the route of the marches. The TUC's rather laggardly efforts in the 1930s to form associations of the unemployed under its own control were generally regarded as fairly ineffective.[7] The TUC in another 'Black Circular' of 1938 advised the exclusion of communists from positions of responsibility in all unions.

There were also recurring inter-union disputes only partially helped by continuing amalgamations. Sixteen further unions – most of them small – merged with the TGWU in the 1930s. These included Northern Irish unions of textile workers and bakers and butchers, the Scottish Busmen's Union, the Scottish Farm Servants' Union and the Scottish Seafarers' Union.[8] The TUC tried to tackle the problem of inter-union disputes by means of the Bridlington Agreement of 1939 which sought to eradicate poaching and lay down clear rules about accepting new members. It was a tactic pushed through by the big general unions in particular to prevent smaller unions such as the National Union of Public Employees (NUPE), which was in a perpetual struggle with NALGO, from recruiting in what they openly talked about as their 'spheres of influence'.[9]

Mining remained an area where disputes were rampant. Between 1927 and 1939 usually something between 40 and 50 per cent of the working days lost through disputes were in mining. In the aftermath of 1926 the MFGB had been badly weakened but had not fallen apart. With district bargaining returning, separate country unions once again regained importance. There was also a great deal of non-unionism: just over half the eligible miners. Scotland was a particularly militant area ten times more strike prone than Lancashire and 20 times more than the Midlands, but, even there, 30 per cent were not in the union in 1938.[10] Employment in the industry had fallen by more than a quarter to under 800 000 between 1927 and 1935. A diversity of relatively small coal companies remained a problem which the Coal Mines' Act of 1930, intended to encourage reorganisation, had done little to solve. The employers' Mining Association refused to meet with the MFGB.

With demand for coal picking up in the second half of the 1930s, conditions did begin to improve. By pressing for their pay claim to go to arbitration they were able to attract public sympathy and louder criticism of the reactionary intransigence of the owners. A threat of a national strike in January 1936 resulted in enough public pressure on the coal owners to force concessions. The MFGB was able to win wage rises in the different districts and to get the owners to meet them to discuss more general problems of the industry. The meetings went some way towards being a national negotiating organisation for which the MFGB had been pressing. In Nottinghamshire, after a bitter and often violent strike at the Harworth colliery at the end of 1936 over the ill-treatment of two boys, and the threat of a national strike by the MFGB, the Spencer Union once again joined up with the Mineworkers' Union, with Spencer as president of the new Nottinghamshire and District Miners' Federated Union. There were signs of a growing confidence, with demands for a closed shop. The South Wales Miners, under Arthur Horner, were able to achieve this by 1939.

In other industries, extending organisation was a struggle. Although there were signs of improvement by the end of the 1930s scarcely more than one worker in three in metals and engineering was organised and just one in five in the chemical industries. Jack Jones, the future general secretary of the TGWU, paints a gloomy picture of the situation when he arrived as a full-time official in Coventry in 1938.

> In factory after factory I found that it was difficult to arouse the workers' interest. . . . Even those who were members were worried lest their workmates found out, because if they did they might pass on the knowledge to the 'boss', the foreman or the charge hand.
>
> The industry was busiest from September to April. Workers were anxious to keep their jobs during this period, working as much overtime as possible and driving themselves flat out on piecework.
>
> . . . In the slack periods many workers were laid off and even the lucky ones worked short time. It was as casual as the old days in the docks. In such circumstances victimisation could be practised with impunity.[11]

New assembly line methods of production meant that a plentiful supply of young unemployed from all over the country could be readily utilised in the different parts of the motor industry and in the government-built aero engine 'shadow' factories being opened. Most established unionists were in poor jobs in older factories.

One group who did make advances in the second half of the 1930s were some women workers. The Civil Service Association, almost entirely confined to the lower ranks of the civil service, began to push for equal pay for equal work. In November 1937 the Shop Assistants' Union, for the first time, got a national wage agreement with the Multiple Shop Proprietors, thanks to the good offices of the Ministry of Labour Conciliation Department. In the same year, a new Factory Act laid down a maximum 48-hour week or 9-hour day for women and young persons under the age of 16, although there was plenty of leeway as regards the amount of overtime that could be asked for. But, according to Sheila Lewenhak, there was mounting frustration among women activists that the TUC was in fact showing less interest in so-called 'women's issues' such as maternal and infant welfare provision, and even less in the issue of equal pay.[12] This despite the fact that by 1939 the number of women in trade unions had crossed the million mark.

By 1939 the whole country was covered by a network of voluntary negotiating bodies and statutory wages regulating authorities. Clegg argues that it is possible to make a distinction between those industries which were relatively sheltered in the domestic market and those which were exposed to the brunt of foreign competition. In the building industry and the railways, for example, a system of collective bargaining, largely built up during the First World War persisted, with ups and downs admittedly, but still well entrenched. In other areas like public administration, in the water and electricity industries and in road haulage, collective bargaining was introduced for the first time between the wars. The industries with really bad industrial relations and a breakdown in collective bargaining procedures were mining and cotton, the two industries which suffered most badly from the economic situation, and both of which required government intervention to restore effective bargaining. Increasing numbers of workers had gained a week's period holiday. The Engineering Employers' Federation agreed to it in the settlement of 1937 and, by 1939, some 23 unions had negotiated such an arrangement. In 1938, a Holidays with Pay Act gave holidays to those workers covered by trade boards and by the Road Haulage and Agricultural Boards.

At official union level respectability oozed from every pore, symbolised by the award of a knighthood to the general secretary of the TUC, Walter Citrine, in 1935. If the function of trade unions is to achieve gradual progress, to institutionalise protest and generally to avoid strikes and to extend the workers' voice into all areas affecting their lives, then the policies pursued after 1926 had been a success. On the other hand, membership figures were not back to levels of 1920 and employers had used the relative weakness of the union position to push for tighter managerial control. This weakness may also have had wider effects. It has been argued that a lack of militancy strengthened a conservatism and inertia in British management. They were prepared to sit out the Depression rather than to invest, innovate and look for new lines. Arthur McIvor's study of cotton employers concludes that 'the spinning employers proved to be unwilling to press for fundamental reforms in work processes, manning levels and the division of labour, made no great effort to promote shift working and more mule working, nor did they openly encourage the more rapid diffusion of the ring frame'.[13] The Depression years also hindered what pressures for change there were within trade unionism. The threat of unemployment, which was ever present in so many areas from the early 1920s, made the craft unions determined to protect the position of their own members at whatever cost. Technological change, which meant reorganisation and the loss of status for the skilled worker or any narrowing of differentials, was resisted.

War Again

By the time war broke out in 1939 it was clear that government had learned some of the lessons of the First World War. As early as 1938 the General Council was consulted about plans for mobilisation and about which workers would be granted reserved occupation status in the event of war. It helped that there was a much wider consensus in 1939 than there had been in 1914 that this was a 'necessary' war against fascism. Only the communists continued to denounce it as an imperialist war until Hitler's invasion of Russia in 1941. This consensus, and the real threat of defeat and invasion in the summer of 1940, created a tolerance of control and direction by government which would have produced uproar in 1914–18. Conscription was operating before war broke out and dilution agreements in key industries were worked out very early on. On the other hand, all the problems which had caused bitterness in the First World War were not avoided. There was an immediate debate on how far wage control should replace collective bargaining. The TUC pressed for price and profits control as a first priority. Churchill's appointment, on Attlee's advice, of Ernest Bevin in May 1940 as Minister of Labour and National Service was an inspired choice. He speedily brought in direction of labour to 'essential work' and restrictions on leaving work, but with the control of the latter in the hands of national service officers, not the employers. Foremen lost much of their power to arbitrarily dismiss workers, while the shortage of skills gave individual workers considerable power to move jobs if they really wanted to. In April 1941, Order 386 effectively allowed the mobilisation of all women and, by the end of 1943, 45 per cent of women were either in the services or at work.

At the same time, Bevin insisted on improved health, sanitary and welfare conditions in factories involved in government work. Personnel managers began to appear as did works canteens. Money was provided to local authorities to develop day nursery provision. Firms which had traditionally pursued anti-union policies came under pressure to change and, for the first time, trade unionism began to make an appearance in some of the smaller engineering firms. Dilutees were expected to become union members. Workers covered by the label 'essential work' were guaranteed a full week's wage. In 1941 certain named trade union officials were permitted to have access to the management of all firms engaged in government work. Bevin also promulgated Order 1305 which, to all intents, banned strikes and lock-outs, but maintained the existing voluntary procedures for settling disputes. A national arbitration tribunal could, however, be used if both sides wanted and its awards were enforceable by law. It also provided for the recording of any departures from customary trade practices to facilitate their restoration at the end of the war. This was something which forced dealings with unions, and required all employers in a district to accept major collective agreements, which had been worked out by joint industrial councils or by negotiations between unions and employers' organisations in their district.

Bevin's new powers and the national crisis also allowed him to act in his own territory of the docks. Throughout his career he had wanted to bring an end to the casual system of dock employment by means of a system of registration of a permanent dock labour force with a guaranteed minimum maintenance pay. Both employers and workers had resisted this. Some registration had taken place in most ports throughout the country in the 1920s and 1930s but there was still deep hostility to making it totally effective. In the summer of 1940, however, registration was made compulsory and dockers were required to move between ports as required. Despite this – or because of it – strikes and absenteeism remained a problem throughout the war. None the less, some of the worst restrictive practices were eliminated.

Order 1305 did not halt strikes. There were more strikes in the 11 years during which the Order operated than in the previous 20 years. There were almost as many in 1940 as in 1939 and each year they continued to rise, but they were of short duration and the days lost were fewer than ever before. Local officials condoned them and employers generally tolerated them without invoking the Order. Mining remained a particularly fraught area, soured by 20 years of bitter industrial relations and frequent unofficial action, and further embittered by the fact that miners' earnings had lost ground compared to other groups of workers. Under the Essential Work Order miners were protected from conscription and guaranteed a weekly wage, but, at the same time, were subject to new disciplinary measures to reduce absenteeism. By the summer of 1941 the demand was such that real efforts were being made to attract former miners back into the industry. None of the measures eradicated persistent industrial stoppages in the industry. But the prosecution of 1000 striking miners at Betteshanger Colliery in Kent[14] in December 1941, which resulted in the imprisonment of three of the branch officials and fines on the 1000 strikers, showed the futility of compulsion. Few fines were paid and were quietly ignored by the authorities and the officials were soon released. It was the last time anyone was imprisoned under the Order. Otherwise strikes were usually confined to a single plant and over issues like changes to piece rates.

As well as seeking ways of avoiding disputes, the Coalition Government was also concerned to avoid the levels of price inflation which had been behind so much of the tension in the First World War. There was strong Treasury pressure for wage control, but Bevin was powerful enough to see off this demand. Instead, the cost of living index was manipulated to underestimate the cost of living and the Treasury was able to block demands from unions like the Post Office Workers for equal pay for women. The TUC was opposed to wage control and some groups of scarce workers made substantial gains. In other cases, there was a readiness to use the bargaining strength of a few key workers to lever up wages and conditions for a wider group, and the main feature of engineering during the war was lightning strikes over some local issue. A strike of engineering apprentices in the spring of 1941 spread from the Clyde to Belfast, Barrow and Manchester before a court of inquiry achieved a settlement, although one which still left the apprentices with grievances.

By 1943–4 it was becoming more difficult for trade union officials to keep in check their members' discontents. Civil service unions were prepared to challenge the 1927 Act by applying for affiliation to the TUC. Long hours, with extensive overtime to maintain war production, and tight controls over the labour market, built up tensions in armaments firms. The need for work practice flexibility allowed the re-emergence of a significant role for shop stewards, who had had a very limited place in the industrial relations system since 1922. Some historians have painted a bleak picture of guerrilla warfare in many areas of munitions.[15] Movement between firms spread knowledge of practices and rates in different sectors of an industry and encouraged attempts to get the best possible rates. Engineering shop stewards began to claw back some of the loss of autonomy which skilled engineers had experienced since the defeat of 1922, often with scant reference to other unions. The AEU insisted that dilutees from other unions had to take out temporary membership of the AEU as well. They were able to impose on the employers the right to hold shop stewards' meetings during working hours.

At the same time, war-time solidarity did bring a revival of Joint Industrial Councils in a few areas. Some 56 of them were established or revived during the war. Also there were attempts, particularly in the blackest days of war, to co-operate to improve production, by finding ways of using machinery, material and work methods more efficiently. There were attractions for some activists in being involved with management in decisions which had formerly been seen as the prerogative of management and there was, once again, talk of workers' control. Jack Tanner, the former syndicalist, who was now president of the AEU, had campaigned for Joint Production, Consultative and Advisory Committees which were established in engineering and shipbuilding. Most workers were, however, suspicious of their representatives becoming spokesmen *for* management and a feeling returned fairly quickly that management would be the main beneficiaries of such ideas.

Shop stewards once again emerged as key figures in dealing with shop-floor reorganisations and in overseeing the improved working and welfare conditions which were being brought in. What was lacking, in contrast to the First World War years, was an effective politicisation of industrial unrest. The CPGB, after 1941, had no doubt about the justice of the war and wanted nothing that would disrupt the flow of supplies to Russia or delay the opening of a second front.[16] And yet, there was a persistent belief on the part of Bevin and others, as patriotic exhortations failed to restrain strikes from reaching their highest incidence since records began, that communists and Trotskyists were behind many of the disputes, especially those on Clydeside, where most of the prosecutions under Order 1305 were, and among miners. In April 1944 Bevin brought in, with TUC support, Regulation 1AA which made *incitement* to strike an offence. In fact, it was never to be used and was repealed immediately the war in Europe ended. The concerns were not entirely unjustified. Some Trotskyists were active in engineering disputes, especially among the apprentice engineers, and, by 1944, the executive of the Electrical Trades Union was firmly in the hands of communists. Frank Foulkes was elected president in 1945; his associate and recent member of the CPGB, Walter Stevens, was made general secretary in 1947. A third key figure, Frank Haxell, was elected as Stevens's assistant. Communists also held key offices in the Miners' Union. There was, however, little sign of anything resembling revolutionary defeatism. Also both employers and government went out of their way to ensure that the power of union executives would not be eroded to the extent that an alternative shop-floor leadership would emerge.

Looking to the Future

From 1944 both government and TUC began to look towards the post-war world. Beveridge's proposals and Butler's Education Act had both pointed in that direction even earlier. The first TUC Report on Reconstruction reiterated support for a gradual transition of the economic system away from private to public control, but argued that, even with continuing private control, there had to be a commitment to the 'abolition of unemployment, the provision of an adequate number of good houses, reduced hours of labour, better working conditions and progressive improvements in the standard of living generally'. It was made clear, at the same time, that full employment could not be achieved at any price and there would be no reduction in trade union rates to achieve it. It was government's duty to create the conditions for full employment by locating industry, regulating imports, retraining workers and replacing private with public ownership.[17] Employers, on the other hand, were keen to get back to some kind of normalcy as quickly as possible. The car firm of Humber Rootes, for example, announced new piecework rates in 1945 strictly in line with national agreements but well below the war-time rates. A go-slow against them resulted in redundancies and an all-out strike.[18] Standard Motors, in contrast, agreed to the maintenance of war-time rates and a five-day week in 1946. A national five-day week for the car industry was agreed from January 1947.

The coal miners prepared for the post-war world by transforming the MFGB into 'One Union', the National Union of Mineworkers, which came into operation on 1 January 1945. Arthur Horner, shrewd and pragmatic communist secretary of the South Wales Miners, and Sam Watson of the Durham Miners, had devised a more effective, centralised organisation for the MFGB at the end of the 1930s. But strong regional particularities remained and they came up against the intransigence of districts. Government control of coal production meant that once again the MFGB was negotiating nationally and the prospect of nationalisation broke down some of that resistance, till only Spencer from Nottingham continued to stand out strongly against it. Symbolically, the founding conference of the National Union of Mineworkers (NUM) was held in Nottingham in August 1944.[19] It fell short of the aims of Horner and Watson, however, and county identity was still largely retained by the counties being made areas of the National Union. The areas were still allowed to control most of their own funds.

During the war, union membership rose by some 1.5 million. Just as with the First World War, this war saw a substantial growth in collective bargaining, to a large extent encouraged by government, but also made possible by the improved bargaining position of workers and the improved profits of employers. By its end the bulk of workers were covered by some kind of collective agreement. Women workers had made some gains in wages and slightly narrowed the gap in pay levels. In some areas of banking and the civil service the bar on married women working had been removed. Even the AEU, which had so long set its face against admitting women, agreed in a low and 'unenthusiastic' postal ballot in 1943 to admit them, rather than to see increasing numbers of them going off to join the general unions. They also decided to campaign for a women's rate that was 95 per cent of the men's one. As early as 1940, the AEU and the EEF had come to an agreement which, in theory, would have given women workers with the necessary skills the same rate of pay as men. In practice, however, both union and employers connived at avoiding paying equal rates, by providing some limited supervision, for example, to show that they were not skilled enough to deserve the 'rate for the job'.[20]

Workers generally had emerged from the war with substantially improved living standards. The population as a whole was generally healthier despite (or was it because of?) food shortages. Pauperism of the kind that was known before 1939 was rare. The average real earnings of those in work, which was all but a small number, were a third higher than they had been in 1913. Families were also smaller than a generation before and this added to improved living standards. That and a policy agreed by both main parties to maintain full employment made post-war austerity tolerable and created an atmosphere for constructive industrial relations.

Labour in Power

Unions could look forward to Attlee's Labour Government, the first with an absolute majority, rewarding their support. It acted quickly with the repeal of the much-resented 1927 Trade Disputes and Trade Union Act. But Order 1305 was continued and the restoration of pre-war practices was delayed. Poorly organised workers got better protection with the Wages

Council Act of 1945, an alternative to the trade boards. It brought minimum wages, for the first time, to the areas of retailing and hairdressing. The Catering Wages Act of 1943 had already extended wage-fixing legislation to catering, something which the 1929–31 Labour Government had tried but failed to achieve, and which Conservative back-benchers continued vigorously to oppose. In the increasingly prosperous farming industry, farm labourers gained something from the Agricultural (Wages) Regulation Act of 1947. The Fair Wages Resolution was strengthened with a clause requiring all those getting government contracts to recognise their workers' rights to join trade unions. No legislation, however, ratified the International Labour Organisation conventions which would have protected workers from anti-union discrimination. It was a sign of the times that, over the protests of courtiers, royal servants joined the Civil Service Union, with the Treasury reminding an angry Palace that 'it is a well recognised practice in this country that employees have a right to represent their grievances to their employer and that if they wish to do so collectively they could get someone to speak on their behalf'.[21]

A Royal Commission on Equal Pay reported in 1946, with only the three women members dissenting, rejecting the claim for equal pay on the grounds that women would lose by it, although it recommended its introduction in the lower ranks of the civil service and in teaching. The arguments from employers were familiar ones, that women did lighter jobs, were more likely to be absent through sickness and could not work such long hours. There was little enthusiasm for it among the majority of male unionists who still clung to the idea of a family wage for men and feared that any weakening of that concept would undermine their bargaining position. Individual women unionists and unions like the National Union of Teachers, NALGO and the Civil Service Clerical Staff Association worked to get the recommendations accepted and to overcome TUC resistance. Not until 1950, however, did the TUC carry its first resolution for equal pay for women outside the public services. Individual trade unions did little to help. In many cases women were organised in separate sections and the National Union of Boot and Shoe Operatives, for example, actually agreed to an *increase* in the differential between men and women's pay in 1947. Many unions passed resolutions supporting the principle of equal pay, while doing nothing to try to achieve it. As Sarah Boston has argued, they only had 'liberty on their lips'.[22] It was left to a Conservative Chancellor, R. A. Butler, to implement equal pay in the civil service in 1955. Overall, however, in the post-war years, women's earnings lost ground in relation to men's, falling to 50 per cent on average by 1961.

Crises Years

By 1947, as the balance of payments situation deteriorated, the austere Chancellor, Stafford Cripps, warned of the country's critical economic position and called for wage restraint as well as increased production. A worsening situation produced a *Statement on Personal Incomes, Costs and Prices* in February 1948, arguing that there 'should be no further general increases in the level of personal incomes without at least a corresponding increase in the volume of production'. A still loyal trade union leadership persuaded the TUC, against considerable rank-and-file opposition, to accept wage restraint as a *quid pro quo* for full employment. But even leaders like Arthur Deakin, Bevin's successor at the TGWU, and committed to making the Labour Government a success, growled at suggestions of a pay freeze. He told the Labour Party conference in 1947, 'Under no circumstances at all will we accept the position that the responsibility for the fixation of wages and the regulation of employment is one for the Government.' Tom Williamson, the equally moderate leader of the GMWU, spelled out the difficulty as the unions saw it: 'Wages policy could do no more than usurp the authority of the trade union movement.' Both believed that the *Statement* was one-sided since it had almost nothing to say about price control.

The miners achieved their long-demanded nationalisation of the coal industry in 1947, and this was seen by the NUM as an opportunity for pushing up wages. Miners were conscious that they had lost ground since 1926 compared with other groups of workers and there was a determination to reverse the position. The leadership in the NUM led resistance to an incomes' policy, other than one which gave preferential treatment to the mining industry in order to attract more labour into mining. The fact that demand for coal greatly exceeded the supply at the end of the 1940s meant that miners had little to fear from unemployment, and, indeed, such was the labour shortage that the NUM agreed to the importation of Polish miners. They were happy to accept the requirement made in all the nationalised industries that negotiating machinery had to be established and union membership made more or less compulsory, something which added to the membership of white-collar unions in particular. Initially, relations between the NUM and the National Coal Board were good, helped by the fairly steady increase in wage rates into the 1950s, largely due to the labour shortages which the industry experienced. On the other hand, not a great deal changed in the way the industry was actually managed and for some there was disappointment that nationalisation had not brought with it some participation of workers in management. The NUM leadership struggled to curb unofficial action, particularly in the most strike-prone areas of Scotland, South Wales and Yorkshire.

Another area of tension was in the docks where there was a series of unofficial strikes. Dockers were also in a strong bargaining position in that there was a desperate desire after the war to get a revival of exports. Their wages and earnings were considerably above the national average.[23] The Government was concerned that there should be no return to pre-war casualisation and war-time regulation was continued until 1947. On the other hand, British exporters were finding it extremely difficult to compete with cheaper foreign competition and austerity made it difficult for imports. Trade was slow to pick up and there was less of a demand for dockers. Before the war ended there were major disputes in Liverpool, Manchester, Newcastle and London and in the autumn of 1945 50 000 had struck at the ports of Birkenhead, Liverpool, Manchester, Hull and London and troops were called in to move cargoes. There were four major dockers' stoppages between 1948 and 1950 and innumerable lesser ones.

Central to the tensions in the docks, as always, was the issue of decasualisation. It had been examined and talked about for more than half a century, but had proved impossible to achieve. Most ports had some system of registration, but a committee of inquiry on port labour in 1931 had failed to come up with anything much beyond that. War-time needs for dock labour had resulted in a gradual erosion of casualisation. In 1941 state regulation of all the docks brought with it compulsory registration and an agreed weekly wage. All registered dockers were now allocated to an employer and, if not required for work, were transferred to a National Dock Labour Corporation which paid attendance money. Union pressure resulted in the scheme being extended until 1947, but attempts by employers and unions to devise a mutually acceptable post-war scheme of decasualisation floundered. Employers did not want the restrictions and costs and even many of the dockers themselves were hesitant to see the advantages of flexible working disappear.

Lacking agreement, in June 1947 the Ministry of Labour imposed the National Dock Labour Scheme. By this, a National Dock Labour Board, with parallel local boards at each port under joint union and employer control, regulated the recruitment, employment and discharging of registered dockers. There was a guaranteed wage, providing a level of security that was quite new to many dockers. It depended upon dockers accepting mobility between employers and ports and flexibility of working time. It depended also on dockers having to sacrifice their age-old freedom of deciding when to work and for whom to work. Now they were required to be in attendance each morning and afternoon and to accept the work available. It did not, however, change the pattern of standing around waiting to be called to work, which had been the feature of the casual system. So old habits and styles did not change and payment by piece rate continued to produce competition for good jobs rather than dirty ones.[24]

In practice, the National Dock Labour Scheme ushered in a whole series of strikes. Moving from employer to employer, dockers had little patience for or understanding of long-drawn-out disputes procedures and embarked on unofficial strike action with apparent zeal over real or imagined grievances. A sense of solidarity among dockers (bound by gang working and by family and community ties in many cases) again and again overrode loyalty to the wider union, the Transport and General.

The involvement of union officials in the administration of the dock scheme meant that the union bore some of the resentment against unpopular decisions and there were always unofficial leaders or the TGWU's rival, the NASDU or 'blue union', to lead the opposition. What overtime meant and how much should be accepted became a particular bone of contention. Under the dock labour scheme it was obligatory but ill-defined and a number of the strikes were over what was perceived as the victimisation of dockers who were refusing to work 'reasonable' overtime. Again and again troops were called in to unload ships, and paradoxically, it was during the left-wing Aneurin Bevan's brief stay at the Ministry of Labour in the spring of 1951 that seven dockers in London and Merseyside were charged with incitement under Order 1305. The jury found them guilty on one charge, but failed to agree on the second and the Government decided not to proceed further.

Further economic difficulties in 1949 led to a sterling crisis, devaluation of the pound and further belt-tightening. Rationing was restored in a number of areas and the TUC General Council declared that it would go along with restraint as long as the Government continued to support the maintenance of voluntary collective bargaining and admitted that wage increases could be justified by increased output. It also asked the government to affirm that the wages of workers whose incomes were below a level to provide a reasonable standard of living should be improved. Finally, it asked the Government to

> recognise the need to safeguard those wage differentials which are an essential element in the wages structure of many important industries and are required to sustain those standards of craftsmanship, training and experience that contribute directly to industrial efficiency and higher productivity.

In other words, as long as little was changed, the TUC was willing to accept some conditional wage restraint. Even this caused resentment and assisted the Communist Party, once again, in making some advances within unions like the Foundry Workers and the Fire Brigades' Union on the basis of resistance to the policy.

On the whole, the TUC had supported the maintenance of Order 1305, despite calls for its repeal by a number of unions. In 1950 Congress had, by a majority of two to one, supported its retention. But its actual use, coupled with mounting internal pressure within unions as inflation began to bite sharply into living standards, produced a dramatic volte face by the General Council. In June 1950 the General Council voted unanimously in favour of an end to the policy of wage restraint. Since devaluation of the pound in 1947 real wages had declined for most workers. The arbitration tribunals took little account of this, with the effect that it undermined the confidence of unions in the independence of the Ministry of Labour and the National Arbitration Tribunal. Bevan's successor, Alf Robens, later in the year, finally withdrew Order 1305 and replaced it with Order 1376. There was now no prohibition of strikes and lock-outs, but compulsory arbitration was retained if either party in a dispute referred the matter to the Minister of Labour.

Despite the short-term crises, the bargaining position of Labour was as strong as it had ever been. There was, for the first time ever, full employment and frequent shortages of skilled labour in key areas. Employers did little to try to remedy the situation, preferring to continue with traditional patterns and processes.[25] The TUC continued to urge unions to reform and to merge, but the pressures for change were not powerful enough to achieve much.

9 Policies and Power, 1951–74

The Churchill Years

The Labour Government in its last years had been looking closely at ways of using legislation to prevent strikes in the essential services and at the possibility of making an extended Order 1305 a permanent feature. The new Conservative Government which came to power in 1951, in contrast, was determined to avoid any politically inspired industrial conflict. As his Minister of Labour Churchill appointed the conciliatory and mild-mannered barrister, Sir Walter Monckton.

Union membership had continued to grow and by 1951 stood at 7 740 000, 1.5 million more than when the war ended. Over one in two men were in unions and around one in four women workers. The outbreak of the Korean war in the summer of 1950, which occasioned a fast rearmament programme, had once again provided trade unions with bargaining opportunities. In industries like engineering, labour demand rose. The Labour Government's efforts to maintain a policy of wage restraint, which had the support of the main trade union leaders, had already crumbled by the time of the Government's defeat. With prices rising more than earnings, wage claims grew. But a policy of concession and compromise and the continuing moderation of leaders like Arthur Deakin of the TGWU, Tom Williamson of the GMWU and Will Lawther of the NUM meant that industrial relations in the early 1950s were fairly tranquil. Churchill and Monkton both made clear their distaste for the anti-union policy pursued by firms like the Dundee-based publishers D. C. Thomson and Co. whose dispute with NATSOPA went to a court of inquiry in 1952. During the early 1950s there were few major official strikes; days lost were little more than in the late 1930s and the early war years; and far and away the majority of strikes were confined to the coal mining industry.

Claims from engineering and shipbuilding unions, involving something like three million workers, were debated through the various negotiating procedures in the summer of 1952. Fifty-three unions were affiliated to the Confederation of Shipbuilding and Engineering Unions and most major employers were in the Engineering and Allied Employers' National Federation and the Shipbuilding Employers' Federation. The employers rejected a £2 wage claim from the engineering unions, but rises above the cost of living were conceded with government approval. In the now nationalised railways industrial peace was purchased by good wage rises, doing something to improve the position of a notably underpaid group of workers. Rather tentative suggestions for a voluntary wages policy were vigorously resisted.

Beneath the relative peace, however, many unions were facing major internal tensions and relations between unions were even more acerbic than usual. The union leaders of the big unions were on the right of Labour Party politics and they infuriated Bevanite supporters by casting doubt on wider nationalisation. The decision of Lincoln Evans of the Steel Workers' Union to sit on the Iron and Steel Board of the once-again denationalised steel industry infuriated many on the left. Ideological battles rumbled on and so too did inter-union pettiness. Rivalry persisted between the National Union of Public Employees, organising the poorer paid council workers, like roadmen, and the general unions. Although politically the moderate Bryn Roberts of NUPE was on the same side as Deakin and Williamson, his union was a red rag to them because of a history of rivalry dating back to at least 1907. The GMWU and the TGWU both persistently tried to exclude NUPE from negotiating bodies such as the Joint Industrial Councils. Calls by Roberts for a fundamental reorganisation of trade unions were persistently blocked. In other words, there was a heavy price to pay for Monckton's emollient attitude in that unions were allowed to ignore the fundamental need for organisational reform.

Equally there was tension within individual unions. Within the ETU the communists now operated a tight control. In the TGWU Arthur Deakin battled to maintain authoritarian control with a mixture of bluster and bullying and a paranoia towards any ideas that came from left-wingers. Since 1949 communists had been banned from holding union office. But it was not always possible to maintain the tight control he would have wished. In 1955, Hull dockers, whose unofficial strike over a local grievance had not been given backing by the TGWU, turned, in defiance of the Bridlington Agreement, to the National Amalgamated Stevedores and Dockers,[1] which had hitherto been confined to the London docks, and eventually nearly 10 000 dockers at different ports followed them. Expulsion of the Stevedores from the industry's National Joint Council and suspension from the TUC did not resolve the problem and there were bitter disputes during 1955 as the stevedores sought to break the monopoly which the TGWU had in port authorities.[2] Hundreds of local disputes continued as dockers in different ports acted with little consultation with either the TGWU or the NASDU. More than half a million working days were lost in London alone in 1955. But as a Devlin Report of 1956 made clear, the dock employers did little to help with their persistent attempts to undermine the working of the National Dock Labour Scheme, which they had never liked because of the extent to which it allowed union involvement in what they regarded as properly management decisions.

The End of Tranquillity

In 1955 the number of disputes reached a higher level than in any year since records began in 1893, and the number of working days lost were the highest since 1933 (1944 excepted). The 'years of peace', when there was talk of the 'withering away of the strike' had given way to a return of strike activity.[3] Over the next three years the number of disputes continued to rise and working days lost peaked in 1958 at over eight million. There had been signs of a renewed unrest for a year or two. The railwaymen had rejected an arbitration award in 1953 and a strike had been narrowly prevented by the promise of something more. In an engineering dispute the following year, neither side proposed arbitration and the unions would not guarantee to accept a judgment by a court of inquiry. A number of the disputes were the result of a revolt by skilled workers against a narrowing of differentials which had taken place between them and the non-craft workers. London newspapers were shut down for three weeks when AEU and ETU members working alongside print workers struck for unilateral bargaining rights. Up until then they had had to accept terms negotiated for them by the powerful print unions. It took weeks to get the unions to come together to agree a settlement with the proprietors. A recurrence of the perpetual rivalry between the NUR and ASLEF led to a four-week rail strike in May 1955 when the footplatemen in ASLEF struck for the restoration of differentials in pay over non-footplate workers, which had been narrowed in previous settlements. It was the first nation-wide strike for 20 years. A state of emergency was declared. An arbitration award conceded a rise, but the legacy of inter-union bitterness was great. There were instances of drivers and firemen from rival unions refusing to speak to one another in the cab and at Taunton ASLEF members of the railway choir refused to sing alongside NUR men.[4] A quarter of a century later the bitterness remained.

Resistance to innovation was also strong within the TUC. When the Ministry of Labour proposed that there should be a mechanism within all negotiating procedures for a final resort to arbitration, the TUC rejected it out of hand, arguing that where it did exist it had not prevented disputes and, indeed, discouraged some employers from looking for settlements. There was also a deep suspicion that government could influence any arbitrators. There were still those who argued for a radical reorganisation of unions along industrial lines, but there was no way that the large general unions were going to tolerate the break-up which such a reorganisation would involve. The big unions continued to be unwilling to subordinate themselves to the General Council.

Employers did not help the situation, although the British Employers' Confederation continued to assert a desire to maintain co-operative relations with the TUC. The British Motor Corporation, a merger of Morris and Austin, for example, grappling to maintain competitiveness, dismissed 6000 workers in 1956 without any warning and with no consultation with the unions. It led to strikes in Coventry and Oxford. It was only since the 1940s that trade unionism had gained a firm foothold in most of the car industry and there were still many non-unionists. The refusal of most of these to strike produced great division and bitterness among the work-force, but it also encouraged a relatively successful drive to extend union membership. Shop stewards began to push for the imposition of a closed shop.[5]

Faced with rising inflation there was a hardening of government attitudes. The replacement of Monckton at the Ministry of Labour by Iain MacLeod quickly showed a newer tone as government tried to curb wage awards. Most unions were not in the mood for restraint, however, and the TUC had lost the moderating tones of Arthur Deakin. His death, quickly followed by that of his successor, Arthur Tiffin, opened the door for the accession of Frank Cousins to the general secretaryship of the TGWU. Cousins rejected all calls for 'wage restraint in any form' and his public rhetoric constantly advocated an aggressive policy, although in practice he tended to caution. By the spring of 1957 there was talk of the possibility of a general strike and a threat of government collapse and devaluation. The Confederation of Shipbuilding and Engineering Unions had put in a claim for a rise in minimum time rates to match the rise in the cost of living. The Employers' Federation refused any rise and in March a nation-wide strike broke out in engineering works, followed quickly by one in the shipyards. But government was the first to blink and prevailed on the engineering and shipbuilding employers and the Railway Board to concede rises to bring strikes to an end. Employers began to complain bitterly of government feebleness. On the other hand, there were genuine efforts being made to improve labour relations. The British Transport Commission, responsible for the railways, introduced joint consultation in 1956 as a way to improve work practices; 'cooperation in practice' they called it. ICI, which had had works councils since the days of Mond, extended the scope of these. The National Coal Board brought in consultative councils, but these were treated with considerable suspicion by many trade union activists, who saw them as being mainly about raising productivity, and union leaders remained obsessed with the annual wage-round battle.

Macmillan's Government tentatively moved towards a wages' policy in 1957 with the Council on Prices, Productivity and Incomes under Lord Cohen. Neither the Employers' Confederation nor the TUC showed any enthusiasm for it. Its first report, which suggested that inflation could best be curbed by letting unemployment rise, convinced the unions to boycott it.[6] The result was also to undermine what remaining faith there was in conciliation and arbitration procedures. A decision in November 1957 to reject Whitley Council proposals for workers in the health service augured badly for the public sector. The Industrial Disputes' Tribunal, which had survived from Order 1305 and offered compulsory arbitration, was abolished under the Terms and Conditions of Employment Act of 1959, leaving only the voluntary industrial court. Government resistance stiffened and Macleod was able to see off a seven-week London bus strike of TGWU members which, despite Frank Cousins's rhetoric, had failed to attract support from other unions. Living standards for many were rising so as to give some validity to Harold Macmillan's election claim in 1959 that 'You have never had it so good' and some breathing space was allowed.

But unions were coming under attack. There was increasingly public criticism, particularly of the role of shop stewards. The readiness to blow the whistle and call everyone out was satirised with devastating effect in the 1959 film *I'm All Right, Jack*, with Peter Sellers, and more harshly in 1960 in Attenborough and Forbes's film *The Angry Silence*, on the treatment of someone refusing to strike. The newspaper proprietors were growing resentful of the tight hold which the printing unions were exerting on them and the press coverage displayed a new hostility. Although they lacked the courage to challenge them directly, they were prepared to cheer others into confrontation. Individual workers were resentful of the extension of the closed shops in many parts of industry, although most big employers liked the stability which this could provide. The courts were querying the protection which unions assumed they had and in *Bonsor* v. *Musicians' Union* upheld the right of an expelled member to sue his union. A great deal of the hostile publicity for unions focused on communist activists and this was made easier when the position of the CPGB was seriously weakened in the aftermath of the Russian attack on Hungary in 1956.

The ETU Saga

The issue of communist influence came to a head in the affairs of the Electrical Trade Union where communists had won most of the chief offices and dominated the executive since the mid 1940s. By 1954, the executive was firmly in the hands of committed communists or what the historian of the union calls 'unargumentative fellow travellers'.[7] The right-wing Labour MP and journalist, Woodrow Wyatt, had been trying to expose the internal workings of the ETU for some years, arguing that officials had falsified voting returns from various branches, at least since 1948, in order to keep out of office an anti-communist candidate, John Byrne. It tied in with academic studies which were showing that apathy among union membership was allowing small coteries of political activists to take control of branches. The role which trade unions played within the Labour Party gave the shaping of union policy on non-industrial issues a particular importance for the politically aware. On the other hand, to many, including leading conservatives, the ETU was seen as having many qualities of which they approved. The leadership worked out firm agreements with the employers and ensured that the agreements were enforced.

Internal conflict gradually came to a head around the education officer, Les Cannon, who ran the union's splendidly appointed and only recently opened residential college at Esher Place. Cannon had been a committed communist but had left the party in 1956. Most of the executive remained loyal to the Communist Party and there were moves to prise out Cannon. There were also major financial difficulties in the aftermath of the 1957 engineering strike in which the ETU had maintained a hard confrontational position and had backed strikes after the main settlement. The closure of the residential college gave the CP leadership a solution to both problems. But Cannon decided to fight back by standing for a place on the executive. The result of the election was not declared, as required, and instead the general secretary, Frank Haxell, announced an inquiry into electoral procedures at various branches, the outcome of which was their votes being declared invalid. As a result, Cannon was declared defeated; but by now he had gone to the press to denounce communist malpractice.

The battles of the union were now fought out in the public domain, doing immense damage to unionism in general. Woodrow Wyatt returned to the attack, but was joined by other, less partisan, journalists. Cannon linked up with some others in the union who had vainly protested against communist tactics in the past and soon after found himself suspended from the union. In 1959 he gained a powerful ally in another ex-communist, Frank Chapple. In December 1959 the veteran anti-communist, John Byrne, once again stood against Haxell and was once again defeated by a narrow majority after many branches were again disqualified. Byrne and Chapple now decided to take the matter to the courts. The union leadership used every tactic, not stopping short of intimidation, to prevent the real situation coming to light. Cannon, Chapple and their supporters toured the branches seeking support and details of procedures. The court case revealed decades of ballot-rigging in union elections by CP members and what the judge called 'pliant sympathisers', designed to keep the communist leadership in power. Byrne was declared elected but faced a hostile executive.

The struggle for control of the union was far from over. Some found it unforgivable that Cannon and Chapple should have taken the issue to the courts in the first place, with all the damaging publicity to the whole trade union movement which that entailed. But the TUC at last decided that it could stand aside no longer and demanded the exclusion of the key figures who had been named in ballot rigging. When the executive of the ETU refused, the union was expelled from Congress. In September 1961 an election, in which only 13 per cent of the membership voted, finally brought an anti-communist majority and two years later Les Cannon won election to the presidency of the union.[8]

Structural Weaknesses

The ETU affair, in particular, led to demands for the internal affairs of unions to be regulated. There were calls for the registration of union rules, which would only be accepted if they met with certain standards. By the early 1960s there was substantial agreement on the weakness of trade union structure. Within individual trade unions it was always extremely difficult to get organisational change. A union like the NUR, for example, tried for more than 20 years to reform structures which had been largely unchanged since 1913. The national executive was made up of members who were elected from different sections in different geographical areas for a period of three years away from their jobs. The role was attractive and not particularly onerous but it meant that neither areas nor sections were willing to give up the perk of representation. Not until the end of the 1970s was some minor reform achieved.

Historical division between unions of craft and unskilled workers, which cut horizontally across industrial boundaries, still bedevilled orderly industrial relations. Most so-called craft unions like the AEU or the Boilermakers or the Vehicle Builders had membership which included supervisory and technical workers, semi-skilled and unskilled workers, even if the 'craftsmen' usually maintained a privileged position within the union organisation. The general unions contained many groups of craft, technical and clerical workers. Apprenticeship as a badge of skill hardly existed. The effect was a proliferation of union representation in the largest industries which bore little relation to the realities of the work-place. Ford's at their Dagenham car works had to deal with nearly two dozen unions.[9] There was some rationalisation through amalgamation, such as between the ETU and the Plumbers' Trade Union into the EETPU in 1968 and the Amalgamated Engineering Union and the Amalgamated Union of Foundry Workers and others into the AUEW in 1971. Pushed by the TUC and with great difficulty, the Boilermakers and the Shipwrights merged in 1963, gradually reducing the demarcations disputes which had been such a feature of the shipyards. But some amalgamations in the 1960s did not always streamline the industrial relations position. Restrictive practices based on past craft traditions remained a problem for industries which increasingly required flexibility. But most employers, unlike many of their contemporaries in the United States, were not prepared to 'buy out' restrictive practices. Few followed the example of Esso at their Fawley refinery of negotiating away at least some of the worst practices through productivity agreements. Here, after lengthy negotiations, restrictive practices had steadily been eroded and labour costs reduced. The labour force had been persuaded to accept new manning scales, greater flexibility on jobs and fewer interruptions of work in return for higher pay, more job security, retraining and better redundancy arrangements.[10] Attractive as it might have been, it had required an immense amount of managerial time and skill to achieve such an agreement and few employers had the will or resources to do something similar.

A second weakness which was identified was the spread of *unofficial* strikes and, as occasionally in the past, there were calls for a ban on these. Such strikes were bedevilling the car industry and the docks, and the Government launched inquiries into both these areas. There was an attempt to bring improvements in job security as a way of easing tensions. In many cases, the existing procedures did nothing to discourage unofficial action. Procedures in engineering after 1957 were governed by the York Memorandum, but the procedures were desperately slow. It took a long time before a dispute was passed up to a conference of unions in the Confederation of Shipbuilding and Engineering Unions and of employers in the Engineering Employers' Federation. Often the outcome of the procedure was to refer the issue back to the factory for settlement. Local unionists had good reason for believing that there were quicker ways of bringing matters to a resolution.

The Minister of Labour vainly tried to persuade the Treasury to concede a system of redundancy payment. It foundered on yet another stop in what had become by now a familiar 'stop, go' economic policy, with a 'pay pause' declared in the summer of 1961, followed by a guideline of 2.5 per cent for future pay rises. An incomes' policy was now officially declared with the objective of keeping 'the rate of increase of incomes within the long-term rate of growth of national production'. Arguments for increases based on the cost of living, on shortage of labour, on the trend of profits or productivity in an industry were no longer to be enough, although some elements of comparability were to be allowed.[11] A National Incomes' Commission was established to review wage claims and to review collective agreements, but it never received trade union support and soon foundered. The TUC, every bit as much as the employers, set its face against too much government intervention in regulating conditions of work, preferring, as always, to rely on collective bargaining.[12] Union leaders did, however, participate in the National Economic Development Council with a broad remit to look at the problems affecting the British economy. It proposed pay guidelines in 1963 and 1964.

It could be argued that there was some success in these policies although sharply rising unemployment, from fewer than 300 000 in the summer of 1961 to over 500 000 in 1962, played its part. The number of stoppages was lower than it had been in 1957 and only in 1962 did the working days lost reach an exceptionally high level of over five million, as opposed to an average of between two and three million. Compared with many other countries, Britain's strike record was not bad. Between 1955 and 1964, an average of 294 days a year for every 1000 workers were lost because of strikes. This compared with 1044 for the USA, 391 for Japan and 336 for France. Only Germany and Sweden among our main competitors had a substantially better record. Strikes were short and, on average, involved only about 500 workers. But 95 per cent of all strikes in the early 1960s were unofficial, nearly two thirds of the days lost. Hence the perception that Britain was a strike-torn country; the unofficial strike was a particular symptom of what the press called the 'British disease'.

What was happening, however, was that the union leadership seemed to be losing control of the rank-and-file members and much of the blame was placed on shop stewards. In most unions their role was still remarkably ill-defined, but with the spread of joint consultation procedures in the workplace, their activities and importance had increased. Since many of them were politically active it was relatively easy to see them as a sinister force. Yet studies of the car industry painted a rather different picture of stewards, with their concern for the maintenance of the 'constitutionality' of procedures often acting as a restraining force on workers. Garfield Clack concluded:

> In short, the conveners and shop stewards' organisation at the factory did not appear as a driving force behind labour unrest, but could more validly be regarded as 'shock absorbers' of the industrial relations' machinery. The suggestions that trade unions should prevent unofficial action by their members by 'disciplining' their shop stewards in some way would be inappropriate in conditions of this kind.[13]

Trade unions received a fright early in 1964 when the House of Lords upheld the case of Rookes against officials of the Association of Engineering and Shipbuilding Draughtsmen, by declaring that their threat to go on strike at British Overseas Airways if Rookes were not dismissed, although there was a no-strike agreement, was illegal. It called into question the immunity from legal action when unions struck to maintain a closed shop, which earlier court decisions seem to have granted. It appeared to go in the face of the 1906 Act and there were demands from the unions for fresh legislation to overthrow the *Rookes* v. *Barnard* decision.[14] Harold Wilson's Labour Government immediately conceded a new Act, the 1965 Trades Disputes Act, but it also set up a Royal Commission into Trade Unions under Lord Donovan, to examine the whole industrial relations' system. The unions were further conciliated by agreeing that the chairman and general secretary of the TUC should be on the Commission along with two employers. The Ministry of Labour's original idea of an entirely independent body had to be abandoned.[15]

Incomes Policies

What did not change was the pressure for wage restraint. Wages were rising faster in Britain than among its competitors and without any comparable improvements in productivity. Investment levels were notoriously low and this was often blamed on the confrontational atmosphere of industrial relations. An economic crisis in 1961 had brought a six months' 'pay pause' for public service employees and for those workers covered by wages councils. Not for the last time, nurses became the focus of protests against the implementation of the policy. Attempts to adjust policy, after strikes had broken its effectiveness, foundered. Government also failed to control the private sector or to regulate prices and, as the Macmillan Government staggered politically under the public glee in the Profumo/Keeler affair, the unions revelled in confrontation with it. Labour scarcity was once again leading to an over-heating of the economy.

By the time the Labour Government came into power in 1964 unemployment had already fallen again to nearly 300 000. Labour costs were continuing to rise while output had stopped expanding. During 1964 and 1965 many unions were able to negotiate a reduction in the working week to near 40 hours[16] but industrial output was rising by less than 2 per cent per year. On the other hand, hourly earnings were at a level that had not been reached since the Korean war boom of 1952. Unions, employers' associations and government had signed a 'Declaration of Intent' at the end of 1964 to improve productivity and George Brown's National Plan proposed a 'norm of 3–3.5 per cent' to keep the growth of wages and salaries in line with inflation. This was to be administered by a National Board for Prices and Incomes (a supposedly significant change of nomenclature from the now abolished National Incomes Commission) under a former Conservative Minister, Aubrey Jones. In the new atmosphere of what was expected to be a planned economy, some union leaders were attracted by the Swedish model of industrial relations, where a powerful centralised union movement negotiated with a similarly powerful and centralised employers' organisation and their conclusions were made legally binding.[17] The emergence in 1965 of the Confederation of British Industry, combining the British Employers' Confederation, the Federation of British Industries, the National Association of British Manufacturers and the Industrial Association of Wales in a single organisation, made this seem feasible.

On the critical issue of an incomes policy, however, the unions were divided. The National Union of General and Municipal Workers, under the moderate leadership of Jack Cooper, and the ETU, under Cannon, were in favour, arguing that 'the living standards and job security of our members can best be pursued through the implementation of a productivity, prices and incomes policy'[18] and that it would in fact 'strengthen our power by demonstrating that we are able to exercise that power with responsibility'.[19] Both, however, also wanted action to curb price rises. Others, particularly from the ranks of the craft unions, argued that to give up collective bargaining would be fatal. Dan McGarvey, the rough-hewn secretary of the Boilermakers' Society, growled to the 1965 TUC that the Boilermakers would concede it to no one. The smoother George Doughty of the Draughtsmen's Association joined him, arguing that the policy was in practice only a control of incomes not prices. George Woodcock, the general secretary of the TUC, did manage to persuade them to submit any new wage claims to a TUC wage-claim vetting committee so that a system of 'early warning' of problems could be established.

There was, nevertheless, growing resistance to the 'norms' and the TUC's attempts to improve the earnings of the low-paid led to what many skilled men regarded as an unacceptable narrowing of differentials. In conditions of severe shortages of skilled workers it was proving impossible to maintain the 'norms'. On the Clyde, for example, shipbuilders were having to turn down orders because the skill shortage was so severe. A rail strike by the NUR was narrowly avoided in February 1966 by Harold Wilson's direct intervention with 'beer and sandwiches' at 10 Downing Street. It was an unprecedented level of prime ministerial involvement, with ministers essentially taking over the negotiations. 'This is going far beyond recognised methods of conciliation,' Alfred Roberts told the Confederation of Shipbuilding and Engineering Unions, 'The next step could very well be intrusion into trade union functions within the negotiating machinery.'[20]

Wilson was, however, unable to prevent a seven-week strike by the National Union of Seamen in the summer of 1966. It was ostensibly over wages and a demand for a 40-hour week, which in theory they had, but in practice, with weekend work, became a 56-hour week. But it was also as much about a union whose leadership was seen to be to too great an extent in the pockets of the employers. The policies and style which Havelock Wilson had established were carried through to the cigar-smoking, Rolls-Royce driving Sir Thomas Yates's general secretaryship in the 1950s and a reform movement within the union had been given scant respect by Yates. Yet the reformers had gained ground in the early 1960s. The employers used the Government's prices and incomes policy to refuse concessions. When political conciliation failed to do the trick, and the report of a court of inquiry which declared the strike 'unjustified' was contemptuously rejected by the NUS executive, Wilson angrily blamed a 'tightly knit group of politically motivated men' for exploiting the grievances of seamen. He saw it as part of a communist conspiracy to take over the NUS and to destroy the Government's prices and incomes policy.

The NUS held out and a number of shipping companies began to break ranks and concede the full demands. At the same time, other unions were pressing the NUS for settlement and the TUC was trying to isolate them. Unity among the seamen's leaders began to crack. A settlement was reached at the end of June, which gave some concessions such as extended leave and an eventual 40 hours, together with a promised inquiry into the 1894 Merchant Shipping Act. It was reluctantly accepted by a majority of the executive.

The Government in other words could still count on a great deal of goodwill and the TUC, albeit reluctantly, in the autumn of 1966, acquiesced in the statutory prices and incomes freeze which the Wilson Government imposed. The Prices and Incomes Act of 1966 was a major turning point, with government, for the first time, imposing criminal sanctions for breach of legislation on employers and unions or union members. The compensation to be paid, it was hoped, would be a more active role for the unions in planning, through such bodies as the National Economic Development Council. Frank Cousins, who had resigned from the Cabinet and returned to the general secretaryship of the TGWU when the prices and incomes freeze was introduced, argued powerfully against penalties on trade unions: 'You cannot have social democracy and at the same time control by legislation the activity of a free trade union movement.' J. E. Newton of the Tailors and Garment Workers likened the Government's policy to that of 'a child trying to eat its parents', but their objections were overruled. The votes of the AEU, the GMWU, the NUM, the ETU and the NUR ensured that support for the policy was pushed through Congress. That same month the British Motor Corporation announced 12 000 redundancies and short time for 40 000 other car workers.

Disputes

Unrest persisted in other areas. There were major strikes in Liverpool and London, largely stemming from both the insecurity and the apparent opportunities created by decasualisation of the docks, which yet another Devlin Report of 1966 had at long last started to bring about. The 1947 registration scheme had done little to change the culture of casualisation in the docks and time-honoured work practices abounded. There were, for example, systems known as 'spelling' or 'welting' in which only half the gang worked at any one time, in a situation where payment to the gang was by time.[21] Devlin was scathing about the conditions in which dockers had to work and the failure of employers to provide basic facilities in toilets and washrooms. He firmly recommended the end of casual labour and the creation of a permanent dock labour force, with workers mainly attached to a single employer. He also recommended that the TGWU appoint shop stewards who could deal with issues on the spot, which were usually over the rates for handling a particular cargo, rather than having to await the arrival of a union official.

The new scheme was eventually brought in in September 1967 and was followed by nearly three years of almost perpetual industrial strife, most of it unofficial, with the TGWU struggling to maintain control over the situation. Even by dockers' standards the level of militancy was unprecedented. This was despite the major boost to dockers' earnings which accompanied the process of modernisation. Since the process of decasualisation was also supposed to be accompanied by the eradication of restrictive practices, the room for conflict was immense and seized with alacrity by some with particular axes to grind. Many in government came to believe that much of the trouble was fomented by an unholy (and, it should be said, unlikely) alliance of communists and Trotskyists. The communist Jack Dash, the unofficial leader in London, emerged as a media hate figure and, while undoubtedly politically motivated, he was able to tap into what the dockers felt were real grievances. Decasualisation and modernisation failed to remove the insecurities of dockers. There were too many on the register, the threat of redundancy was ever present and in a declining economy many dock companies were going bankrupt. Dockers faced the prospect of long-term unemployment, even if they were registered. The casual system had always held out the prospect of some work and flexibility to look for other jobs. Decasualisation meant a new discipline. The dock strikes played a part in the forced devaluation of the pound at the end of 1967.

There were difficulties elsewhere. The Barbican development in the City of London and other major building contracts in London were held up by a whole series of unofficial strikes from 1964 onwards. The Cameron Inquiry had no doubt that they were fomented by the communist-led London Building Workers' Joint Sites Committee. Attempts by George Smith, general secretary of the Amalgamated Society of Woodworkers, to expel the leaders of the committee were overthrown by the Union's lay general council. The Building Workers' Committee in turn had links with the London Dockers' unofficial movement around Jack Dash and were in turn linked up with other militant groups in the communist-led Liaison Committee for the Defence of Trade Unions.

A. J. (Jack) Scamp, the chairman of the Motor Industry Joint Labour Council, at the end of 1966, painted a picture of some motor factories not far from a state of anarchy, with 'minority groups [in] the selfish pursuit of immediate sectional advantage'.[23] Disputes, while not getting longer (most lasted less than a day; two thirds were over in a few hours) and often involving only a handful of workers, were getting more frequent. He claimed that in 600 stoppages in eight firms in the first six months of 1966, all but five were unofficial and in many cases the disputes' procedure had not been used at all or abandoned at an early stage. There were many explanations offered for the strike proneness of the car industry. Some suggested that the repetitive nature of the work led to boredom and frustration and short strikes broke the tedium of the day. As the employers pointed out, however, the union representatives had never raised boredom and tedium as an issue in negotiations. Others argued that short bursts of expansion of the industry had brought in people who had no experience of engineering and of the customary disputes' procedures. Scamp also identified managerial failure to impose discipline. 'Is it always wise,' he asked, 'to permit men who have walked out without warning to resume work again at their own pleasure?' He also blamed the complex wage structures which had evolved. Unions pursued sectional claims, but a concession to one immediately brought demands from another, with a constant 'jacking up' of earnings without regard to productivity. He was also highly critical of the unions', usually the TGWU, the AEU and the NUVB, failure to cooperate. Attempts to set up a joint works committee at Rover's at Solihull had failed because the eight unions could not agree on who should serve on the workers' side.

A report on the Fleet Street newspaper industry, commissioned from the Economist Intelligence Unit, also revealed an archaic and often anarchic situation there, which was blocking the introduction of new technology. Agreed basic rates bore little relationship to actual earnings and earnings bore little relationship to the amount of work involved in a job. On the production side, sons followed fathers into the trade and there was little recognition of the changes taking place outside the industry. Drunkenness was a problem which was rarely confronted. *Daily Telegraph* and *Observer* workers ran a bar overnight, as well as having their own drinking club. Workers had time on their hands during shifts to run a host of private enterprises.[24] Restrictive practices proliferated because unions controlled the labour process to an extent far beyond what occurred elsewhere. But the report noted that such practices were not the cause of the newspaper industries' problems, but 'the outward symptom of more serious and deep-rooted faults', most of which stemmed from weak management. There was, however, frequent animosity between the 'craft' members of the National Graphical Association (NGA) and the machine-minding Society of Graphical and Allied Trades (SOGAT) members. The NGA had been formed in 1964, linking nine long-established printing unions, including the various Typographical Associations. SOGAT was formed two years later by an amalgamation of NUPB&PW and NATSOPA. The SOGAT amalgamation failed to eradicate the traditional divisions between the two groups of workers and it fell apart in 1970 accompanied by legal action.[25] Particular acrimony arose between NGA and SOGAT people since some so-called 'craft' jobs required less skill than non-craft jobs and, in many cases, non-craftsmen could earn as much as craft workers for fewer hours. In some cases, operatives automatically received overtime payments for attendance only, even if they did not work. In other cases absenteeism was covered up or ignored. Technological developments were also forcing changes which threatened both letter-press craft workers and others. There were fears on the part of SOGAT that the NGA was trying to monopolise control of the new lithographic technology. The introduction of web-offset machines, which were not covered by collective agreements, continued to give ample opportunity for inter-union disputes.

The newly renationalised steel industry faced comparable problems. There the main process workers' union, the 120 000 strong Iron and Steel Trades Confederation, would not share negotiations with the 12 craft unions, led by the Boilermakers and AEU.

There were some successes. Productivity conferences were held. Some of the lessons of the Fawley productivity agreements were filtering through and, to stimulate this, the Government agreed that the 'norms' could be exceeded if accompanied by genuine productivity agreements. The result was many phoney deals cobbled together to get around the restrictions, but the Prices and Incomes Board believed that most did involve genuine productivity gains, although later commentators have been less convinced.[26]

Donovan

Meanwhile, the Royal Commission under Lord Donovan undertook the most extensive inquiry into industrial relations since the 1890s. It reported in the summer of 1968, having published various research papers before then. The Commission did not regard Britain's strike record in terms of working days lost as any worse than the average of other major industrial countries. On the other hand, the number of short stoppages was high and put Britain near the worst in the league, alongside Australia and New Zealand. As one historian suggests, what was unusual was not the strike record in Britain, but the media attention devoted to it in the 1960s,[27] kept alive by a flow of press releases and pamphlets from right-wing groups such as the Economic League.

The Donovan Report reiterated what was already well known: for example, that alongside the formal procedures for bargaining which had grown up between national trade union officials and national employers' organisations, there existed informal structures and practices in the work-place based on unwritten understandings and customs and practice. It paid much attention to the role of shop stewards, who spent a great deal of their time negotiating with management and yet were rarely referred to in any formal agreements. It found that 'unwritten understandings and "custom and practice" predominate'. The result was that there was a wide and growing gap between nationally agreed rates of pay and actual earnings and endless potential for conflict between the formal and informal systems. For some time there had been growing concern over wage drift, the gap between agreed and actual earnings. The report also documented numerous examples of the persistence of restrictive practices, 'rules and customs which unduly hinder the efficient use of labour', and of increasingly artificial divisions between so-called craft grades and semi-skilled grades which, they argued, held back technological innovation. Studies of strikes confirmed that these were overwhelmingly unofficial and unconstitutional, breaching both disputes procedures and the decision-making procedures of unions. Out of more than 2000 disputes each year between 1964 and 1966 fewer than a hundred had official sanction.

The report gave little credence to the popular media view that much of the trouble was created by political activists (probably wrongly, judging from some recent work). Employers were criticised for failing to develop adequate management policies to devise rational wage structures and unions were criticised for their failure to deal with inter-union rivalries and to control effectively what was happening in the work-place. It encouraged developments on the lines of the agreement at Esso's Fawley Refinery, which had been strongly publicised by the academic industrial relations' specialist, Alan Flanders.

Donovan's solutions were somehow to transfer the core of collective bargaining away from industry-wide agreements and down to the shop-floor, with the informal system properly incorporated. Under the existing system the informal pattern was not 'developing into an effective and orderly method or regulation'. As so often in the past, the concern was to get union leaders to take control of their membership and particularly of the shop stewards. But, the report argued, the voluntary system should remain without the sanction of law, the British system's 'outstanding characteristic which distinguishes it from systems of many comparable countries'. Only the writer on economics, Andrew Schonfield, in a note of reservation, clearly argued for collectively bargained agreements to be made legally binding, enforceable contracts. 'In industrial relations' the main report argued, '"law and order" can be created only by adequate collective bargaining arrangements.'

The Donovan Report had many of the features of a disinterested academic report, analysing in great detail the problems of the system, but offering few practical solutions. It called for a cultural change which would take years or decades to bring about, without suggesting any mechanisms for instigating it. Nevertheless, it *did* have some effect. Agreements in the 1970s were apparently 'more extensive and more detailed than those concluded previously'.[28] The number of shop stewards in all unions increased until the end of the 1970s, reflecting continuing developments in plant negotiations, but so too did the number of full-time officers.

Events and politics, however, were overtaking the report even before it was published and politicians were making up their own minds about the causes and remedies for industrial strife. The Conservatives had already published *Fair Deal at Work*. Its analysis was the same as Donovan but its prescription was different. It proposed a role for law within the system, a new comprehensive legal framework regulating industrial behaviour. The Conservatives proposed to legislate to require a 60-day 'cooling off period' before a strike could take place and then only after a strike ballot; and collective agreements would have the force of law. In addition the National Board for Prices and Incomes would have productivity added to its responsibilities and it would have as its main task the removal of restrictive practices. A Commission on Industrial Relations was to push and prod the parties to reform their institutions and disputes' procedures.

Search for a Policy

The Labour Government, increasingly beleaguered by sterling crises, battled to maintain an incomes policy based on 'norms', interspersed with wage freezes and severe restraint, but the rhetoric bore little relation to the realities of what, in many areas, was a wage explosion. Devaluation of the pound in 1967 undermined the price stability which was the precondition of incomes' restraint. The TUC was finding it difficult to maintain the system of early warning of potential disputes, particularly as new, left-wing figures came to the leadership of their unions. Hugh Scanlon succeeded the right-wing Bill Carron in the Engineering and Foundry Workers' Union and Jack Jones was in the process of taking over from Frank Cousins at the TGWU.[29] Keen to show their mettle these new people proved much more amendable to unofficial pressures. Early in 1969, for example, the TGWU and the Amalgamated Union of Engineering and Foundry Workers gave official recognition to an unofficial dispute at Fords against their own, recently negotiated agreement on the grounds that the workers did not fully understand the settlement.[30] Ford had tried to buy out restrictive practices by offering to provide a guaranteed week for workers laid off by strikes in other parts of the industry, a £20 holiday bonus and equal pay for women. They insisted, at the same time, that workers involved in 'unconstitutional' action should forfeit their bonus. Ford sought the backing of the courts, but it was reaffirmed that collective agreements were not enforceable in law. Other employers, like the motor manufacturers, were pressing the government to legislate to curb unofficial strikes.

Both the large unions were launched on a determined show of will against another, with left-wing credentials equally impeccable to their own – Barbara Castle, who was now Secretary of State for Employment and Productivity. Her White Paper, *In Place of Strife*, published in January 1969 and committed to legislating to reform a system which had 'failed to prevent injustice, disruption of work and inefficient use of manpower', was greeted with dismay and bitterness. There were 'sweeteners' for the unions, such as their right to have more information from employers, and promised help to get more workers' representatives on to company boards. Mechanisms were to be provided to prevent employers refusing to recognise unions, to safeguard against unfair dismissal. There were even to be government grants and loans for trade union development. But against that, unions and employers' associations were to be required to register and some of the protection of the 1906 Trade Disputes Act was to be removed. The Secretary of State could impose a 28-day cooling-off period before a strike (official or unofficial) or lock-out could take place and the defiance of such an order could lead to strikers being fined. In certain circumstances the Secretary of State could require a strike ballot and order strikers back to work until the agreed procedures had been exhausted. Yet another difficult area for the unions was the proposal that an industrial board would have powers to decide on inter-union disputes with the possibility of fining unions who rejected a board decision.

There were some among the union leadership, such as Jack Cooper of the GMWU and George Lothian of the Bricklayers, who saw attractions in what was being offered and were prepared to negotiate with government. But the big battalions of the AUEW and TGWU were determined on a trial of strength, which probably had as much to do with influence within a divided Labour Party as concern about industrial relations. A special TUC in June came out strongly against any legal penalties being imposed in a dispute. Its model was Donovan and the voluntary reform of collective bargaining. Even the appointment of George Woodcock, the secretary of the TUC, to chair the new Commission on Industrial Relations did nothing to mollify the opposition and it meant the replacement at the TUC of a shrewd and experienced unionist who had long operated at the centre of power with a much less experienced and less effective successor, Victor Feather.

In the end the Government backed down, with the face saver of a 'solemn and binding' declaration that the TUC would take disciplinary action against unions which did not act vigorously to maintain negotiations. Few believed that 'Solomon Binding' (as it was jokingly referred to by Dennis Healey) was going to achieve much. To be fair, Feather did put in a great deal of effort to settle disputes, but the numbers continued to rise and working days lost in 1970 were more than double that of the previous year. In the docks, for example, there were 373 strikes in 1969 with the loss of nearly a quarter of a million working days; in 1970, 374 strikes lost 656 000 working days, with a national strike shutting almost all the county's main ports for the first time since 1926.[31]

The Labour Government duly paid the price with defeat in the June 1970 election. One parting gift in the last hours of government brought the termination of a battle fought by women for decades, with the passage of the Equal Pay Act. Women could now claim the same level of pay as men for the same or closely similar job. Collective agreements could no longer have male and female pay rates. Women's pay in any agreement had to be brought up to at least the level of the lowest skilled men. Of course, there was, as always, a gap between what the legislation said and what happened in practice. Gains under the Act had to be fought for without generally the support of male-dominated unions. It did not help that women still had major difficulties in gaining positions of any authority within unions, some of whom were not particularly good employers of their own office staff. In 1982 the AUEW, with a female membership of 14 per cent, had no women on its executive committee. But then neither did COHSE, where 78 per cent of the members were women. The Union of Shop, Distributive and Allied Workers, also with an overwhelmingly female membership, had only two women among its 120 officials; the TGWU nine out of 500 officials.[32]

The trade unions paid the price of having contributed to the Government's defeat, with the immediate end to the Prices and Incomes Board, as market forces were to be given free rein, and the passage of an Industrial Relations Act in 1971, which implemented most of the policies spelled out in *Fair Deal at Work.* Every collective agreement made in writing under the Act became legally binding, unless there was a provision in the agreement to the contrary. Up until now it had been impossible to make legally binding agreements. The right *not* to belong to a trade union was enshrined in law alongside the right of belonging, thus, in theory, eliminating the pre-entry closed shop. To deal with the complaint about so-called 'free riders' who took the gains without paying their dues, there was, in certain circumstances, a requirement by which all employees could be required to contribute to the union, even if not a member.[33] In such a situation employers and a majority of workers could agree to union recognition and those with conscientious objection could make a payment to charity. In order to get recognition and legal protection, unions were required to register with the Registrar. A National Industrial Relations Court was established as a new division of the High Court, which could impose a 60-day cooling-off period or a ballot of members before a major strike and which could act if written collective agreements were breached. Legal immunities in sympathetic strikes for unions were removed.

A key aspect was the establishment of the new civil wrong of an unfair industrial practice. This meant that in certain circumstances anyone responsible for industrial action might be sued for compensation or subjected to an order by the court to stop what was being done and not repeat it. Only an authorised official could induce anyone to break a contract as part of an industrial dispute. It was a direct outcome of the analysis of Donovan that the official leadership needed to get control of their shop stewards. What the Act did was to put unofficial strike leaders in breach of the law, unless they gave equivalent to that notice given by a worker if he were resigning from a job. At the same time, there was an accompanying Code of Practice which was intended to improve management practice as well as trade union practice. Employers could only get legal redress if they had conformed to the code. Whereas previous governments had generally tried to buy concessions from unions over industrial relations by extending welfare legislation, it was a sign of changing attitudes that this government amended social security legislation to make it more difficult for strikers' families to receive state support. It also conspicuously failed to consult the TUC before introducing the measure, in sharp contrast to what had been an established pattern since 1945.

Protests failed to stop the measure getting through and, pushed by Hugh Scanlon of TGWU, the TUC then instructed unions not to register and those, like the ETU, which had already done so, to de-register. In the end the Act was little used. Most unions did de-register. Those which did not, some 32, mainly small craft unions, but also including the Confederation of Health Service Employees and the National Union of Bank Employees, were expelled from the TUC. Even the National Union of Seamen and the actors' union, Equity, both of whom depended for survival on the maintenance of the closed shop, were expelled for their failure to de-register. The NGA, while supporting the policy of non-registration, claimed that technical reasons prevented their de-registration and resigned. Few employers turned to the Industrial Relations Court. The only use of the 60-day cooling-off period was over a railway dispute in the spring of 1972. The rail union boycotted the court, but a 14-day cooling-off period was imposed together with a ballot. The railwaymen duly voted overwhelmingly for industrial action; the British Rail Board quickly settled.

Meanwhile, the failure to appear before the court caused the TGWU to receive a £50 000 fine and the TUC policy of complete boycott had quickly to be modified. The Industrial Relations Court ruled that a union had to take responsibility for the action of its shop stewards (in this case in Liverpool docks) even if they were acting in defiance of official instructions. The alternative was to expel them from the union. On appeal, however, Lord Denning overruled this and declared that a union could not be held responsible for stewards acting outside their delegated authority. The Government now found itself having to go to great lengths to ensure that shop stewards and pickets were not turned into martyrs by the court.

They were not entirely successful, and five East London dockers found themselves in Pentonville prison in the summer of 1972 for defiance of the National Industrial Relations Court. There was the threat of a one-day general strike by the TUC. A timely decision from the House of Lords overthrew Denning's ruling, upheld that of the Industrial Relations Court, and the TGWU had the fine reimposed together with substantial costs.

The freeing of the 'Pentonville Five' cooled feelings a little, although tension continued at the docks as containerisation was revolutionising the role of the traditional docker. The costs of defying the court were now made clear to the AUEW, who found themselves facing mounting fines when a branch tried to exclude one of its members. Attempts to force recognition on a firm resulted in another £100 000 fine plus £75 000 for costs. Despite these actions, the attempts to apply the 1971 Act were only succeeding in heightening the rhetoric of defiance from the unions, politicising most disputes and bringing few gains. Something like 3 300 000 working days were lost during the three years of the Heath Government in protests against the Industrial Relations Bill and Act.[34] The Act conspicuously failed to achieve any of the ends for which it had been intended. By 1974, most commentators were agreed that the Industrial Relations Act had been a disaster, which had achieved little at the cost of much embittered industrial relations.

Upper Clyde Shipbuilders

The once huge Clyde shipbuilding industry had found itself increasingly beleaguered by foreign competition and not helped by a failure to invest. Disputes over pay had been increasing throughout the 1960s. Survival pointed towards rationalisation of yards, which inevitably meant the loss of jobs. In 1965 the large Fairfield yard in Govan looked set for closure, but an intervention by a group of business people, some of whom wanted a new approach to industrial relations, others of whom felt threatened by the rationalisation policies being urged by the big firms, saved the day, backed with government money. The so-called Fairfield experiment had union investment and union representation on the board of management and a relaxation of many customary work practices. Workers gained from higher earnings, dependent upon increased productivity. There was plenty of suspicion, but even the reluctant Boilermakers' Union eventually agreed, with pay compensation, to relax some of its deeply entrenched protective practices. But this, of course, had major implications for the other shipyards, as earnings at the Fairfield yard rose. It was given little time to be tested and folded after 20 months, but there were only limited signs of its producing any fundamental changes in attitude among different groups of workers, and battles to maintain differentials bedevilled the experiment. The yard was now incorporated into the Upper Clyde Shipbuilders' (UCS) consortium and demarcation battles continued with little sign of improved productivity.

By 1970 union officials had only limited control over negotiations being conducted at yard level by a powerful group of shop stewards – one of the products of productivity bargaining. A year later the UCS was on the verge of bankruptcy and this time there was to be no state bailing out of what the Conservative Government regarded as a 'lame duck' industry. A meeting of shop stewards on 12 June 1971 hit on the idea of a work-in, which came into play when the liquidation of the Fairfield yard was announced. Coming as it did at a period of intense political debate about Scotland's future within the UK, and at a time of rapidly rising unemployment, the work-in caught the public imagination and attracted widespread support from press and pulpit. They were helped by shrewd leadership from James Airlie, chairman of the Co-ordinating Committee, and by the charismatic verbosity of Jimmy Reid. Eventually, a year later, a rescue package for the yard was worked out between government and the Marathon company. It was soon in difficulty again and later nationalisation did little to help. It survived ultimately by being bought out by a private Norwegian company.

Strikes

National strikes now made a reappearance. By 1970–2 disputes were becoming more protracted and working days lost were hitting levels not reached since the 1920s. A 1970 strike at the formerly paternalistic firm of Pilkingtons in St Helens lasted seven weeks. It was organised by shop stewards in a rank-and-file strike committee of the branch of the GMWU but failed to get official backing. A so-called 'parsons' poll' carried out for the GMWU showed a small majority in favour of a return to work, but this was rejected by the strike committee. A court of inquiry proved equally ineffective, but eventually Vic Feather of the TUC succeeded in mediating a settlement between the three parties. The dispute left behind workers deeply at odds with their union.[35] The TGWU called its first national dock strike since 1926. In January 1971 a localised strike for a pay claim had spread to every Ford plant in the country and 45 000 workers were out for nine weeks, making it one of the largest strikes since the 1930s.[36]

Wage rises of as high as 15 per cent were being conceded and inflation was rising fast. The Government proved unable to devise a policy other than a curb in the public sector, which it was hoped would be a model for the private sector. The result was strikes of public service workers. Electricity supply workers put in a claim for a 25 per cent increase and settled for something near 15 per cent. There was no evidence of private industry emulating the attempted government hard line and, after the nine-week strike, Fords conceded a substantial rise, although there were fears that the company was trying to push out the more militant shop stewards. The Government, on the other hand, sat out a national postmen's strike, the first such national strike by the Union of Post Office Workers and an indication of how strikes were spreading to industries which in the past had been largely immune from such action. After 47 days, with the union's resources used up, the postmen had to settle for a little above the original offer which they had been made.

In the docks there were numerous disputes as the process of containerisation undermined the demands for the 'skills' which dockers had in dealing with different kinds of cargo. Employers increasingly pushed the new technology to ports, like Felixstowe, not included in the dock registration scheme. Liverpool and London ports went into rapid decline. The Dock Labour Scheme was finally abolished in 1989.

The coal industry, second only to the dockers in its history of disputes, had in fact gone through a period of relative calm in the late 1960s, despite the fact that in the old mining heartlands of Durham, Scotland and South Wales the industry was experiencing massive cuts. The bargaining position of miners had started to deteriorate after 1957 when demand for coal began to fall sharply. Over the next years, 264 pits were closed and the number of miners fell by 39 per cent. In South Wales alone the number of pits fell from nearly 200 at nationalisation to 55 in 1969 and the number of miners from 106 000 to 40 000.[37] Morale and militancy in mining areas had both been dissipated. A day-work system of payment, which got rid of piecework and, therefore, the wage differences between coalfields, had been phased in since 1966 and, in 1967–8, coal output lost through disputes was dramatically reduced. But this was accompanied by changes in the work process. Miners were increasingly being directed and supervised by managers. By 1968 there was one under-official to every 4.5 face workers compared with 1 to 6.5 ten years before.[38] Mechanisation too was rapidly changing the work environment, with an increase in the number of accidents. With falling demand for labour, earnings fell as did the miners' place in the league table of earnings. Between 1945 and 1970 they fell from first to twelfth place.

Since the war communists had achieved a high profile in the leadership of the NUM, although making up less than a quarter of the National Executive. Arthur Horner was general secretary from 1944 to 1958 and Will Paynter from 1958, both from South Wales. On Paynter's retirement in 1968 he was succeeded by Laurence Daly, a Fife area official. He too had Communist Party backing although he had left the party in 1956. On the other hand, the presidency of the union was usually in the hands of someone from the right and, in 1971, Joe Gormley of the Lancashire area had beaten off a left challenge. CP activists were, however, well represented at area level – Dai Francis in South Wales, Michael McGahey in Scotland, Jack Dunn in Kent and Jock Kane in Yorkshire – and keen to alter union policy to a more confrontational stance against closures. Their success reflected a revival of militancy in many areas and unofficial strikes spread after 1969, when for the first time for a decade demand for coal picked up. Those miners left in the industry were embittered by the fact that their earnings were failing to keep pace with those of workers in manufacturing industry and that despite the pit closures and redundancies of the 1960s the wages and the security of the remaining miners had not improved.

After an overtime ban in pursuit of a wage claim for an increase from £30 to £35 for a face worker and £18 to £24 for a surface worker, which had reduced the coal stocks at power stations, the NUM in January 1972 launched their first national strike since 1926. Under the leadership of Arthur Scargill of the Yorkshire area, a system of 'flying pickets' effectively, and often violently, prevented open-cast coal being moved. Power stations, steelworks, ports and coal depots, the major coal users, were all picketed to prevent their stocks being replenished. A court of inquiry under Lord Wilberforce, set up after the strike had run for more than a month, recommended increases, but these were rejected by the union. In February 1972 a state of emergency was declared, and major companies were forced to curb production to save fuel. There were restrictions on electrical heating in public buildings, with dire warnings that soon all industry would have to close. The Government, caught unprepared, eventually conceded. Talks at Downing Street resulted in improvements on the Wilberforce offer and the miners were awarded something like a 20 per cent wage rise. For some mining communities at least it was sweet retribution for the defeats of the 1920s and the Government's attempt gradually to push down the level of each wage settlement had been shattered.

Before the deal had run its course, the miners returned for more. The success of 1972 had strengthened miner solidarity and increased militancy. Left-wing candidates tightened their hold within the leadership. In September 1973 a new bid was submitted, taking advantage of a rise in oil prices (by fivefold in 1973) and growing demands for coal. The National Coal Board made complicated efforts to find a way around the Government's pay code to give the miners something like a 13 per cent rise. But in some ways it was too generous and gave no room for manoeuvre and few more concessions for the miners' leadership to 'win'. The offer was rejected and the miners once again began an overtime ban. The Prime Minister, Edward Heath, announced a three-day week from the start of the new year, to save fuel and, presumably, to get across the implications of miners' action. Power cuts followed, the country shivered in the gloom and people were told to brush their teeth in the dark. In February the miners voted for an all-out strike (81 per cent of those voting supporting it). Before the strike started, the Conservative Government called a general election on the issue of 'who governs Britain?'. Joe Gormley urged suspension of the strike until after the election, but was overruled by twenty votes to six. It did not help the Government's case that the Pay Board announced that their calculation of miners' wages revealed that they were in fact substantially less well paid than workers in manufacturing industry. Heath went down to defeat. The irony was that by all accounts Heath had, more than many other prime ministers, been willing to discuss matters with the unions. Harold Wilson returned, much to his own surprise, with a minority administration and some unionists felt that they could begin calculating how many industries would be nationalised.[39]

10 Decline and Fall? 1974–98

The Social Contract

The Labour Party had already made it clear that there would be no statutory incomes policy. Instead, what was offered as an answer to rising inflation, the balance of payments crises and anarchic industrial relations was the 'Social Contract', a trade union agreement to curb wage rises to no more than the increase in the retail price index in return for a government commitment to social policies, including improved employee protection. The Government started to deliver. Michael Foot at the Department of Employment quickly brought the month-long miners' strike to an end. The 1971 Industrial Relations Act was repealed, thus ending the National Industrial Relations Court, the Commission on Industrial Relations and the process of registration. The Advisory, Conciliation and Arbitration Service (ACAS) took over the role of the Department of Employment's long-established conciliation service, but with the intention of its being free from government interference. It was also expected to encourage union recognition by employers and develop good codes of practice in industry. Its director, Jim Mortimer, had long advocated that British trade unions should be pressing for the legal right to recognition.

The 1974 Trade Union and Labour Relations Act restored some of the immunity which unions had against legal action for inducing a breach of contract and protected employers from actions on unfair dismissals for sacking non-union members of a closed shop. The Employment Protection Act of 1975 allowed a trade union to refer a recognition issue to ACAS and ACAS was required to investigate and report. Protection against unfair dismissal was extended and companies were compelled to provide maternity pay for women and to keep their jobs open, to give longer notice of redundancy and to allow union officials to carry out their duties. Employers were obliged to consult with unions before announcing redundancies. A 1976 Trade Union Amendment Act narrowed the protection of non-unionists in closed shops only to those whose religious beliefs precluded union membership. Where the closed shop operated, individual workers had little option but to accept union membership or lose their jobs. It was probably, in the long run, one of the most damaging developments to the public image of unions. Opinion polls in the 1980s revealed very real hostility to the closed shop even among trade unionists.[1] The government delivered, the unions, on the other hand, could not or would not deliver.

It was a time of great union confidence. Not only had they 'their own' government in power, but union membership was reaching peaks never before achieved. After a long period of stability, union density had begun to rise in the late 1960s and, in 1974 for the first time ever, it crossed the 60 per cent mark for men, and the 50 per cent mark overall, and was to continue to rise until 1979. Such a figure was far above what had been achieved in the previous peaks of 1920 and 1948.[2] It encouraged unions to seize the moment. So-called catch-up increases and demands for earlier pay rises to be incorporated into basic pay led to pay rises of 35 per cent and more. The miners in March 1975 won a 35 per cent wage increase and power-workers' earnings climbed by over 50 per cent. Postmen's earnings rose by 38.5 per cent and an arbitration award gave railwaymen 27.5 per cent, only to be rejected by the NUR on the grounds that it did not maintain their position in the league table *vis-à-vis* the miners.

Once again the calls for restraint in the aftermath of a threatened sterling crisis, led to a 'voluntary' £6 across-the board increase in July 1975 for those on incomes of less than £8500, with a parallel constraint on prices and dividends. The persuasive arguments of Jack Jones of the TGWU had got this through an unenthusiastic TUC General Council. It particularly helped the less well-paid. The next year brought a second phase, 5 per cent with a maximum of £4, but compensated by tax cuts. This time the AEU's Hugh Scanlon's dire warnings persuaded the TUC to go along with it. But inflation continued to rise and reached 16 per cent by the end of 1977. The standard of living was falling as earnings failed to keep up with inflation and demands began to grow for the restoration of the differentials which the flat-rate increases had eroded. The miners declared that their aim was £100 a week, nearly a 50 per cent rise.

On the other hand, the evidence of growing economic problems was plain to see. The car industry was finding it increasingly difficult to maintain its markets. A reputation for poor quality and poor delivery was undermining British Leyland (as BMC had become). It had to be rescued by nationalisation. There was a much greater readiness by management to confront and to try to weaken the hold that shop stewards had been able to build up in the 1960s. The British Steel Corporation, in 1975, faced with massive losses, announced plans which would have involved the cutting of 20 000 jobs and demanded changes in the work-place allowing greater flexibility.

A key issue became the right of workers to have their union recognised. This was tested in the courts in the dispute at the Grunwick Processing Laboratories in North London which broke out in the summer of 1976. The company refused to co-operate with ACAS in the testing of employees' views on union membership and the Court of Appeal ruled that without the testing of the opinion of all the workers ACAS could not insist on recognition. Despite the support from the TUC and many thousands from different areas of the trade union movement, the unions found that they could do nothing to overcome company resistance. However, ACAS intervention did result in recognition in very many cases and, by 1980, it claimed that as many as 65 000 workers had been accorded recognition thanks to its actions.[3] On the other hand, as the decade progressed, more small employers put obstacles in the way of recognition. Bigger employers still, on the whole, seemed happy to go along with the post-entry closed shop.

The period also saw a speeding-up in the growth of white-collar unionism which had been gaining momentum since the 1960s. NALGO, with 700 000 plus members was the fourth largest union in the TUC. Other public sector unions also grew, such as the Civil and Public Services Association and the Inland Revenue Staff Association. By the end of the 1970s, over 80 per cent of public sector workers were unionised. The loquacious Clive Jenkins had built up, largely by mergers, the Association of Scientific, Technical and Managerial Staffs (ASTMS) to nearly half a million members, doubling its membership in four years in the mid-1970s. White-collar unionism was always difficult with so many of the potential members closely tied to management or with aspirations to become part of management. There were many staff associations which sometimes offered substantial benefits in return for a ban on trade union membership. It required legislation to prevent new unionists losing the contributions they had made to staff associations. But changes were taking place. Government policies had generally made companies readier to recognise unionism among their white-collar staff and George Bain found this to be the single most important factor in explaining the growth of white-collar unionism. But the reorganisation of many companies through mergers and takeovers was also threatening supervisory and managerial people who had always believed that their jobs were relatively secure and who had also seen the differentials narrowed between themselves and manual workers.[4]

The Social Contract worked for a time and inflation fell sharply to 13 per cent in the first year. Unions also gained a clear sense of being one of the main estates of the realm and there were those who hoped that what was happening would be a prelude to regular annual agreements between the TUC and government on 'the whole social and economic fabric of national policy'.[5] But, in a dramatically symbolic gesture, the TGWU conference of 1977 voted for the abolition of all wage restraint, against the advice of their general secretary, Jack Jones, the main architect of the Social Contract. The Government tried to impose a rigid – and without TUC agreement unworkable – 5 per cent maximum on earnings' increases in the autumn of 1978, and was faced with what the press labelled as the 'winter of discontent'. Even normally 'moderate' figures such as Gavin Laird of the AUEW, reflecting the views of his craft members, declared that they were 'not prepared to accept any more and certainly not a 5 per cent norm', although Sidney Weighell of the NUR argued that the alternative was 'the philosophy of the pig trough – those with the biggest snout get the biggest share'.

The public service workers in NUPE, although they had probably been gainers from the Social Contract, led the way with demands for a 40 per cent rise. NUPE had gone through a period of rapid reorganisation in the 1970s, attracting many more workers from the public sector, including large numbers of women workers. It also integrated shop stewards, district officers and central union officials much more effectively than most other unions and had become more militant. Tales of the dead lying unburied and of pickets deciding who could or could not get in and out of Great Ormond Street Children's Hospital were grist for a press determined to break both unions and government. The Miners' Union also had already declared the Social Contract dead and had called for a return to free collective bargaining and they easily broke the 5 per cent barrier at the beginning of 1979. During a lorry drivers' strike in January, the new TGWU secretary, Moss Evans, rejected the concept of norms: 'It is not my responsibility to manage the economy. We are concerned with getting the rate for the job.'[6] Both were reflecting growing rank-and-file pressure against restraint, as both government and unions failed to reduce workers' expectations.

Despite it all, the trade union movement ended the decade at a peak. It had grown to over 13 million members, far and away the 'largest and most representative voluntary and democratic movement in the UK' and, according to a confident Clive Jenkins in 1979 was 'changing from the moribund "carthorse" image of Low [the cartoonist] to a more dynamic and thoughtful movement'.[7] Trade unions bargained on behalf of at least 5 million workers and in a work-force of 23 million had achieved their highest ever penetration of 55.4 per cent of the potential membership. Many of these were now white-collar workers, who made up more than 40 per cent of British trade unionists by 1979. Three out of ten were women workers, although there was still a failure on the part of almost all unions to set out to attract these. Linked with this was the failure to show enough concern about part-time workers, which many women workers were, although this was to be the employment growth area in the following decade. Union members had, as Colin Crouch suggests, fairly decisively in the 'winter of discontent' rejected the concept of incorporation into the processes of government in favour of the traditional free-for-all of the voluntarist system of wage negotiation.[8] The Labour Government paid the price in electoral defeat.

Conservative Governments

The new Government made clear that its priority was to reduce and control inflation, not to try to recover full employment. But Margaret Thatcher's arrival did not make an immediate difference, except that the TUC found that it was no longer invited to Downing Street for informal discussions on the economy. The Conservative Party's manifesto had promised action on the closed shop, on picketing and on democracy within unions, and many Conservatives, including the Prime Minister, remembered the humiliation of the last Conservative Government by the miners. But James Prior, the Employment Secretary, like previous Conservative ministers, wanted to find ways of maintaining industrial peace and to move away from the existing 'trench warfare', as he described it. Like his predecessors, he did not necessarily want to weaken the unions, but rather to strengthen the trade union leadership so that they could control their rank and file. His 1980 Employment Act made secondary strike action illegal and picketing lawful only if carried out by workers at their own place of work. But he still allowed a closed shop if 80 per cent of the workers covered by the arrangements approved it by ballot and he was prepared to provide funds for a union to conduct strike ballots. Yet, within months, there was a 'Day of Action' because 'we cannot talk to this Government'. With unemployment going up fast, and as manufacturing industry was being rapidly decimated both by the Government's monetarist policies and by another hike in oil prices, the Day was hardly a great success and by the end of the year unemployment had crossed the two million mark.

The bargaining position of workers was speedily deteriorating. There was a three months' strike in the nationalised steel industry early in 1980, by far and away the biggest in the history of the steel industry. It involved not only the main unions, the ISTC and the National Union of Blastfurnacemen, but the craftsmen in the AUEW and the EETPU. Profitability and production in the steel industry had been in rapid decline throughout the previous decade. The Beswick Plan of 1975 proposed a further programme of plant closures. The result was that steelworkers' wages plummeted in the wages' league. Conciliation machinery began to crumble. Closures in Hartlepool, Lanarkshire and South Wales were bought off quite quietly, with good redundancy payments, but the abrupt closure of the Shilton and Bilston works and the threat to Corby – all much newer places – led to resistance. Negotiations over a wage increase brought demands from groups of workers at these plants for a rejection of all productivity deals. The Government would not agree to any further subsidy of the British Steel Corporation. Meanwhile, the threat to extend strike action to the private sector of the industry brought an injunction, which was overturned by the House of Lords, and in February the strike spread. Flying pickets with mass picketing led to clashes with the police and with non-strikers. Prior refused a court of inquiry, but a committee of inquiry, jointly agreed on by the BSC and the unions, eventually offered 15.95 per cent, which was nearly twice what the union leadership would have settled for in January. It was quickly accepted in April although some steel workers wanted to hold out for 20 per cent. The price paid was the ousting of the chair of the BSC and his replacement by a Scot, Ian MacGregor, whose business experience had largely been in the USA. His plan for the industry involved substantial restructuring and around 25 000 redundancies. He persuaded the workers to accept it, even if the Iron and Steel Trades' Confederation opposed it. The strike lost the industry nearly a tenth of its markets to other countries where over-capacity also existed. To give MacGregor his due, the industry *did* regain its market share, but the world market for steel was shrinking fast.

The squeeze on government finance of British Rail also inevitably aggravated the industrial relations system there. ASLEF and the NUR blithely continued their long-established animosity and antagonised the public with separate strikes.

Attempts to get flexibility of time rosters and flexibility in train manning led to ASLEF disputes which gave fodder to Thatcher's already well-known hostility towards the industry.

Efforts to revive a triple alliance of steelmen, railwaymen and miners came to very little in the harsh climate of constraint on the nationalised industries. They were killed off by the retirement of Joe Gormley early in 1982 and his replacement by Arthur Scargill with whom both Bill Sirs of the ISTC and Sidney Weighell of the NUR found it impossible to work. Unemployment had been rising sharply since 1978 when it had been 1.4 million. By the summer of 1982 it was 3.2 million. Manufacturing was particularly badly bit, although all areas were affected. In metal manufacturing employment fell by more than a third, in textiles by 30 per cent and in shipbuilding, clothing and footwear by a fifth. The old core areas of shipbuilding, vehicle building, steel and consumer durables, were losing their significance within the economy compared with the new, and usually foreign-owned, computer assembling and electronics industries. Many of these new firms were employing women in preference to men. The other employment growth area was in the service sector which has always proved notoriously difficult to recruit.

The tone of Prior's successor at the Ministry of Employment, Norman Tebbit, was very different. A former union national official himself, amongst airline pilots, he was now determined to curb union power permanently. Backed by the Prime Minister, he did not believe, unlike many other Conservatives, that to confront a major union would lead to the Government's humiliation. He attacked 'the most privileged trade union movement in the world, commanding a huge conscript army in the closed shop' for having failed its members and left them at the bottom of the European productivity league and, therefore, 'led them into unemployment'.[9] A 1982 Employment Act banned pre-entry closed shops, required 85 per cent approval for post-entry ones, required union compensation for any workers who would not accept a closed shop and gave employers the right to sue for damages and to get court injunctions to halt industrial action. It was quickly tested when the National Graphical Association tried to enforce a closed shop and existing agreed employment conditions in provincial newspapers at a Warrington newspaper printing works by the use of mass picketing. ACAS conciliation could not persuade the newspaper owner to take back the six dismissed employees. When the union defied two court injunctions, restraining it from putting pressure on advertisers and from secondary picketing, it found itself fined first £50 000 and then £100 000 and then had its funds sequestered. The attempt to call a national newspaper strike in sympathy was declared illegal and strikers threatened with dismissal. Other newspapers took out writs against the NGA. A further fine of £525 000 and clear signs that the TUC General Council would not support continued action and the NGA had little alternative but to pay up, so that it could survive to represent the bulk of its membership who were not in newspapers.[10]

One sees a fundamental change in political strategy from that of the previous 60 years. Since at least the First World War unions had been increasingly incorporated into the political system, becoming one of the 'estates of the realm'. From now on that was to be replaced by a deliberate policy of exclusion aimed at reducing both union and worker power, at strengthening individual rights at the expense of the unions, at undermining collective bargaining and at rejecting any idea of extending workers' involvement in management.

Meanwhile strikes in the motor car industry continued unabated. In the first 198 days of 1980 Ford experienced 254 disputes.[11] Often these involved no more than 20 workers who were being asked to move to some new job, or to try some new process. The struggling British Leyland had a new, tougher managerial style in the person of the South African Michael Edwardes. He sacked Derek Robinson, the convener of shop stewards, whom the press had identified as 'Red Robbo'. He next imposed a wages' settlement. A further offer in November 1980 was below the going rate, but thanks to the intervention of Terry Duffy, the president of the AUEW, the shop stewards' advice for rejection was not accepted. The financially much stronger Ford Company proposed a new plan to discipline unofficial strikers.

For a time union density, if one excludes the unemployed, held up quite well despite the increasingly hostile environment. But they were facing major problems. Manufacturing industry was pounded from many different directions in the early 1980s. New firms coming in, often building on green field sites, and using a high proportion of female labour and in many cases part of American combines, were determinedly anti-union. Studies of 133 American-owned plants in Scotland in 1983 found that 44 per cent were non-union, but when one looked at the newer ones in electronics, oil-related firms or health care the figure rose to 63 per cent, 73 per cent and 86 per cent respectively. Firms, often offering high pay and good working conditions, demanded a flexibility from management and work-force and generally adopted less adversarial and (to be blunt) class-ridden attitudes than had been typical in older British firms. Government, of course, encouraged employers to resist union pressure and gave no encouragement to its own employees to participate.

There was division among the unions on how to respond to the legislation. The rhetoric of many on the left was for direct confrontation and defiance of the law. Working-class defiance of 'bad' laws in the past was frequently cited. On the other hand, others rejected any idea of breaking the law, no matter how much they disliked it. An increasingly confident government moved to a further onslaught. Trade unions (mainly the moderate and immensely respectable Civil and Public Services Association) were banned at the Government Communications' Headquarters at Cheltenham, the beginning of a process of branding trade unions as potentially a threat to the state, 'the enemy within', as they were soon to become.[12] The Government moved cautiously but persistently, and despite another 'day of action' the last union members were sacked in November 1988 and not until 1997 was the right to union membership at GCHQ partially restored.

The Miners' Strike

The Government was also preparing for a symbolic battle with the NUM. For many in the Conservative ranks the triumphalism of the miners after the defeat of the Heath Government in 1974 rankled deeply and there was a deliberate policy of ensuring that coal supplies at power stations were kept at a high level. In the years after 1974 the NUM president, Joe Gormley, had used his considerable authority to check both militancy and left-wing influence. He argued against trying to use the union to challenge government: 'You are going to produce an ogre that none of you will be able to control. You will produce something that will destroy the Labour and Trade Union Movement in Britain.'[13] But on Gormley's retirement in 1982 it was Arthur Scargill who succeeded him. In the following year, Lawrence Daly took early retirement and his successor as general secretary was another figure from the left, the Derbyshire leader, Peter Heathfield. For the first time, the left controlled both the key posts in the union. There was growing alarm in mining areas at talk of pit closures. Scargill had tried to persuade the miners to strike in 1982 and again in 1983 in protest at the closures, but on both occasions the ballot had gone against strike action.

The coal industry was facing major competition not just from cheap coal imports, but from the nuclear energy programme which the Government was encouraging. At the Coal Board, the conciliatory Derek Ezra had given way to Ian MacGregor. He announced cuts involving some 20 000 jobs (most of which could be achieved by voluntary redundancies). Few doubted that MacGregor's appointment was a deliberate step to taking on the NUM. Scargill had made his reputation as leader of the flying pickets who had played such a part in the effectiveness of the 1972 strike. He, with the backing of his fellow communist vice-president, the Scottish miners' leader Michael McGahey, seem to have entertained few doubts that a miners' challenge to the Government could again be successful, and to have assumed that the miners could count on mass support from other workers. Their position was, however, fatally undermined by their refusal to hold a strike ballot, which was a requirement of the NUM's rules before a national strike could be called, (presumably because of a fear that it would not achieve the necessary support) and to rely on mass picketing to bring out reluctant pits.[14]

The trigger for the strike was the closure of Cortonwood Colliery in March 1984, with MacGregor confident that the miners would again reject strike action. This brought out Scargill's own area, Yorkshire, and most other areas came out in sympathy. On the other hand, the varying responses demonstrated clearly how far the NUM had failed to eradicate entirely the district divisions and loyalties of the old MFGB. The failure to bring out the Nottingham miners proved crucial. There, many of the pits were new and efficient and therefore not threatened with closure; loyalty to the national union had always been weaker there since the bitter divisions of 1926. It was not possible to present a united front and it was not possible to justify the legitimacy of the action. In addition, the timing was wrong, as spring turned to summer and adequate coal stocks were available and as unemployment in other industries continued to rise. And finally, a determined government used force, which more than once got out of control, to break up mass picketing.

The miners' leadership assumed that it was the 'duty' of other unions to support them, with little effort to persuade. Steelmen, power station workers, dockers, fearful for their jobs and their union resources, all failed to provide anything beyond rhetorical aid, and even that tended to evaporate after experiencing the vituperation of a mass picket at a steel works or a power station. As Bill Sirs of the ISTC said, he 'was not prepared to allow my industry to be sacrificed on someone else's altar'.[15] In Scotland the ISTC was struggling to stop the closure of the large steel plants at Hunterston and Ravenscraig. The STUC was appalled at the idea that a lack of coal because of the strike might be the excuse for shut down. At Scunthorpe lack of coke was threatening the viability of the furnaces and the survival of another plant. It was the attempt to stop coke coming from Orgreave to Scunthorpe that produced the most extreme and violent confrontations between pickets and police. Meanwhile, the courts happily agreed to fines and seizure of union funds for contempt and set off in pursuit of them through the European banking system.

The miners' leaders appeared to have learned nothing from the 1920s and chose to ignore the TUC. Talk of using the strike to bring down the Government was fantasy, as the miners' leaders were duly warned by some other unions.[16] But any other objective was never made entirely clear. Few union leaders dared to speak out openly, however, to make clear to the miners that they could not expect support. Those who did were abused, threatened and even physically attacked. There was little attempt to win over public opinion, despite sympathy for the suffering families – but relying for financial support on collecting cans in the streets was not a strategy which could work for long. By the end of 1984 the hopeless isolation into which the miners had been led was more than apparent and, despite heroic efforts, particularly by miners' wives, to alleviate real hardship in the mining villages through communal activities, unity was breaking and a drift back to work began. Not until March 1985, though, did the Mineworkers' conference overrule Scargill and agree formally to a return to work. Misguided expectations that winter would swing circumstances in the miners' favour kept some going. But the power stations had no difficulty in meeting demand from their extensive stocks and TGWU lorry drivers were regularly crossing the picket lines. The immediate repercussions were devastated and embittered families and communities, and a divided union as the Nottingham and South Derbyshire miners broke to form the Union of Democratic Miners, with threatened splits in moderate areas like Durham and Lancashire. Defeat also produced a vindictively triumphalist Ian MacGregor and Margaret Thatcher. 'People are now discovering the price of insubordination and insurrection. And boy, are we going to make it stick,' MacGregor declared.[17]

For some years after 1984 there were still many stoppages in mining. Without a negotiated settlement there were numerous local issues to be disputed. But the longer term result was that neither unions nor communities were in a position to resist effectively the wave of mine closures which largely killed off the coal industry in the early 1990s. The miners, with substantial debts after a year's loss of pay, were keen for bonus payments and they increased output dramatically. By the early 1990s British Coal was profitable enough to be privatised, but the demand for coal was plummeting as new power stations converted to the cheaper natural gas. The resistance to further extensive closures was token. By 1995 the industry employed fewer than 2 per cent of what it had 50 years before.

More Legislation

The failure of the miners to hold a ballot was particularly inept in view of the fact that the Government had been focusing on the issue of ballots as evidence that unions were essentially undemocratic organisations. It was a difficult line of attack for the unions to counter. There is little doubt that in many unions electoral mechanisms were open to abuse. In the NUR, for example, the election of the National Executive was by the block votes of branches. In other words, a branch meeting, where the decision might be taken by a dozen people attending, could deliver the votes of a few hundred branch members. Given the normally poor attendance at branch meetings in all unions it was perfectly possible for half a dozen activists to manipulate the election. The Trade Union Act of 1984 required properly run, secret ballots for union elections, and legal immunity from damages claims during industrial action was only maintained for those who had held secret ballots four weeks before industrial action. The requirement that unions should ballot their members on maintaining their political funds, however, backfired badly on the Government. It was so clearly a party-political gesture and a skilful trade union campaign ensured that all the ballots which were held on the political fund issue came out in favour of maintaining such a fund. The revenge was the 1988 Employment Act which allowed individual union members to ignore a majority ballot decision on industrial action and, among other things, made action to bring about or maintain a closed shop illegal. All ballots, both for the elections of officers and on the political fund had to be postal. The next year a further Act weakened the right of workers to claim unfair dismissal before industrial tribunals and removed that protection altogether from workers who had not worked for an employer for more than two years. The 1990 Employment Act put further obstacles in the way of unions. All industrial action had to be confined to the immediate contractual employer. Where a dispute covered more than one employer then each had to be regarded as a separate dispute requiring a separate ballot before proceeding. Unions were responsible for any unofficial actions by their members unless they specifically disavowed such action in writing. Employers who made employment contingent on union membership could be sued and those workers who were participants in unofficial disputes had no protection from dismissal.

Wapping

There was one last attempt at the use of the mass picketing weapon when in 1986 Rupert Murdoch moved his News International[18] operation from Fleet Street (actually Bouverie Street and Gray's Inn Road) to new premises in Wapping, in East London. He used the move as a way of breaking the bonds of restrictive practices with which the printing unions had bound the national newspaper industry for nearly a century. The semi-skilled and non-craft unions in printing had again merged into the Society of Graphical and Allied Trades (SOGAT 82). Both SOGAT and the craft NGA had seen the speed at which new computer-based technology was changing their industry. The man against whom the Warrington strike of 1983 had taken place, Eddie Shah, launched a new newspaper, *Today*, using the new technology and non-union labour. Journalists could now bypass the jobs of most printers. SOGAT members feared that they would be marginalised completely between NGA and EETPU members. It tried fruitlessly to get News International to agree to lifelong job security for its members in Fleet Street. The printing unions were prepared to make major concessions, but News International was determined to break their hold. As John Gennard has shown, the dispute was not about working new technology. The actual technology at Wapping was not new. It was about management authority. The printers were presented with an ultimatum which was essentially a charter for management and included:

(i) no local negotiations; no recognition of chapels or branches, or of union rights to represent supervisory grades;
(ii) no strikes or any other form of industrial action, and instant dismissal for anyone taking part; union repudiation of any such action;
(iii) no closed shop; union representatives 'warned' under the disciplinary procedure to lose office;

(iv) complete flexibility and no demarcation lines;
(v) total acceptance of management's 'right to manage' including changes in working methods; introduction of new technology; staffing levels; the hiring, classification, transfer and promotion of employees; disciplinary, laying off or dismissing employees;
(vi) legally binding contracts.[19]

There was an equally fruitless attempt to get a united front between the five unions involved, SOGAT, NGA, AUEW, EETPU and the NUJ. When the printing unions called a strike in January 1986 more than 5000 strikers were sacked and the remaining operations were moved to a well-prepared and well-fortified plant at Wapping. New employees, secretly recruited, were already in place organised in the EETPU. A year of often bitterly violent clashes at the gates of the plant failed to stop the papers being produced and distributed.[20] The printers and the AUEW conspicuously failed to persuade the electricians to come out. Once again legal powers were used ruthlessly. By early February 1987 SOGAT's funds had been sequestered, its officials' cars seized and its offices threatened with closure. Police quite regularly sealed off whole areas of Wapping to ensure that the distribution trucks could get out. The TGWU was unable to prevent its members crossing picket lines. After 13 months the print unions reluctantly agreed to accept compensation terms from News International.

The print unions pressed hard for the expulsion of the EETPU from the TUC, but, with a threat of legal action from the Electricians, the General Council backed away. However, the EETPU continued to defy TUC directives and to breach the Bridlington Agreement on recruitment and was eventually expelled.

New Directions

The defeat of the miners and of the Fleet Street workers was crucial in persuading the unions that confrontation with government and police and the repetition of unsuccessful picketing tactics was going to achieve nothing, and that a more effective response would be to accept the legislation and learn to operate it. A number of unions, led by the Electrical Workers and the Amalgamated Union of Engineering Workers came round to accepting the state funding on offer under the 1980 Act for conducting union postal ballots. Both had long made use of secret postal ballots for elections. Attempts to expel them from the TUC, even after they had tested their members' opinions, were eventually dropped.

Union membership appeared to be in a downward spiral which was, if anything, gathering momentum. The TUC lost three million affiliated members between 1980 and 1987. Membership was back to the level of the late 1960s, and, more alarmingly, was becoming increasingly concentrated in the public sector. The TUC, with the affable Norman Willis as general secretary, seemed to offer little leadership. But gradually the brake was applied and a number of the ablest union leaders began to learn from their counterparts abroad that survival required change. A 1989 TUC policy document *Organising for the 1990s* urged unions to set out to attract white-collar, professional and, most important, the growing force of women workers. The TUC itself reorganised its General Council to allow 18 women members among its 53 members.

There were signs that some union leaders recognised that new directions were necessary. The EETPU, as early as 1981, had worked out an agreement with Toshiba which gave them single-union recognition in return for a no-strike policy. It also involved workers' participation in the running of the company, through an advisory board which received financial and investment information. Disputes that could not be negotiated away were to be settled by what was known as 'pendulum arbitration', which prevented a 'splitting the difference' approach and required instead that an arbiter chose either the union claim or the employers' final offer. The implications of such agreements, which spread to other Japanese-owned companies, was fundamentally to challenge the principles of the 1939 Bridlington Agreement, which protected the negotiating rights of unions against 'poaching'. Under single-union deals, other unions had to lose out. It was yet another reason for expelling the EETPU from the TUC. The agreements also generally involved the end of class distinctions in the work-place in terms of hours, welfare provision and eating arrangements. To replicate them in the rest of industry would have involved a massive cultural adjustment. Few British companies were prepared to even try and, in practice, such single-union agreements have in fact been rare.

For some employers the weakness of unions was seen as an opportunity and many, including some public sector bodies, withdrew from employers' associations and instead pursued a policy of bargaining on their own, even at plant level. Others felt strong enough to impose new terms and conditions unilaterally.[21] A study in 1981 found that in manufacturing single employer bargaining was the main means of wage determination for two thirds of manual workers[22] and later studies confirmed the trend. It paralleled trends in management involving decentralising decision-making and pushing down responsibilities to profit centres within companies. Government gave every encouragement to these trends. The Wages Act of 1986 reduced the role of wages councils and abolished the concept of Fair Wages Resolutions which had existed since the 1890s. A 1988 White Paper called for a completely new approach on the part of employers and unions, abandoning concepts like 'the going rate' or 'comparability'. They argued for local variations in wage rates which took account of local markets, seeing this as a way in which unemployment could be reduced in particularly badly hit areas.

Most trade union officials were wary of changes which might weaken their power and influence and sought to defend national negotiations. NALGO in 1991 had a national strike to resist a deal which would have allowed local variations of the national minimum. But the AUEW came round to accepting the end of national wage negotiations. Moves towards performance-related pay also undermined the traditional incremental pay structures which unions negotiated. Many others came to recognise that the climate of industrial relations might have changed fundamentally as more and more industries became globalised. Unions began to show a greater willingness to accept changes in managerial relations, in how work and the working day were organised, in return for higher earnings and shorter hours. Probably the most significant change of the 1980s was the agreement between the Engineering Employers' Federation and the CSEU. After more than three years of negotiation it was agreed in 1987 that, in return for a reduction in hours from 39 to 37.5, there would be flexibility in the work-place and that 'workers will perform any task within their capabilities regardless of whether or not the task form part of their normal work, and regardless of whether or not the task is traditionally performed by members of another union'. It pointed towards single-union bargaining which, not surprisingly, aroused the fears of some of the smaller unions in engineering who were concerned that they would lose out to the AUEW. But the pressures for greater flexibility have proved immensely powerful. The TGWU conference in 1991 agreed to participate in negotiations over team working and quality control. Industrial relations gave way to human resource management which was intended to get the workers to identify more closely with the company's goals. How far this has been successful only time and research to get behind the rhetoric of the enthusiasts will tell. But none of these changes has meant the end of unionism.

The 1993 Trade Union Reform and Employment Rights Act placed further obstacles in front of trade unions. It required seven days' notice of a strike to be given; tightened control over the conduct of ballots for industrial action; granted individuals the right to join the union of their choice, thus undermining the Bridlington Agreement; and required employees to agree in writing each year to the deduction (the check-off) of their union dues from their wages. The powers of the certification officer to investigate union finances were further increased and ACAS no longer had any duty to promote the extension of collective bargaining. Wages councils were abolished, removing the final protection for the lowest-paid workers. With the hopes of a Labour Government shattered in the 1992 election and deepening recession, union morale was at a low point. Unemployment reached 2.8 million at the most conservative estimate.

The policy of deliberately excluding unions from any role in civil society was continued, with the Secretary of State for Employment declaring in 1992 that the 'traditional pattern of industrial relations, based on collective bargaining and collective agreements, seems increasingly inappropriate and are [sic] in decline'. By 1990 only 54 per cent of employees were covered by collective bargaining agreements compared with 71 per cent in 1984. A number of areas moved to derecognising unions' rights to negotiate. Banks, insurance companies and the chemical and pharmaceutical areas were particularly bad in this respect. That said, however, it has tended to be smaller companies with fewer than 200 employees who have gone along this route. A 1990 survey showed that there had been 'no overall decline in either union membership or recognition of collective bargaining in the largest work-places', and that seven out of ten companies with more than 200 employees still recognised unions.[23] But the proportion of work-places where unions were recognised was only 53 per cent and most of these were in the public sector. The fall in the proportion in private manufacture was from 65 per cent in 1980 to 44 per cent in 1990. In private service industries the figures went down from 41 per cent to 36 per cent. Unions tended to find themselves excluded from new developments on greenfield sites even when there was union recognition in other parts of a company. In private industry, only 41 per cent of employees were covered by collective bargaining in 1990, compared with 52 per cent in 1984.

The price to be paid for the collapse of unionism in many areas has been a heavy one for many of the weakest members of British society. Those areas where effective unionism has been lost are often the ones where pay, health and safety, job security, grievance procedures, systems of consultation and communication are at their worst.[24] Management, even where unions continue to operate, has had 18 years of a virtual free hand in reducing and reorganising the labour force. New technology, new payment methods, new procedures have been brought in with the minimum of consultation and the minimum of consequences for employers. Unions have been unable to resist in a world of large-scale unemployment.[25] The number of working days lost in any year since 1985 has only once exceeded four million, back to the levels below those experienced in the 1930s, and in the 1990s the average has been less than 0.75 million. Unions have also found it very difficult to adjust to a labour market which involves increasing amounts of part-time work, freelance work and short, fixed-term contracts.

Amalgamations

The one area where there has been massive reorganisation has been in the number of unions. Amalgamations have gathered pace as unions have responded to changes in the workplace, to their own financial difficulties and to the need to reduce their own administrative costs while at the same time improving the services which they offer their members. The need for many of the hundreds of small unions to merge had been recognised for decades. A TUC Report in 1943 had recommended this, but change was difficult to achieve and came very slowly. Negotiations between unions often went on for decades. The Trade Union (Amalgamation) Act of 1964 made merger easier, requiring only a majority of those voting. It also facilitated transfer of members between unions to create more rational structures. More than 50 mergers followed in the next decade and another 40 in the 1970s. These included the building unions in UCATT and various engineering unions in AUEW.

The process continued in the 1980s. Over 22 years between 1967 and 1989, 244 transfers and 87 mergers created 36 new unions. In 1982 the skilled craft unionists of the Amalgamated Society of Boilermakers, Shipwrights, Blacksmiths and Structural Workers joined with the GMWU to form GMBATU, becoming the GMB in 1989 when APEX merged with it. The modern GMB can trace its roots to some 100 earlier unions. In 1988 ASTMS and the TASS section of the AUEW combined to form MSF (Manufacturing, Science and Finance). In 1990 there were still 323 unions but 23 of these covered over 81 per cent of trade unionists.

This continued in the 1990s. In 1990 the NUR and NUS joined in the National Union of Rail, Maritime and Transport Workers. In 1991 the NGA and SOGAT amalgamated in the Graphical, Printing and Media Union. In 1992 AEU and EETPU came together in Amalgamated Engineering and Electrical Union (AEEU). This was the end of long-drawn-out negotiations which were finally brought to fruition by the two right-wing leaders, Gavin Laird of the AUEW and Eric Hammond of the EETPU, with the latter smoothing the process of merger by retiring. In 1993 three public service unions,

COHSE, NALGO and NUPE merged to form the country's largest union, UNISON. In 1996 the Civil Service Unions, IRSF and NUCPS, amalgamated into PCS (Public and Commercial Services' Union). The TGWU and the GMB continued to talk. The result is that the TUC's 6.7 million membership in 1998 is now represented by only 75 trade unions.

Winds of Change

There are many other signs of a rapidly changing trade union movement at the end of the 1990s. One area of dramatic change has been in attitudes towards Europe. In 1974 only a tiny handful of union leaders campaigned in favour of British membership of the European Common Market and hostility continued into the 1980s. By the end of the decade there had been a sea change, with all the major unions going out of their way to emphasise their Europeanness and leading calls for early membership of the European Monetary Union. Deprived of a role at home, the TUC found itself accepted as a representative institution in the corridors of power in Europe. Just as Conservative legislation was trying to destroy collective bargaining, the Europeanisation of companies was bringing new approaches to industrial relations involving greater consultation with workers. Growing knowledge of the practices of other member states revealed conditions of work which British workers, with the longest working hours in Europe, could only envy and hope to emulate. As Dennis McShane has argued, by the 1990s there was 'a new European ideology and practice . . . stemming from common experiences, a convergence of economic, political and social problems, and a sense that Europe, as much as the nation, was the playing field for effective trade unionism in the future'.[26] The coming of a single internal market in the EU required moves towards a uniformity of social rights. All but Britain accepted the goals laid down in the Community Charter of Fundamental Social Rights, the Social Chapter, which committed member states to working towards closer co-operation between employers and workers 'so that economic and social change take place in a socially acceptable manner'. Not surprisingly, the trade unions have made the acceptance of the Social Charter by the British Government a central goal and see European-wide action as the way to tackle employment problems. The Amsterdam Treaty of October 1997 further extended the EU's role in social welfare and trade union rights with little room for British exceptionalism. British companies operating in Europe and European companies operating in Britain are increasingly adopting uniform patterns of communication and consultation in line with the Social Charter.

As opportunities for manoeuvre in industrial activities have become limited, many unions have set out to recruit and retain members by offering a range of benefits and personal and financial services. Credit cards, insurance, discount schemes are all on offer to the union member. In an increasingly insecure world of employment the provision of legal advice for individual members has grown in importance. Unions such as the GPMU and UNISON have been involved in establishing training schemes for their unemployed members. Inspired by American and Australian examples of union organising, the TUC at the end of 1997 launched a major campaign to increase membership, with new, specially trained young organisers. Their activities are aimed particularly at newer industries and those areas where there is no tradition of union membership, and at young workers, women workers and those from ethnic minorities.

The coming to power of a majority Labour Government in May 1997 held out some prospect of a more sympathetic ear for the trade unions. Ken Jackson, the general secretary of the AEEU, put it bluntly that trade unions had put £200 million into the Labour Party over the 18 years since 1979 and 'like any sensible investors we want some return on it. Not in the form of favours or special treatment but recognition of the importance, and continuing importance, of that contribution.' But the trade unions have undoubtedly lost much of their weight within the Labour Party as it transformed itself into New Labour. By the end of the 1980s the Labour leadership had made very clear that there would be no extensive repeal of Conservative trade union legislation. The unions' influence over Labour Conference decisions was reduced just as the power of conference to influence policy was also diminished. Despite the evidence that hostility to the unions had had negligible effect on the elections of 1987 and 1992 the Labour leadership continued to try to distance themselves. Trade unions lost their role in the selection of parliamentary candidates and had their part in the election of party leader reduced to an equal third with MPs and constituency parties. The union vote had to be backed up by membership ballots. Tony Blair, newly-elected as party leader in 1994, showed himself keen to avoid any tainting of New Labour's image by association with trade unionism and seemed determined to further weaken the party's links with the unions. He consistently warned that a Labour Government would be even-handed between employers and unions and his new Government enthusiastically set about recruiting businessmen, some of whom had shown little regard for their employees' collective demands, into key advisory positions.

New Labour's manifesto in the general election of May 1997 promised a national minimum wage, the European Social Chapter, rights of union recognition and the restoration of trade union membership at GCHQ. The last was delivered within a fortnight of the election; the others left plenty of room for debate on detail. There was no consensus on what the level of minimum wage ought to be and there was soon pressure from employers for exemptions and for age and regional variations. The Low Pay Commission which was established to set the rate in May 1998 came up with the figure of £3.60 an hour, which was well short of some union hopes, which were targeted as high as £4.50, but above the CBI hopes of £3.20. Even more controversially it recommended a youth rate for 18–20-year-olds of only £3.20. The effect was somewhat cushioned by the publication of the Government's White Paper, *Fairness at Work*. Its commitment to new work-place and union rights went further than most unionists had hoped. In firms of more than 20 employees, where more than 50 per cent of a particular bargaining unit or group of workers are unionised, then the employer will be bound to recognise the union's right to negotiate. In other cases, union recognition can be achieved if a work-place ballot produces a minimum of 40 per cent of the work-force vote in favour. But all workers will have the right to be represented by a union official in

disciplinary proceedings. In addition the White Paper promises a reduction in the qualifying period during which workers can claim unfair dismissal from two years to one. The right to claim for unfair dismissal will apply to workers who are sacked for taking part in a legal industrial dispute. Discrimination against or blacklisting of trade unionists is to be outlawed. Contracts which require workers to be available for work without any guarantee of work, so-called zero-hours contracts, or contracts which require workers to sign away their legal rights, are to be reviewed and 12 weeks' parental leave in line with the Social Chapter is to be introduced and maternity leave is to be extended to 18 weeks.

These and other signs indicate that the coming of a new government has helped to change the atmosphere. Derecognition of unions has been reduced to a trickle and recognition campaigns have been increasing in success. The rate of union membership loss has slowed down. The unions now project an image of efficiency far removed from the cart-horse caricature that bedevilled them for the previous half-century. They have shown an ability to respond to the greatest crisis of their history and to adapt to rapidly changing circumstances. There is much talk of new unionism and of 'social partnership' in the work-place with 'employers and trade unions working together to achieve common goals such as fairness and competitiveness' and of employers and unions 'making common cause wherever possible'.[27] Perhaps, most significantly of all, there is a recognition among union leaders that the future of unionism will be based on a policy of inclusion of all kinds of workers and less on the protective sectionalism which for so long was the defining feature of trade unionism. The successful revival of unionism, however, will depend on a cultural change which once again brings a recognition that in an uncertain world security comes from collective action.

Notes

(Place of publication is London unless otherwise stated.)

1 Learning the Game

1. A. E. Musson, *British Trade Unions, 1800–1875* (Basingstoke, 1980) is the worst offender, but see also E. H. Hunt, *British Labour History, 1815–1914* (1981).
2. Adrian Randall, 'The Industrial Moral Economy of the Gloucestershire Weavers in the Eighteenth Century' in John Rule (ed.), *British Trade Unionism 1750–1850. The Formative Years* (London, 1988), p. 33.
3. H. A. Turner, *Trade Union Growth, Structure and Policy* (1962), p. 51.
4. John Rule, *The Experience of Labour in Eighteenth Century Industry* (1981), p. 159.
5. These and other examples can be found in W. Hamish Fraser, *Conflict and Class. Scottish Workers 1700–1838* (Edinburgh, 1988), pp. 42–4.
6. Ibid., p. 48.
7. E. J. Hobsbawm, *Labouring Men. Studies in the History of Labour* (1964), p. 36; R. A. Leeson, *Travelling Brothers. The six centuries' road from craft fellowship to trade unionism.* (1979) paints a very different picture.
8. Fraser, *Conflict and Class*, p. 45.
9. C. R. Dobson, *Masters and Journeymen. A Pre-History of Industrial Relations* (1980).
10. Randall, 'The Industrial Moral Economy', pp. 32–3.
11. *Edinburgh Evening Courant*, 27 August 1754.
12. Ibid., 23 July 1764.
13. For these and similar disputes see Fraser, *Conflict and Class*, Chapter 3.
14. Rule, *The Experience of Labour*, pp. 182–3.
15. Ibid., p. 105.
16. Ibid., p. 187.
17. James Moher, 'From Suppression to Containment: Roots of Trade Union Law to 1825' in Rule, *British Trade Unionism*, p. 76.
18. Glasgow weaving employers in 1787.
19. Fraser, *Conflict and Class*, pp. 75–80 for more examples.
20. Ibid., p. 82.
21. J. B. Jefferys, *The Story of the Engineers 1900–1945* (n.d.), p. 12.
22. Ibid., p. 16.

23. Moher, 'From Suppression to Containment', pp. 90–3.
24. There was, for example, an Association of Colliers of Scotland in 1825–6, A. Campbell, 'The Scots Colliers' Strikes of 1824–26: the Years of Freedom and Independence' in Rule, *British Trade Unionism*, pp. 143–61.
25. Richard Price, *Masters, Unions and Men. Work control in building and the rise of labour 1830–1914* (Cambridge, 1980), pp. 22–34.
26. W. Hamish Fraser, *Alexander Campbell and the Search for Socialism* (Manchester, 1996), pp. 32–40.
27. W. H. Oliver, 'The Consolidated Trades Union of 1834', *Economic History Review*, xvii, 1, 1964.
28. W. Hamish Fraser, 'The Glasgow Cotton Spinners, 1837' in J. Butt and J. T. Ward (eds), *Scottish Themes* (Edinburgh, 1976), pp. 80–97.
29. *Manchester Guardian*, 24 August 1842.
30. R. Harrison (ed.), *Independent Collier. The Coal Miners as Archetypal Proletarian Reconsidered* (Hassocks, 1978).
31. Jefferys, *Story of the Engineers*, p. 25.

2 The Rise of National Unions, 1850–80

1. The official birth date of the ASE was 6 January 1851.
2. For a summary of some of the questioning see A. E. Musson, *Trade Union and Social History* (1974).
3. D. Blankenhorn, '"Our Class of Workmen": The Cabinetmakers' Revisited' in R. Harrison and J. Zeitlin, *Division of Labour: Skilled Workers and Technological Change in Nineteenth Century England* (Hassocks, 1985), p. 25.
4. Keith Burgess, *The Origins of British Industrial Relations. The Nineteenth Century Experience* (1975), Chapter 1.
5. Sidney and Beatrice Webb, *Industrial Democracy* (1902 ed.), p. 16.
6. Takao Matsumura, *The Labour Aristocracy Revisited. The Victorian Flint Glassmakers 1850–80* (Manchester, 1983), p. 1; Hobsbawm, *Labouring Men* (1964), p. 274.
7. Royden Harrison, *Before the Socialists. Studies in Labour and Politics, 1861–1881* (1965), pp. 14–15.
8. H. Pelling, 'The concept of the labour aristocracy' in *Popular Politics and Society in Late Victorian Britain* (1968), p. 61.
9. Musson, *Trade Union and Social History*, p. 21.
10. Quoted in R. V. Clements, 'British trade unions and popular political economy', *Economic History Review*, 14, 1960–1, p. 102.
11. E. F. Biagini, 'British Trade Unions and Popular Political Economy, 1860–1880', *Historical Journal*, 30, 4 (1987), pp. 811–40.
12. For Gast see I. Prothero, *Artisans and Politics in Early Nineteenth Century London. John Gast and His Times* (1979).
13. *Reynolds's Newspaper*, 28 August 1859.

14. *Bee-Hive*, 26 March 1864.
15. For the importance of these links see especially Harrison, *Before the Socialists* and W. Hamish Fraser, *Trade Unions and Society. The Struggle for Acceptance* (1974).
16. *The Times*, 25 August 1859.
17. For a discussion of the changes in political economy see E. F. Biagini, 'British Trade Unions and Popular Political Economy 1860–1880', *Historical Journal*, 30, 4 (1987), pp. 811–40 and Fraser, *Trade Unions and Society*, Chapter 7.
18. The campaign eventually led to a modified Master and Servant Act in 1869.
19. The Scottish Registrar of Friendly Societies had always declined to receive the rules of unions because he believed that they were illegal on the grounds that they were in restraint of trade.
20. John V. Orth, *Combination and Conspiracy. A Legal History of Trade Unionism, 1721–1906* (Oxford, 1991), pp. 105–6.
21. S. Higgenbottam, *Our Society's History* (Manchester, 1939), p. 37.
22. The original summons was addressed mainly to trades councils hence the *Trades'* Union in the title.
23. C. G. Hanson, 'Craft Unions, Welfare Benefits, and the Case for Trade Union Law Reform, 1867–75', *Economic History Review*, 2nd ser., XXVIII, 2, May 1975, pp. 243–59; an effective qualification of Hanson's views is to be found in Pat Thane's 'Comment' in *Economic History Review*, XXIX, 4, 1976, pp. 617–25.
24. E. Allen, J. F. Clarke, N. McCord and D. J. Rowe (eds), *The North-East Engineers' Strikes of 1871* (Newcastle upon Tyne, 1971), pp. 144–7.
25. E. F. Biagini and A. Reid (eds), *Currents of Radicalism: popular radicalism, organised labour, and party politics, 1850–1914* (Cambridge, 1991), p. 229.
26. E. Gordon, 'The Scottish Trade Union Movement, Class and Gender, 1850–1914', *Scottish Labour History Society Journal*, 23 (1988), p. 37.
27. Sian Reynolds, *Britannica's Typesetters. Women Compositors in Edinburgh* (Edinburgh, 1989), p. 40.
28. M. A. Woodgate, 'The National Agricultural Labourers' Union and the Politicisation of Farm Workers in North Essex 1872–1894', unpublished M.Phil. thesis, University of Essex, 1993, pp. 6–11.
29. T. Wright, *Our New Masters* (1873), p. 283.
30. Eleanor Gordon, *Women and the Labour Movement in Scotland 1850–1914* (Oxford, 1991), p. 87.
31. E. Taplin, *Liverpool Dockers and Seamen, 1870–1890* (Hull, 1974), p. 25.
32. F. Harrison, 'The Good and Evil of Trade Unions', *Fortnightly Review*, III, Nov. 1865, p. 34.
33. J. Cronin, 'Strikes and Power in Britain, 1870–1920', *International Review of Social History*, 32, 1987.

3 The Coming of Collective Bargaining, 1850–80

1. R. Harrison, *Before the Socialists. Studies in Labour and Politics, 1861–1881* (1965), p. 14.
2. ASCJ, *Monthly Report*, July 1869.
3. G. Potter, 'Trades' Unions, Strikes and Lock-outs: A rejoinder', *Contemporary Review*, XVII (1871), p. 529.
4. R. Postgate, *The Builders' History* (n.d.), p. 152.
5. Takao Matsumura, *The Labour Aristocracy Revisited. The Victorian Flint Glass Makers 1850–80* (Manchester, 1983), p. 130.
6. ASCJ, *Annual Report*, 1867.
7. There is an excellent study of this strike, H. I. Dutton and J. E. King, *'Ten Per Cent and No Surrender'. The Preston Strike, 1853–54* (Cambridge, 1981).
8. Matsumura, *Labour Aristocracy Revisited*, pp. 130–48.
9. J. Cronin, 'Strikes and the Struggle for Union Organisation in Britain and Europe' in Mommsen and Husung (eds), *The Development of Trade Unionism in Great Britain and Germany 1880–1914* (1985), p. 57.
10. A. McIvor, *Organised Capital. Employers' associations and industrial relations in northern England 1880–1939* (Cambridge, 1996), p. 43.
11. Matsumura, *Labour Aristocracy Revisited*, pp. 130–43.
12. Richard Price, *Masters, Unions and Men. Work control in building and the rise of labour 1830–1914* (Cambridge, 1980), pp. 49–53.
13. J. E. Mortimer, *History of the Boilermakers' Society*, I, (1973), pp. 57–71.
14. E. Allen, J. F. Clarke, N. McCord and D. J. Rowe, *The North-East Engineers' Strikes of 1871* (Newcastle upon Tyne, 1971).
15. Jefferys, *Story of the Engineers*, 96–7.
16. J. Stirling, *Trade Unionism*, (Glasgow, 1869).
17. Quoted in C. G. Hanson, 'Craft Unions etc', *Economic History Review*, XXVIII, 2, May 1975, p. 253.
18. T. Brassay, *Lectures on the Labour Question* (1878), p. 72.
19. The Blackburn List was agreed in 1853.
20. H. Broadhurst, *Henry Broadhurst, M.P. The Story of His Life from Stonemason's Bench to the Treasury Bench. Told by Himself* (1901), p. 44.
21. Alan Fox, *History and Heritage. The Social Origins of the British Industrial Relations System* (1985), pp. 126–8. Patrick Joyce, *Work, Society and Politics: The Culture of the Factory in Later Victorian England* (1980).
22. G. C. Halverson, 'Development of Railway Relations in British Railways since 1860'. Ph.D. London, 1952, pp. 69–70.
23. E. J. Hobsbawm, *Labouring Men. Studies in the History of Labour* (1964), p. 272.
24. R. W. Postgate, *The Builders' History* (1923), heading to Chapter 9.
25. W. Hamish Fraser, *Trade Unions and Society. The Struggle for Acceptance* (1974).

26. Chris Fisher and John Smethurst, 'War on the Law of Supply and Demand: the Amalgamated Association of Miners and the Forest of Dean Collier' in Harrison (ed.), *Independent Collier*, pp. 141–8.

27. V. L. Allen, *The Sociology of Industrial Relations* (1971), p. 81.

28. *Capital and Labour*, 31 December 1873.

4 Revival and Confrontation, 1880–98

1. Sidney Pollard, 'New Unionism in Britain: its Economic Background' in W. J. Mommsen and Hans-Gerhard Husung, *The Development of Trade Unionism in Great Britain and Germany, 1880–1914* (1985), pp. 47–8.

2. A. E. P. Duffy, 'New Unionism in Britain, 1889–90: a reappraisal', *Economic History Review*, 14 (1961–2), pp. 306–19, effectively demolished the older chronology.

3. Alastair Reid, 'Employers' Strategies and Craft Production. The British Shipbuilding Industry 1870–1950' in S. Tolliday and J. Zeitlin (eds), *The Power to Manage? Employers and Industrial Relations in Comparative Historical Perspective* (1991), p. 40.

4. All figures for union density are taken from G. S. Bain and R. Price, *Profiles of Union Growth* (1980).

5. Raymond Brown, *Waterfront Organisation in Hull 1870–1900* (University of Hull, 1972), pp. 20–3.

6. The first had been in 1858.

7. Perhaps best remembered for the fact that it organised the strippers and grinders.

8. Hull Trades Council, *Annual Report 1886.*

9. Duffy, 'The New Unionism', p. 309.

10. Formerly the Women's Protective and Provident League.

11. G. Evans, 'Farm Servants' unions in Aberdeenshire', *Scottish Historical Review*, XXI, 1952.

12. See George Shipton's comments to Beatrice Webb at the 1889 TUC in B. Webb, *My Apprenticeship* (1926), pp. 20–1. At the same time the Trades Council had reason to be suspicious of dockers' unions since there had been a number of bogus ones over the years.

13. John Lovell, *Stevedores and Dockers. A Study of Trade Unionism in the Port of London, 1870–1914* (1969), pp. 92–112.

14. E. J. Hobsbawm, 'New Unionism Reconsidered' in Mommsen and Husung, *Development of Trade Unionism*, p. 17.

15. Brown, *Waterfront Organisation*, pp. 66–98.

16. J. Lovell, *Stevedores and Dockers*, p. 91.

17. E. Taplin, *The Dockers' Union. A Study of the National Union of Dock Labourers, 1889–1922* (Leicester, 1985), p. 160.

18. A. Clegg, A. Fox and A. F. Thompson, *A History of British Trade Unions since 1889*, I, (Oxford, 1964), pp. 106–11.

19. J. E. Mortimer, *History of the Boilermakers' Society*, I, (1973), p. 119.

20. Jefferys, *The Story of the Engineers 1900–1945* (n.d.), p. 106.
21. Keith Burgess, 'New Unionism for Old?' in Mommsen and Husung (eds), *Development of Trade Unionism*, p. 167.
22. A. E. P. Duffy made most of these points in his 'New Unionism in Britain'.
23. See Henry Pelling, 'The Working Class and the Origins of the Welfare State' in *Popular Politics and Society in Late Victorian Britain* (1968), pp. 1–18.
24. R. Price, 'The labour process and labour history', *Social History*, 8 (1983), p. 69.
25. J. E. Cronin, 'Strikes and the Struggle for Union Organisation' in Mommsen and Husung (eds), *Development of Trade Unionism*, p. 60.
26. *Cotton Factory Times*, 17 March 1893, quoted in Clegg, Fox and Thompson, *British Trade Unions*, I, p. 116.
27. *Labour Elector*, 18 January 1890.
28. The effect was to exclude both Keir Hardie and Henry Broadhurst.
29. Ross M. Martin, *TUC: The Growth of a Pressure Group 1868–1896* (Oxford, 1980), pp. 79–81.

5 The Intervening State, 1893–1914

1. John Burnett, the general secretary of the ASE, was appointed as the Board's Labour Correspondent.
2. E. Wigham, *Strikes and the Government 1893–1981* (1982, 2nd edition), pp. 8–9.
3. N. McCord, 'Taff Vale Revisited', *History*, 78, June 1993, pp. 243–60.
4. Clegg, Fox and Thompson, *British Trade Unions*, I, pp. 374–6.
5. Later Lord Merthyr, he was the Marquis of Bute's agent in South Wales.
6. A. V. Dicey in an introduction to a new edition of his *Law and Public Opinion in England* (1914). A recent examination of the background to the measure is John Saville, 'The Trade Disputes Act of 1906' in *Historical Studies in Industrial Relations*, No.1, March 1996, pp. 11–46.
7. K. D. Ewing, *Trade Unions, the Labour Party and the Law. A Study of the Trade Union Act 1913* (Edinburgh, 1982), p. 40.
8. R. Davidson, 'The Board of Trade and Industrial Relations 1896–1914', *Historical Journal*, 21, 3 (1978), p. 576.
9. Clegg et al., *British Trade Unions*, I, pp. 362–3.
10. H. F. Gospel, 'Employers and Managers: Organisation and Strategy' in Chris Wrigley (ed.), *A History of British Industrial Relations 1914–1939* (Brighton, 1987), pp. 163–4.
11. Ken Coates and Tony Topham, *The Making of the Transport and General Workers' Union: the emergence of the Labour Movement* (Oxford, 1991), p. 247.

12. E. H. Phelps Brown, *The Growth of British Industrial Relations* (1989), p. 186.
13. Clegg et al., *British Trade Unions*, I, pp. 189–90.
14. Ibid., pp. 194–6.
15. J. Hodge, *From Workmen's Cottage to Windsor Castle* (1931), p. 91.
16. H. Braverman, *Labor and Monopoly Capitalism. The Degradation of Work in the Twentieth Century* (1974).
17. R. Price, *Labour in British Society* (1986), pp. 93–130.
18. Alice Prochaska, *History of the General Federation of Trade Unions, 1899–1980* (1982), p. 16.
19. Clegg et al., *British Trade Unions*, I, pp. 342–3.
20. Craig R. Littler, *The Development of the Labour Process in Capitalist Society* (1982), pp. 50–1.
21. Wayne Lewchuk, 'Fordism and British Motor Car Employers, 1896–1932' in Howard F. Gospel and Craig R. Littler, *Managerial Strategies and Industrial Relations* (Aldershot, 1983), pp. 84–5.
22. Ibid.
23. Jefferys, *Story of the Engineers*, p. 132.
24. J. Zeitlin, 'Industrial Structure, Employer Strategy and the Diffusion of Job Control in Britain, 1880–1920' in Mommsen & Husung, *Development of Trade Unionism*, p. 327.
25. A. Reid, 'Employers' Strategies and Craft Production. The British Shipbuilding Industry 1870–1950' in S. Tolliday and J. Zeitlin (eds), *The Power to Manage?* (1991), pp. 35–6.
26. Littler, *Development of the Labour Process*, p. 84.
27. Clegg et al., *British Trade Unions*, I, pp. 476–9.
28. R. Price, 'The New Unionism and the Labour Process' in Mommsen & Husung, *Development of Trade Unionism*, p. 138.
29. R. J. Price, *Masters, Unions and Men* (1980), pp. 228–9.
30. Clegg et al., *British Trade Unions*, I, p. 430.
31. Joseph L. White, 'Lancashire Cotton Textiles' in Wrigley, *History 1875–1914*, p. 223.
32. Roy Church, 'Edwardian Labour Unrest and Coalfield Militancy, 1890–1914', *Historical Journal*, 30, 4 (1987), p. 850.
33. M. J. Daunton, 'Down the Pit: Work in the Great Northern and South Wales Coalfields, 1870–1914', *Economic History Review*, XXXIV, 4, November 1981, pp. 578–97.
34. Charles Stanton quoted by C. Williams, '"The hope of the British proletariat", the South Wales Miners, 1910–1947' in A. Campbell, N. Fishman and D. Howell, *Miners, Unions and Politics 1910–47* (Aldershot, 1996), p. 124.
35. Clegg, *British Trade Unions*, II, p. 35.
36. See G. Bain, *Profile of Union Growth* (Oxford, 1980).
37. Glasgow Labour History Workshop, *Militant Workers. Labour and Class Conflict on the Clyde, 1900–1950* (Edinburgh, 1992), eds Robert Duncan and Arthur McIvor, pp. 84–6.
38. Eleanor Gordon, *Women and the Labour Movement in Scotland 1850–1914* (Oxford, 1991), pp. 209–12.

39. Roy Church, 'Edwardian Labour Unrest', pp. 847–8.

40. Clegg, *British Trade Unions*, II, p. 26.

41. Robert Smillie, 'The Triple Industrial Alliance' in *The Labour Year Book* (1916).

42. Tom Mann, 'Prepare for Action', *The Industrial Syndicalist*, 1, no. 1 (July 1910).

43. Bob Holton, *British Syndicalism, 1900–1914. Myths and Realities* (1976); J. E. Cronin, *Industrial Conflict in Modern Britain* (1979); R. Price, *Labour In British Society: An Interpretative History* (1986), pp. 153–7.

44. J. Schneer, *Ben Tillett. Portrait of a Labour Leader* (1982); E. A. and G. H. Radice, *Will Thorne, Constructive Militant* (1974).

6 Workers, War and the State, 1914–21

1. A. Fox, *History and Heritage: The Social Origins of British Industrial Relations* (1985), p. 286.

2. James Hinton, *The First Shop Stewards' Movement* (1973), p. 115.

3. Joseph Melling, 'Whatever Happened to Red Clydeside?', *International Review of Social History*, XXXV (1990), p. 14. More than 3000 workers were brought before tribunals for breach of the Act within the first five months.

4. H. A. Clegg, *A History of British Trade Unions since 1889, Vol. II, 1911–1933* (Oxford, 1985), p. 148; J. Foster, 'Strike Action and Working-Class Politics on Clydeside 1914–19', *International Review of Social History*, XXXV (1990), p. 49.

5. Hinton, *The First Shop Stewards' Movement*.

6. Iain McLean, *The Legend of Red Clydeside* (Edinburgh, 1983).

7. G. Rubin, *War, Law and Labour* (Oxford, 1987), *passim*.

8. Foster, 'Strike Action and Working-Class Politics on Clydeside 1914–19', p. 48.

9. McLean, *Legend*, p. 90.

10. Arthur J. McIvor, *Organised Capital. Employers' associations and industrial relations in northern England, 1880–1939* (Cambridge, 1996), p. 150.

11. N. Soldon, *Women in British Trade Unions* (Dublin, 1978), p. 84.

12. R. Hyman, 'Rank and File Movements and Workplace Organisation' in C. J. Wrigley (ed.), *A History of British Industrial Relations*, Vol. II *1914–1939* (1987), p. 132.

13. Clegg, *British Trade Unions*, II, p. 168.

14. Soldon, *Women in British Trade Unions*, p. 191.

15. Clydeside, however, could not be stirred.

16. TUC, *Annual Report, 1916*.

17. The National Union of Clerks had 28 000 members, the Union of Post Office Engineers, 15 000, the Musicians' union 16 000 and the National Union of Teachers, 7000.

18. Ken Coates and Tony Topham, *The Making of the Transport and General Workers' Union, 1870–1922* (Oxford, 1991), I, p. 697.

19. Soldon, *Women in British Trade Unions*, pp. 85–91.

20. Sarah Boston, *Women Workers and Trade Unions* (1987), pp. 132–53.

21. Clegg, *British Trade Unions*, II, p. 242.

22. Wayne Lewchuk, 'Fordism and British Motor-Car Employers, 1896–1932' in Howard F. Gospel and Craig R. Littler, *Managerial Strategies and Industrial Relations* (Aldershot, 1983), p. 104.

23. Alan Fowler, 'Lancashire Cotton Trade Unionism in the Inter-War Years' in J. A. Jowitt and A. J. McIvor (eds), *Employers and Labour in the English Textile Industries* (1988), p. 112.

24. McLean, *Legend*, p. 115. The national agreement had abolished the older pattern of 6 a.m. to 1 p.m. with a 9.15 break in favour of 7.30 to 12 without a break.

25. A. Campbell, N. Fishman and D. Howell, *Miners, Unions and Politics 1910–47* (1996), p. 103.

26. For a recent discussion of the debate see Terry Brotherstone, 'Does Red Clydeside Really Matter Any More?' in R. Duncan and A. J. McIvor, *Militant Workers: Labour and Class Conflict on the Clyde 1900–1950* (Edinburgh, 1992), pp. 52–80.

27. Quoted in David F. Wilson, *Dockers. The Impact of Industrial Change* (1972), p. 77.

7 The Industrial Relations of Depression, 1921–33

1. NUR Central Strike Committee, Edinburgh District, *Strike Bulletin* (12 April 1921).

2. C. Wrigley, *Lloyd George and the Challenge of Labour: The Post-War Coalition 1918–22* (Hemel Hempstead, 1990), p. 281. J. H. Thomas was secretary of the NUR from 1916 until 1931.

3. H. A. Clegg, *A History of British Trade Unions since 1889, Vol. II, 1911–1933* (Oxford, 1985), p. 325.

4. Ian MacDougall (ed.), *Militant Miners* (Edinburgh, 1981), pp. 60–3.

5. Arthur J. McIvor, *Organised Capital. Employers' associations and industrial relations in northern England, 1880–1939* (Cambridge, 1996), pp. 183–8.

6. Ross H. Martin, *TUC: The Growth of a Pressure Group 1868–1976* (Oxford, 1980), pp. 180–3.

7. Lord Citrine, *Men and Work. An Autobiography* (1964), p. 87.

8. R. J. Price, *Masters, Unions and Men* (1980), pp. 253–4.

9. Clegg, *British Trade Unions*, II, p. 202.

10. These were the Dockworkers, Riverside and General Workers' Union (Tillett and Bevin's union); the Lightermen's Union (Gosling); the Labour Protection League, the National Amalgamated Labourers' Union (largely Tyneside based), the North of England Trimmers, the Dock and Wharves' Shipping Staff, the Ships Clerks, the United Vehicle Workers, the Amalgamated Carters, Lorrymen

and Motormen, the National Union of Vehicle Workers, the National Amalgamated Coal Workers' Union, the North of Scotland Horse and Motormen's Union, the Amalgamated Association of Carters and Motormen.

11. Ken Coates and Tony Topham, *The Making of the Transport and General Workers' Union*, I, p. 773.

12. V. L. Allen, *Trade Union Leadership. Based on a Study of Arthur Deakin* (1957), p. 49.

13. T. Topham, 'The Unofficial National Dock Strike of 1923: the TGWU's first crisis', *Historical Studies in Industrial Relations*, Sept. 1996, pp. 27–64.

14. Ibid., p. 34.

15. Steam Engine Makers' Society, United Machine Workers, Amalgamated Smiths and Strikers, Associated Brassfounders, North of England Brass Turners, London United Metal Turners, East of Scotland Brassfounders, Amalgamated Toolmakers. Two unions which tried but failed to achieve the necessary 50 per cent for amalgamation were the ETU and the United Patternmakers. The Boilermakers and the Ironfounders declined to participate in the negotiations.

16. H. F. Gospel, 'Employers and Managers: Organisations and Strategy 1914–39' in C. J. Wrigley (ed.), *A History of British Industrial Relations*, Vol. II, 1914–1939 (1987), pp. 170–1; J. Zeitlin, 'The Internal Politics of Employer Organisation: The Engineering Employers' Federation 1896–1939' in S. Tolliday and J. Zeitlin (eds) *The Power to Manage?* (1991).

17. This had grown out of an organisation of London County Council workers established in 1894.

18. Clegg, *British Trade Unions*, II, pp. 317–36.

19. The former was formed on Clydeside in August 1912, the latter in Liverpool in 1909.

20. E. Wigham, *Strikes and the Government 1893–1981* (1982), p. 59.

21. J. A. Jackson, J. W. Leopold and K. Tuck, *Decentralization of Collective Bargaining. An Analysis of Recent Experience in the UK* (1993), p. 8.

22. N. Fishman, *The British Communist Party and the Trade Unions, 1933–45* (Aldershot, 1995), p. 96

23. John Lloyd, *Light and Liberty. A History of the EETPU* (1990), p. 80.

24. A. Fox, *History and Heritage: The Social Origins of British Industrial Relations* (1985), pp. 333–4.

25. James E. Cronin, *Industrial Conflict in Modern Britain* (1979), p. 128

26. Hywel Francis and David Smith, *The Fed. A History of the South Wales Miners in the Twentieth Century* (1980), p. 84.

27. D. Gilbert, 'The Landscape of Spencerism: Mining Politics in the Nottinghamshire Coalfield 1910–1947' in Campbell et al., *Miners, Unions and Politics 1910–47* (1996), p. 180.

28. MacDougall, *Militant Miners*, pp. 118–36.

29. Clegg, *British Trade Unions,* II, p. 453.

30. R. Lowe, 'The Government and Industrial Relations' in Wrigley, *History*, Vol. II, 1914–1939, p. 195.

31. The phrase was A. J. Cook's.

32. The TUC eventually gave support not to European Union but to Imperial (now becoming Commonwealth) economic union.

33. K. Middlemas, *Politics in an Industrial Society* (1979), pp. 218–27.

34. Howard F. Gospel, 'Employers and Managers: Organisation and Strategy, 1914–1939' in Wrigley, *History*, Vol. II, 1914–1939, pp. 173–5.

35. A. J. Cook, *Mond's Manacles. The Destruction of Trade Unionism* (1928).

36. Alan Bullock, *The Life and Times of Ernest Bevin*, Vol. I (1960), pp. 392–416.

37. Quoted Clegg, *British Trade Unions*, Vol. III, 1933–1931 (Oxford, 1994), p. 463.

38. Wigham, *Government and Strikes*, pp. 74–5.

39. H. Gospel and C. R. Littler (eds), *Managerial Strategies and Industrial Relations* (Aldershot, 1983); S. Tolliday and J. Zeitlin (eds), *The Power to Manage?* (1991).

40. C. Littler, *The Development of the Labour Process in Capitalist Societies* (1982), pp. 105–28.

41. Lewchuk, 'Fordism and the British Motor Car Industry', pp. 88–9.

8 Renewal, Regulation and Consolidation, 1933–51

1. R. Hyman, *Strikes* (1972), p. 29.

2. 1934 statement quoted in W. Brown, 'The Contraction of Collective Bargaining in Britain', *British Journal of Industrial Relations*, 31:2, June 1993, p. 191.

3. A. Fowler, 'Lancashire Cotton Trade Unionism in the Interwar Years' in J. A. Jowitt and A. J. McIvor (eds) *Employers and Labour in the English Textile Industries* (1988), p. 116.

4. P. Smith, 'The Road Haulage Industry 1918–1940: The Process of Unionization, Employers' Control and Statutory Regulation' in *Historical Studies in Industrial Relations*, No.3, March 1997, p. 74.

5. V. L. Allen, *Trade Union Leadership* (1957), p. 63.

6. Alan Clinton, *The Trade Union Rank and File. Trades Councils in Britain, 1900–1940* (Manchester, 1977), p. 152.

7. Ibid., pp. 160–6.

8. For the full list see J. T. Ward and W. H. Fraser (eds), *Workers and Employers. Documents on Trade Unions and Industrial Relations in Britain since the Eighteenth Century* (1980), pp. 267–8.

9. NALGO was not affiliated to the TUC but was supported by the GMWU and the TGWU, both of whom had substantial numbers of local government members.

10. R. Church, Q. Outram and D. N. Smith, 'British Coal mining Strikes 1893–1940: Dimensions, Distribution and Persistence', *British Journal of Industrial Relations*, 28:3 (1990), p. 340.

11. Jack Jones, *Union Man: An Autobiography* (1986), p. 89.

12. S. Lewenhak, *Women and Trade Unions. An Outline History of Women in the British Trade Union Movement* (1977), pp. 228–34.

13. A. McIvor, 'Cotton Employers' Associations' in Jowitt and McIvor, *Employers and Labour*, p. 18.

14. This newish coalfield was one where many miners, blacklisted in Scotland and the North after 1926–7, were sent to find work, often under assumed names.

15. R. Croucher, *Engineers at War, 1939–1945* (1982); R. T. Buchanan, 'The Shop Stewards' Movement 1935–47', *Scottish Labour History Society Journal*, 12, 1978, pp. 34–55.

16. J. Hinton, *Shop-floor Citizens. Engineering Democracy in 1940s Britain* (Aldershot, 1994), pp. 33–48.

17. TUC, *Interim Report on Post-War Reconstruction* (1944).

18. Jones, *Union Man*, p. 122.

19. H. Francis in Campbell *et al.*, *Miners, Unions and Politics 1910–47* (1996), p. 267.

20. Lewenhak, *Women and Trade Unions*, p. 237.

21. It was agreed that the arrangement should be kept secret. *Guardian*, 10 January 1998.

22. Sarah Boston, *Women Workers and Trade Unions* (1987), pp. 233–42.

23. Allen, *Trade Union Leadership*, p. 187.

24. J. Phillips, 'Decasualisation and Disruption: Industrial Relations in the Docks, 1954–70' in C. J. Wrigley (ed.), *A History of British Industrial Relations*, Vol. III, 1939–79, pp. 166–76.

25. H. Gospel, 'The Management of Labour' in Wrigley, *History*, Vol. III, 1939–1979, p. 87.

9 Policies and Power, 1951–74

1. Generally known as the 'Blue Union' it was made up of groups who had refused to come into the TGWU and of breakaways from the TGWU.

2. An attempt to force members back into the TGWU was tested in court in the case of *Spring* v. *NASDS*. The court upheld Spring's right to belong to the union of his choice.

3. R. Hyman, *Strikes* (1972), p. 198.

4. P. S. Bagwell, *The Railwaymen. The History of the National Union of Railwaymen* (1963), p. 651.

5. D. Lyddon, 'The Car Industry, 1945–79: Shop Stewards and Workplace Unionism' in C. J. Wrigley (ed.) *A History of British Industrial Relations*, Vol. III, 1939–1979, p. 192.

6. N. Whiteside, 'Industrial Relations and Social Welfare 1945–79', ibid., p. 116.

7. J. Lloyd, *Light and Liberty. A History of the EETPU* (1990), p. 375.
8. Ibid., p. 463. Cannon died in 1970 at the age of 50.
9. PEP, *The Structure and Organisation of British Trade Unions* (1963).
10. Alan Flanders, *The Fawley Productivity Agreements. A case study of management and collective bargaining* (1964).
11. *Incomes Policy: The Next Step.* Cmnd. 1626.
12. E. Wigham, *Strikes and the Government* 1893–1981 (1982), p. 127.
13. Garfield Clack, *Industrial Relations in a British Car Factory*, University of Cambridge Department of Applied Economics, Occasional Papers, 1967.
14. Other court decisions quickly followed which also undermined the immunities which trade unions believed they had.
15. Wigham, *Strikes and the Government*, p. 133.
16. The AEU had vainly campaigned for this in the 1940s, but a breakthrough had come in 1959 when a dispute involving most of the printing unions had led to a phased move towards 40 hours.
17. Jack Cooper, *Industrial Relations: Sweden Shows the Way*, Fabian Research Series, No. 235 (1963).
18. GMWU, *Productivity, Prices and Incomes* (Esher, 1966).
19. Lloyd, *Light and Liberty*, p. 503.
20. *The Times*, 22 June 1966.
21. J. Phillips, 'Decasualization and disruption: industrial relations in the docks, 1945–79' in Wrigley, *History*, Vol. III, 1939–1979, p. 171.
22. *The Times*, 8 September, 1967.
23. *The Times*, 22 December, 1966.
24. J. Gennard and P. Bain, *SOGAT. A History of the Society of Graphical and Allied Trades* (1995), pp. 100–3.
25. The name SOGAT was retained by the NUPB&PW section. For the details see ibid.
26. D. Metcalfe, 'Water Notes Dry Up: the Impact of the Donovan Reform proposals and Thatcherism at work on Labour Productivity in British Manufacturing Industry', *British Journal of Industrial Relations*, 27:1 (1989), pp. 1–31.
27. Hyman, *Strikes*, p. 35.
28. Stephen Dunn and Martin Wright, 'Maintaining the "Status Who"? An Analysis of the Contents of British Collective Agreements 1979–1990', *British Journal of Industrial Relations* 32:1, (March 1994), p. 26.
29. Jones was elected as general secretary in December 1968 but Cousins did not retire until September 1969.
30. Wigham, *Strikes and the Government*, p. 148.
31. D. F. Wilson, *Dockers. The Impact of Industrial Change* (1972), p. 294.
32. N. Soldon, *Women in British Trade Unions*, p. 186; Sarah Boston, *Women Workers and Trade Unions* (1987), p. 332.
33. This was intended to cover what were regarded as the special cases of the actors' union, Equity, and the National Union of Seamen.

34. Wigham, *Strikes and the Government*, p. 165.
35. T. Lane and K. Roberts, *Strike at Pilkingtons* (1971).
36. Hyman, *Strikes*, p. 13.
37. H. Francis and D. Smith, *The Fed. A History of the South Wales Miners in the Twentieth Century* (1980), p. 452; V. L. Allen, *The Militancy of British Miners* (1981), p. 41.
38. Ibid., p. 92.
39. Sidney Weighell, *On the Rails* (1983), p. 23.

10 Decline and Fall? 1974–98

1. S. Dunn and J. Gennard, *The Closed Shop in British Industry* (1984), p. 165.
2. P. B. Beaumont, *The Decline of Trade Union Organisation* (1987), p. 5.
3. Ibid., p. 60.
4. G. S. Bain, *The Growth of White-Collar Unionism* (Oxford, 1970).
5. Sidney Weighell, *On the Rails* (1983), p. 36.
6. G. Arnold, *The Unions* (1981), p. 97.
7. Clive Jenkins and Barrie Sherman, *White-collar Unionism: The Rebellious Salariat* (1979), p. 1. Low, the cartoonist of the *Evening Standard*, regularly caricatured the TUC as a cart-horse.
8. C. Crouch, 'Review Essay: Atavism and Innovation: Labour Legislation and Public Policy since 1979 in Historical Perspective', *Historical Studies in Industrial Relations*, September 1996, pp. 111–24.
9. Dunn and Gennard, *Closed Shop*, p. 2.
10. John Gennard, *A History of the National Graphical Association* (1990), pp. 485–92.
11. Arnold, *The Unions*, p. 178.
12. Ironically, in 1989 the Certification Officer refused to accept the Government Communications Staff Federation as a *bona fide* union because it was too much under the control of the director of GCHQ.
13. D. Howell, *The Politics of the NUM. A Lancashire View* (Manchester, 1989), p. 70.
14. The Trade Union Act of 1984, which made pre-strike ballots compulsory if unions wished to retain immunity, had not completed its passage through Parliament when the miners' strike began.
15. Bill Sirs, *Hard Labour* (1985), p. 28.
16. See, for example, Eric Hammond of the EETPU's letter to Peter Heathfield, the general secretary of the NUM, quoted in J. Lloyd, *Light and Liberty. A History of the EETPU* (1990), pp. 609–10.
17. Howell, *Politics of NUM*, p. 175.
18. Publishers of the *Sun*, the *News of the World*, *The Times* and the *Sunday Times*.
19. John Gennard and Peter Bain, *SOGAT. A History of the Society of Graphical and Allied Trades* (1995), pp. 605–6.

20. Picketing of the Wapping plant was illegal since the place of work of the strikers was not Wapping but Gray's Inn Road and Bouverie Street.

21. M. P. Jackson, J. W. Leopold and K. Tuck; *Decentralization of Collective Bargaining. An Analysis of Recent Experience in the UK* (1993), pp. 1–2.

22. W. Brown, *The Changing Contours of British Industrial Relations* (Oxford, 1981).

23. G. Gall and S. McKay, 'Trade Union Derecognition in Britain 1988–1994', *British Journal of Industrial Relations*, 32:3, 1994, p. 447.

24. Brown, *Changing Contours*, p. 198.

25. Sue Kessler, 'Procedures and Third Parties', *British Journal of Industrial Relations* 31:2, 1993.

26. Denis MacShane, 'British unions and Europe' in Ben Pimlott and Chris Cook (eds), *Trade Unions in British Politics. The First 250 Years* (1991), p. 296.

27. TUC, *Partners for Progress, Next Steps for the New Unionism* (1997).

Select Bibliography

[The place of publication is London unless otherwise stated]

General Works

Bain, G. and Price, R., *Profile of Union Growth* (Oxford, 1980)
Boston, Sarah, *Women Workers and Trade Unions* (1987)
Clegg, H. A., Fox, A., Thompson, A. F., *A History of British Trade Unions since 1889, Vol. I, 1889–1910* (Oxford, 1964)
Clegg, H. A., *A History of British Trade Unions since 1889, Vol. II, 1911–1933* (Oxford, 1985); *Vol. III, 1933–1951* (Oxford, 1994)
Cronin, J. E., *Industrial Conflict in Modern Britain* (1979)
Fox, A., *History and Heritage: The Social Origins of British Industrial Relations* (1985)
Laybourn, Keith, *A History of British Trade Unionism* (Stroud, 1992)
Lovell, John, *British Trade Unions 1875–1933* (1977)
Musson, A. E., *British Trade Unions 1800–1875* (1972)
Pelling, Henry, *A History of British Trade Unionism* (1987)
Price, R., *Labour in British Society: An Interpretative History* (1986)
Ward, J. T. and Fraser, W. H. (eds) *Workers and Employers. Documents on Trade Unions and Industrial Relations in Britain since the Eighteenth Century* (1980)
Wrigley, C. J. (ed.), *A History of British Industrial Relations, Vol. I, 1875–1914* (1980); *Vol II, 1914–1939* (1987); *Vol III, 1939–1979* (1996).

Before 1850

Dobson, C. R., *Masters and Journeymen: A Pre-History of Industrial Relations* (1980)
Fraser, W. Hamish, *Conflict and Class. Scottish Workers 1700–1838* (Edinburgh, 1988)
Prothero, I., *Artisans and Politics in Early Nineteenth Century London: John Gast and His Times* (Folkestone, 1979)
Rule, John, *British Trade Unionism 1750–1850* (1988)

1850–1914

Allen, E., Clarke, J. F., McCord, N., Rowe, D. J., *The North-East Engineers' Strike of 1871* (Newcastle, 1971)

Brown, Raymond, *Waterfront Organisation in Hull, 1870–1900* (Hull, 1974)
Burgess, Keith, *The Origins of British Industrial Relations. The Nineteenth Century Experience* (1975)
Davidson, R., *Whitehall and the Labour Problem in Late Victorian and Edwardian Britain* (1985)
Dutton, H. I. and King, J. E., *Ten Per Cent and No Surrender: The Preston Strike, 1853–54* (Cambridge, 1981)
Fraser, W. Hamish, *Trade Unions and Society: The Struggle for Acceptance, 1850–1880* (1974)
Gordon, Eleanor, *Women and the Labour Movement in Scotland 1850–1914* (Oxford, 1991)
Gray, Robert, *The Labour Aristocracy in Nineteenth Century Britain* (1981)
Harrison, R., (ed.), *Independent Collier: The Coal Miner as Archetypal Proletarian Reconsidered* (Hassocks, 1978)
Harrison, R., and Zeitlin, J., *Divisions of Labour: Skilled Workers and Technological Change in Nineteenth Century England* (Hassocks, 1985)
Hobsbawm, E. J., *Labouring Men. Studies in the History of Labour* (1964)
Holton, Bob, *British Syndicalism 1900–1914: Myth and Realities* (1976)
Joyce, Patrick, *Work, Society and Politics* (1982)
Lovell, John, *Stevedores and Dockers: A Study of Trade Unionism in the Port of London, 1870–1914* (1969)
Matsamura, Takao, *The Labour Aristocracy Revisited* (Manchester, 1983)
Mommsen, W. and Husung, H. J. (eds), *The Development of Trade Unionism in Great Britain and Germany* (1985)
More, Charles, *Skill and the English Working Class, 1870–1914* (1980)
Penn, Roger, *Skilled Workers in the Class Structure* (Cambridge, 1985)
Phelps Brown, E. H., *The Growth of British Industrial Relations* (1965)
Price, R. J., *Masters, Unions and Men* (1980)
Reynolds, Sian, *Britannica's Typesetters. Women Compositors in Edinburgh* (Edinburgh, 1989)
Taplin, E. L., *Liverpool Dockers and Seamen, 1870–1890* (Hull, 1974)
White, J. L., *The Limits of Trade Union Militancy: The Lancashire Textile Workers, 1910–1914* (New York, 1978)
Yapp, Yvonne, *The Air of Freedom: the Birth of New Unionism* (1989)

1914–45

Duncan, R., and McIvor, A. J., *Militant Workers: Labour and Class Conflict on the Clyde, 1900–1950* (Edinburgh, 1992)
Campbell, A., Fishman, N. and Howell, D., *Miners, Unions and Politics 1910–47* (1996)
Hinton, James, *The First Shop Stewards' Movement* (1973)
Hinton, James, *Shop-Floor Citizens. Engineering Democracy in 1940s Britain* (Aldershot, 1994)
McLean, Iain, *The Legend of Red Clydeside* (Edinburgh, 1983)
Martin, Roderick, *Communism and the British Trade Unions, 1924–1933* (Oxford, 1969)

Phillips, G. A., *The General Strike. The Politics of Industrial Conflict* (1976)
Renshaw, P., *The General Strike* (1975)
Rubin, G., *War, Law and Labour* (Oxford, 1987)

Since 1945

Allen, V. L., *The Militancy of British Miners* (1981)
Bain, G. S. *The Growth of White-Collar Unionism* (Oxford, 1970)
Brown, W., *The Changing Contours of British Industrial Relations* (Oxford, 1981)
Flanders, Alan, *The Fawley Productivity Agreements. A Case Study of Management and Collective Bargaining* (1964)
McIlroy, John, *Trade Unions in Britain Today* (second edition, Manchester, 1995)
Minkin, Lewis, *The Contentious Alliance. Trade Unions and the Labour Party* (Edinburgh, 1992).
Moran, Michael, *The Politics of Industrial Relations* (1977)
Taylor, R., *The Future of the Trade Unions* (1994)
Wrigley, Chris, *British Trade Unions 1945–1995* (Manchester, 1997)
Wilson, David F., *Dockers. The Impact of Industrial Change* (1972)

Histories of Trade Unions

Allen, V. L., *Trade Union Leadership. Based on a Study of Arthur Deakin* (1957)
Arnot, R. Page, *The Miners: a History of the Miners Federation of Great Britain, 1889–1910, I* (1949)
Arnot, R. Page, *The Miners: Years of Struggle: A History of the Miners' Federation of Great Britain* (1953)
Bagwell, Philip, *The Railwaymen. The History of the National Union of Railwaymen* (1963)
Clegg, H. A., *General Union. A Study of the National Union of General and Municipal Workers* (1954)
Clinton, Alan, *The Trade Union Rank and File. Trades Councils in Britain, 1900–40* (Manchester, 1977)
Clinton, A., *Post Office Workers* (1984)
Coates, Ken and Topham, Tony, *The Making of the Transport and General Workers' Union: the emergence of the labour movement 1870–1922* (Oxford, 1991)
Fox, Alan, *A History of the National Union of Boot and Shoe Operatives* (Oxford, 1958)
Francis, Hywel and Smith, David, *The Fed. A History of the South Wales Miners in the Twentieth Century* (1980)
Gennard, John, *A History of the National Graphical Association* (1990)
Gennard, John and Bain, Peter, *SOGAT. A History of the Society of Graphical and Allied Trades* (1995)

Howell, David, *The Politics of the NUM. A Lancashire View* (Manchester, 1989)
Hyman, Richard, *The Workers' Union* (Oxford, 1971)
Jefferys, J. B., *The Story of the Engineers 1800–1945* (n.d)
Lloyd, J., *Light and Liberty. A History of the EETPU* (1990)
Lovell, John, *A Short History of the TUC* (1968)
Martin, Ross H., *TUC: The Growth of a Pressure Group 1868–1976* (Oxford, 1980)
Mortimer, J. E., *History of the Boilermakers' Society, I* (1973)
Musson, A. E., *The Typographical Association. Origins and history up to 1949* (Oxford, 1954)
Postgate, R., *The Builders' History* (1923)
Prochaska, A., *History of the General Federation of Trade Unions, 1889–1980* (1982)
Spoor, Alec, *White-Collar Union. Sixty Years of NALGO* (1967)
Taplin, E. L., *The Dockers' Union: A Study of the National Union of Dock Labourers* (Leicester, 1986)
Turner, H. A., *Trade Union Growth, Structure and Policy* (1962)
Wilson, D. F., *Dockers. The Impact of Industrial Change* (1972)

Biographical Material

Bellamy, J. M. and Saville, J. (eds), *Dictionary of Labour Biography* (various volumes)
Bullock, Alan, *The Life and Times of Ernest Bevin. Vol I, Trade Union Leader* (1960)
Citrine, Lord, *Men and Work – An Autobiography* (1964)
Craik, W. W., *Bryn Roberts and the National Union of Public Employees* (1955)
Jones, Jack, *Union Man: An Autobiography* (1986)
Radice, G. and L., *Will Thorne, Constructive Militant* (1974)
Schneer, Jonathan, *Ben Tillett: Portrait of a Labour Leader* (1982)
Sirs, Bill, *Hard Labour* (1985)
Weighell, Sidney, *On the Rails* (1983)
Wilson, Gordon M., *Alexander McDonald, Leader of the Miners* (Aberdeen, 1982)

Aspects of Industrial Relations

Foster, John and Woolfson, Charles, *The Politics of the UCS Work-In* (1986)
Gospel, H., and Littler, C. R. (eds), *Managerial Strategies and Industrial Relations* (Aldershot, 1983)
Hartley, Jean, Kelly, John and Nicholson, Nigel, *Steel Strike. A Case Study in Industrial Relations* (1983)
Harvey, Charles and Turner, John, *Labour and Business in Modern Britain* (1989)

Jackson, M. P., Leopold, J. W. and Tuck, K., *Decentralization of Collective Bargaining. An Analysis of Recent Experience in the UK* (1993)
Jowitt, J. A. and McIvor, A. J. (eds), *Employers and Labour in the English Textile Industries* (1988)
Lane, Tony and Roberts, Kenneth, *Strike at Pilkingtons* (1971)
Littler, Craig R., *The Development of Labour Process in Capitalist Societies* (1982)
McIvor, Arthur J., *Organised Capital. Employers' associations and industrial relations in northern England, 1880–1939* (Cambridge, 1996)
Sobel, Charles F., *Work and Politics. The Division of Labor in Industry* (Cambridge, 1982)
Tolliday, S. and Zeitlin, J. (eds) *Shop Floor Bargaining and the State* (Cambridge, 1985)
Tolliday, S. and Zeitlin, J. (eds) *The Power to Manage?* (1991)
Wigham, E., *Strikes and the Government 1893–1981* (1982)

Index